D1344397

Thomas Hardy's
Tess of the d'Urbervilles

A tragic tale of cruel fates, touching on rape, illegitimate birth and murder, Thomas Hardy's *Tess of the d'Urbervilles* (1891) shocked its early audiences, but has proved to be one of the most enduring and influential works of English literature.

Taking the form of a sourcebook, this guide to Hardy's crucial novel offers:

- extensive introductory comment on the contexts and many interpretations of the text, from publication to the present
- annotated extracts from key contextual documents, reviews, critical works and the text itself
- cross-references between documents and sections of the guide, in order to suggest links between texts, contexts and criticism
- suggestions for further reading.

Part of the *Routledge Guides to Literature* series, this volume is essential reading for all those beginning detailed study of *Tess of the d'Urbervilles* and seeking not only a guide to the novel but a way through the wealth of contextual and critical material that surrounds Hardy's text.

Scott McEathron is Associate Professor of English at Southern Illinois University, Carbondale.

Routledge Guides to Literature*

Editorial Advisory Board: Richard Bradford (University of Ulster at Coleraine), Jan Jedrzejewski (University of Ulster at Coleraine), Duncan Wu (St Catherine's College, University of Oxford)

Routledge Guides to Literature offer clear introductions to the most widely studied authors and literary texts.

Each book engages with texts, contexts and criticism, highlighting the range of critical views and contextual factors that need to be taken into consideration in advanced studies of literary works. The series encourages informed but independent readings of texts by ranging as widely as possible across the contextual and critical issues relevant to the works examined and highlighting areas of debate as well as those of critical consensus. Alongside general guides to texts and authors, the series includes 'sourcebooks', which allow access to reprinted contextual and critical materials as well as annotated extracts of primary text.

Available in this series

Geoffrey Chaucer by Gillian Rudd
Ben Jonson by James Loxley
William Shakespeare's The Merchant of Venice: A Sourcebook edited by S.P. Cerasano
William Shakespeare's King Lear: A Sourcebook edited by Grace Ioppolo
William Shakespeare's Othello: A Sourcebook edited by Andrew Hadfield
John Milton by Richard Bradford
John Milton's Paradise Lost: A Sourcebook edited by Margaret Kean
Alexander Pope by Paul Baines
Mary Wollstonecraft's A Vindication of the Rights of Woman: A Sourcebook edited by Adriana Craciun
Jane Austen by Robert P. Irvine
Jane Austen's Emma: A Sourcebook edited by Paula Byrne
Jane Austen's Pride and Prejudice: A Sourcebook edited by Robert Morrison
Mary Shelley's Frankenstein: A Sourcebook edited by Timothy Morton
The Poems of John Keats: A Sourcebook edited by John Strachan
Charles Dickens's David Copperfield: A Sourcebook edited by Richard J. Dunn
Charles Dickens's Bleak House: A Sourcebook edited by Janice M. Allan
Herman Melville's Moby-Dick: A Sourcebook edited by Michael J. Davey
Harriet Beecher Stowe's Uncle Tom's Cabin: A Sourcebook edited by Debra J. Rosenthal
Walt Whitman's Song of Myself: A Sourcebook and Critical Edition edited by Ezra Greenspan
Robert Browning by Stefan Hawlin
Henrik Ibsen's Hedda Gabler: A Sourcebook edited by Christopher Innes

* Some books in this series were originally published in the Routledge Literary Sourcebooks series, edited by Duncan Wu, or the Complete Critical Guide to English Literature series, edited by Richard Bradford and Jan Jedrzejewski.

Thomas Hardy's
Tess of the d'Urbervilles
A Sourcebook

Edited by Scott McEathron

Routledge
Taylor & Francis Group

LONDON AND NEW YORK

First published 2005 by Routledge
2 Park Square, Milton Park, Abingdon, Oxon, OX14 4RN

Simultaneously published in the USA and Canada
by Routledge
711 Third Avenue, New York, NY 10017

Routledge is an imprint of the Taylor & Francis Group

Editorial material and selection © 2005 Scott McEathron

Typeset in Sabon and Gill Sans by RefineCatch Limited, Bungay, Suffolk

British Library Cataloguing in Publication Data
A catalogue record for this book is available from the British Library

Library of Congress Cataloging in Publication Data
Thomas Hardy's Tess of the d'Urbervilles : a sourcebook / edited by
Scott McEathron.
     p. cm. – (Routledge guides to literature)
   Includes bibliographical references and index.
   1. Hardy, Thomas, 1840–1928. Tess of the d'Urbervilles.
I. McEathron, Scott, 1962– II. Series.
   PR4748.T463 2005
   823'.8–dc22   2004017640

ISBN 0–415–25527–9 (hbk)
ISBN 0–415–25528–7 (pbk)

Contents

2: Interpretations   45

Critical History   47

Early Critical Reception   56

Modern Criticism   64

The Character of Tess   64

Hardy's Philosophical Views   81

Tess and Sexuality   87

Hardy on Nature and Society   97

4: Further Reading   185

Illustrations

Annotation and Footnotes

Annotation is a key feature of this series. Both the original notes from reprinted texts and new annotations by the editor appear at the bottom of the relevant page. The reprinted notes are prefaced by the author's name in square brackets, e.g. '[Robinson's note]'.

Acknowledgements

I wish to extend my sincere thanks to Duncan Wu, the series editor, and to Liz Thompson, Fiona Cairns and Kate Parker, at Routledge, for their help in the preparation of this book. I owe special gratitude to Professor William Morgan of Illinois State University, who generously shared his knowledge of Hardy's poetry. My deepest thanks are due to Anne Chandler, both for her patience and for her innumerable improvements to the typescript.

I wish to thank the following for permission to reprint material under copyright:

The British Library, for the illustration of Hardy's manuscript of *Tess of the d'Urbervilles*.

Dorset County Museum, for the photographs of Thomas Hardy, Max Gate and Gertrude Bugler.

Kobal Collection, for the photograph of Nastassja Kinski in the film *Tess* (1979).

The Library of Congress, for the photograph of Minnie Maddern Fiske in the New York stage production of *Tess*, and for the illustration of Stonehenge.

The Thomas Hardy Association of America, for the photograph of Hardy's map entitled 'Tess's Country'.

P. Boumelha, *Thomas Hardy and Women: Sexual Ideology and Narrative Form*. © 1984 Penny Boumelha. Used by permission of Pearson Education Limited.

Kristin Brady, 'Tess and Alec: Rape or Seduction' in N. Page (ed.), *Thomas Hardy Annual*, vol. 4, 1986, Humanities Press, NJ, reproduced with permission of Palgrave Macmillan.

William A. Davis, Jr, 'The Rape of Tess: Hardy, English Law, and the Case for Sexual Assault', *Nineteenth Century Literature*, vol. 52, no. 2. © 1997 The Regents of the University of California. Used by permission of publisher.

Janet Freeman, 'Ways of Looking at Tess', from *Studies in Philology*, vol. 79. © 1982 by the University of North Carolina Press. Used by permission of the publisher.

Ian Gregor, *The Great Web: The Form of Hardy's Major Fiction.* © 1974 Faber and Faber Ltd. Used by permission of the publisher.

Adam Gussow, 'Dreaming Holmberry-Lipped Tess: Aboriginal Reverie and Spectatorial Desire in *Tess of the d'Urbervilles*', *Studies in the Novel*, vol. 32, no. 4 (Winter 2000), © 2000 by the University of North Texas. Reprinted by permission of the publisher.

Irving Howe, *Thomas Hardy*, 1967, Macmillan. Reproduced with permission of Palgrave Macmillan.

Mary Jacobus, 'Tess's Purity', *Essays in Criticism*, vol. 26 (1976). By permission of Oxford University Press.

Bruce Johnson, ' "The Perfection of Species" and Hardy's *Tess*' from U.C. Knoepflmacher and G.B. Tennyson (eds), *Nature and the Victorian Imagination*, © 1977 The Regents of the University of California. Used by permission of the publisher.

Michael Millgate, *Thomas Hardy: His Career as a Novelist* (© Michael Millgate 1971). Quoted by permission of PFD on behalf of Professor Michael Millgate.

Lisa Sternlieb, 'Three Leahs to Get One Rachel', *Dickens Studies Annual*, vol. 29, © AMS Press, 2000. Used by permission of AMS Press.

Tony Tanner, 'Colour and Movement in Hardy's *Tess of the d'Urbervilles*', *Critical Quarterly*, vol. 10 (1968). By permission of Blackwell publishers.

Peter Widdowson, 'Moments of Vision' in Charles Pettit (ed.), *New Perspectives on Thomas Hardy*, 1994, Macmillan. Reproduced with permission of Palgrave Macmillan.

Merryn Williams, *Thomas Hardy and Rural England*, 1972, Macmillan. Reproduced with permission of Palgrave Macmillan.

Every effort has been made to trace and contact copyright holders. The publishers would be pleased to hear from any copyright holders not acknowledged here so that this section may be amended at the earliest opportunity.

Introduction

Thomas Hardy was an enormously productive writer of fiction. Of his fourteen published novels – a remarkable tally in itself – fully five attained during his lifetime a 'classic' status that has been enhanced, if also continually redefined, through decades of interpretation. The titles *Far from the Madding Crowd* (1874), *The Return of the Native* (1878), *The Mayor of Casterbridge* (1886), *Tess of the d'Urbervilles* (1891) and *Jude the Obscure* (1895) have come to signify a particular kind of novelistic portrayal at which Hardy excelled – that of making the protagonist almost completely defined by his or her 'native' locale, while at the same time painfully alienated from it. This essential conflict is simultaneously portrayed in his work as a conflict between historical eras, with his characters caught between rural traditionalism and the enticements, and potential dangers, of the modern and urban. Perhaps because the quest for stability amidst stunning technological and social change is felt as urgently now as it was in the late Victorian era, Hardy's great novels have acquired an aura of inevitability that spreads beyond the academic canon: it almost seems as if they *had* to be written. And with *Tess of the d'Urbervilles*, that sense of historical impetus or destiny is given artistic balance by Hardy's creation of a truly singular heroine, Tess Durbeyfield, who seems at once to embody these historical conflicts and to stand wholly apart from them. Indeed, one of the most remarkable aspects of *Tess* is its continuing capacity to inspire emotional attachment to its title character, as if she were an actual person. Yet in giving themselves over to this kind of identification, readers are simply following the lead of Hardy himself, who would thoroughly approve the degree to which the very name 'Tess', for today's audiences, still seems invested with a mixture of yearning and enchantment.

But Hardy's success with *Tess of the d'Urbervilles* did not come easily. The manuscript was submitted to several family magazines for serial publication, and repeatedly rejected because it employed inflammatory topics – rape, fornication, illegitimacy, religious scepticism and even murder – in ways that problematized conventionally 'absolute' categories of moral judgement. Beyond this, the tragic storyline was couched in, and funnelled through, descriptions of the natural world that left a 'general impression', as one cautious reader put it, of 'rather too much succulence'. The editor of *Macmillan's Magazine* was here borrowing a term from Hardy's own descriptions of a lush West Country valley, central to the plot of *Tess*; and in so doing, he astutely registered not just the novel's frank evocations of sexual desire but also its appeals to a 'natural' law of morality that might, under certain circumstances, override the formal dictates of church and society. These aspects of *Tess* became, for Hardy, a double bind. After reluctantly altering the narrative to minimize its hints of moral relativism, he found himself accused of inauthenticity and strained argumentation: the novelist Margaret Oliphant, for example, saw *Tess* as an 'elaborate and indignant' attempt on Hardy's part to make 'Vice' seem like 'Virtue'. Hardy complained bitterly about such reactions, but he could hardly have been surprised by them, since *Tess* seems to have been conceived precisely as a challenge to prevailing sexual mores. Grounded in the heroine's successive betrayals by two very different men – the first time through cruel caprice, and then, even more damagingly, through false scruples – the story combines the structure of classical tragedy with scathing social criticism of the 'double standard' in men's and women's sexual behaviour. Hardy's willingness to confront prudish hypocrisy is also apparent in the fact that, when making his final pre-publication revisions, he added the subtitle 'A Pure Woman, Faithfully Presented by Thomas Hardy'. Years later, he professed to wish these words unwritten (*'Melius fuerat non scribere'*), as they had provided hostile reviewers with such an obvious target – yet the fact remains that sympathetic readers over the decades (as will be seen in this volume's selections of modern criticism) have seen this subtitle as crystallizing something important about the novel's sense of purpose. There is widespread agreement that Hardy earnestly wished, through his portrayal of Tess, to complicate and enlarge people's notions of 'purity', especially, though not exclusively, in relation to 'womanhood' – and that he also wanted readers to engage with the narrative processes by which an imaginary individual might be 'faithfully presented'.

To understand these objectives about which Hardy cared so deeply, we need to appreciate the depth of his impulse to view the individual's life course as embedded within massive frameworks of historical and even geographic change – nested contexts extending beyond that individual's comprehension but none the less impinging on his or her identity. As with all of Hardy's novels, readers of *Tess* frequently feel themselves pulled in two directions: urged to sense the characters' individual presences in almost physical, certainly emotional ways; and yet told that these presences lives are fleeting, soon to be forgotten, perhaps even futile, if viewed within a grander scheme of time and space. One famous expression of this tension, in *Tess*, is Hardy's strategy of placing the denouement of the tragedy at Stonehenge (see Key Passages, p. 182). We feel the personal poignancy of Tess's resting on a fallen pillar, her husband keeping her warm with his coat, as the authorities arrive to arrest her for murder; and we also perceive the historical irony of Tess's having at last found safe harbour in a place of pagan sacrifice, just before she must meet her fate with modern, 'civilized' institutions of justice. Indeed, Hardy's fascination with antiquity was fostered through practical experience, long before he began writing fiction. Enlarging upon the career expectations of his father, a stonemason, Hardy was at the age of sixteen apprenticed to an architect who specialized in the restoration of churches, and for the next fifteen years he would be employed in architecture and building design. Though the success of his writing – especially the early novel *Far from the Madding Crowd* – enabled him to put aside architecture as a paid profession in 1874, Hardy would fill his fiction and poetry with stone ruins, venerable churches, monuments, graveyards and other traces of the distant past. These artefacts do not simply provide local colour or window-dressing for Hardy's plots, nor do they have traditional literary associations of romantic melancholia or gothic horror. They operate more subtly, at the back of characters' minds, to remind them (and us) that they are treading ancient ground.

Hardy's commitment to this idea is such that he spends a great deal of time narrating the landscape itself, at a level 'above' that of plot and character developments. People are defined through their environment; the environment rolls on, regardless. And yet that very independence from human affairs, paradoxically, gives landscape in Hardy's eyes a kind of vitality worth exploring. Thus, a common thread in Hardy's major novels is the progressive mapping of a semi-fictional region he calls Wessex. Many of the towns and scenic markers of this region are recognizably those of Dorset, the area of south-central England that Hardy inhabited all his life; Hardy exercises artistic licence in dwelling upon, and in some ways reinventing, subregions of 'Wessex' to suit the themes of particular novels. Fittingly, as Hardy well knew, 'Wessex' is an archaic term for Dorset, dating from the era of Anglo-Saxon rule in the early Middle Ages. The wealth of detail Hardy gives us about present-day life in the region is very much framed by this conceit – as, by extension, are his many stone ruins dwarfed by natural formations of earth and rock. Consider, for example, the description of Egdon Heath with which Hardy opens his novel *The Return of the Native* (1878), in a chapter titled 'A Face on Which Time Makes but Little Impression': 'Every night its Titanic form seemed to await something; but it had waited thus, unmoved, during so many centuries, through the crises of so many things, that it could only be imagined to await one last crisis.' Here the paradox of an impassive, yet somehow expectant landscape is especially clear. And when Hardy adds human beings to such a picture, he seems often to be asking us to transfer the idea of a 'story' – as a chronicle of significant change – from people to their surroundings, and back again. In *Tess*, then, even the edenic Valley of the Dairies has its story, larger in scale but perhaps not essentially different from the stories of its inhabitants: 'Thus they all worked on, encompassed by the vast flat mead which extended to either slope of the valley – a level landscape compounded of old landscapes long forgotten, and, no doubt, differing in character very greatly from the landscape they composed now' (Chapter 17). Our minds work too frenetically and self-interestedly to know all that the earth knows; yet there is value in perceiving, even subconsciously, that we are 'encompassed' by its silent history.

As broad and unshakeable as this truth may seem, however, Hardy also calls our attention to the more contentious nature of 'history' at a personal and local level. In *Tess*, as in much of Hardy's work, the protagonists seem peculiarly trapped, or arrested, relative to the passage of time. The world of the twentieth century beckons to them, but they dwell in a world still dependent on agrarian crafts and trades, where an itinerant 'reddleman' marks the sheep with red dye (*The Return of the Native*), the local 'conjuror' is consulted when the butter-churn fails (*Tess*, Chapter 21) and folkloric customs govern the calendar year. Our first view of Tess (Chapter 2; see Key Passages **p. 120**) shows her participating in the may-day ceremony of her village: the evident honourableness of this ancient tradition is placed in sharp contrast to the unexpected vision of her drunken father in a hired coach, indulging in fantasies of his aristocratic lineage. Tess's two suitors also find themselves repeatedly brought up short as they try to revise traditional class distinctions to fit their present interests. Alec d'Urberville, a shift-less *nouveau riche* whose family has bought an ancient name, temporarily renounces his life of dissipation for a strain of Evangelical Christianity associated with workers' movements of the earlier nineteenth century – but, on unexpectedly seeing Tess after several years' separation, feels compelled to resume the role of abusive privilege that led to her original seduction and ruin. Angel Clare spurns the very idea of nobility, and his aspiration to be a neo-traditionalist farmer fits surprisingly well with his aggressive intellectual modernism – yet he harbours a royal-watcher's fascination with the fate of the real d'Urbervilles (Chapter 30), and, on learning Tess's connection to that family, hopes to startle his own into fully accepting the dairymaid by playing 'the grand card', as he puts it to himself, of her lineage (Chapter 33). (Shortly thereafter, of course, he reverts wholly to the age-old patriarchalist obsession with female 'purity'.) The title *Tess of the d'Urbervilles* (changed from the working title *Too Late, Beloved!*) is itself laden with irony. Tess Durbeyfield's connection to the d'Urberville bloodline is genuine, yet her attempt to reclaim that connection is turned to personal advantage by the fraudulent possessor of the name. It becomes a debatable point whether her fami-ly's poverty or Alec's predatory attraction to her is the worse imprisonment. The noble family is reputed by legend to be 'cursed'; it is Angel, ironically, who explains Tess's momentary panic at the sight of their wedding-carriage with a joking reference to 'the legend of the d'Urberville Coach' (Chapter 33). Implicitly, Hardy offers us the idea that identifying oneself with the pedigree, or internalizing it, may be the true curse of the d'Urbervilles.

The difficulty, but also the desirability, of *integrating* the old and the new is a theme repeatedly borne out in various aspects of Hardy's life. His quasi-anthropological approach to farm and village life – seen, for example, in the country-dance episode at Chaseborough, just prior to the fateful sexual encounter between Tess and Alec – stems partly from his parents' conscious efforts to keep local traditions alive through storytelling (in his mother's case) and the perform-ance of folk music (in his father's). The house in Dorset Hardy later designed for himself, called Max Gate, incorporated neo-gothic, neo-classical and modern elements; it was located in a spot isolated enough to command panoramic vistas, but still close enough to the Hardy family cottage at Higher Bockhampton to enable frequent contact with his parents and the village society he had always known (see p. **19**).

The phases of Hardy's writing career, while shaped by personal and economic circumstances, can also make good sense to us if we correlate them with the revolutions in thought that took place in late nineteenth- and early twentieth-century British culture. Hardy was a publishing writer for almost sixty years, the first thirty primarily as a novelist, and the last thirty primarily as a poet. His first novel, *Desperate Remedies*, appeared in volume form in 1871, the year following Britain's first statutory provision for universal, compulsory schooling; his later volumes of verse reflect upon the more cataclysmic social (and spiritual) changes of the early twentieth century, including of course those attendant upon the First World War. It is generally agreed that his fourteen novels are ever more thor-oughly pessimistic, with his last, *Jude the Obscure* (1895), often seen as singu-larly, almost perversely dark. There, significantly, the agrarian folk culture that brings Tess such a mixture of joy and sorrow is for the stonemason Jude Fawley a pernicious form of societal malingering. But Jude's dream of enlightenment and self-improvement in the great university city of Christminster is played out as a slow, painful dismantling of all he finds important in life. In Hardy's seven collections of lyric poetry, dating from 1898 to a posthumous publication of 1928, we see not so much an overarching progression of mood as an oscillation between two modes: highly localized (many, autobiographical) sketches of love and loss; and much more abstract, quasi-mythological considerations of the historical and indeed cosmic ironies that *encompass* human tragedy. Many of Hardy's volumes of poetry contain a blend of old and new verse, with some poems dating as far back as the middle 1860s; scholars interpret Hardy's choices for inclusion, in each case, as potentially relating to what was currently uppermost in his emotional life. The thematic interplay of poems seems to have been more important to him than a strictly chronological presentation. If Hardy's career as a publishing poet has a culminating moment of pessimism such as we see in *Jude the Obscure*, it is probably best located in *The Dynasts*, an epic verse-drama published in three segments (1904–8). Here Hardy used the Napoleonic Wars, which had dominated British public consciousness at the turn of the prior century, as a vehicle for philosophic arguments against the efficacy of individual free will, and against a providential view of the universe in which a loving, interventionist deity governed human affairs. Hardy arrived at his scepticism honestly, over several decades; like many of his generation, he was influenced by the debates surrounding the work of the naturalist Charles Darwin, and his own gradual loss of religious faith may be seen, in many of his poems, as a subtext for other stories of loss.

Closely related to Hardy's sense of historical transition, and equally important to our understanding of *Tess*, is the nagging conflict of class expectations with which he contended throughout his life. His background was not one of privilege, and, while his parents were friendly toward education in the manner of the aspirant lower middle class, they reasonably expected their first child to capitalize on known quantities. His progression from a national school to a commercial academy, and thence to the apprenticeship at the architectural firm, made eminent sense considering his own aptitudes and his father's business connections; the liberal arts, apart from the smattering of languages he received at the academy, were viewed mainly as leisure pursuits. But the sensible progression did not work out exactly as planned. Hardy had nurtured hopes of a university education, and of a career in the church that would directly complement his scholarly and literary interests. Though successful in design work, he did indeed spend the leisure moments of twenty years in serious, independent study. Whenever he saw opportunities to shift from architecture to writing as a source of income, he took them. It was not so much this further remove from his father's trade, however, as his choice of a life partner that made his professional status a source of friction in Hardy's own family. Emma Livinia Gifford, whom he met while restoring a church in Cornwall, was at once vivacious and bookish, and in many ways a help to Hardy in the production of his early novels; but she was also socially ambitious, and eager for the reflected glory of Hardy's literary reputation, in ways that alienated his parents and particularly his mother, to whom he was very close. This tension only grew over the course of Hardy's nearly forty-year marriage to Emma. At the same time, Hardy's self-made literary credentials also drew fire in the public realm: there was an undercurrent of snobbery in many reviews of his work, proceeding from the assumption that his magisterial, highly allusive style (see, for example, the Key Passage Chapter 20, p. 146) was not a genuine entitlement, because not the product of a university education. Such responses were a constant sore spot for Hardy, and when we read his novels it is crucial to bear in mind the paradigmatic nature of class distinctions in late Victorian Britain. If we are asked to see Angel Clare's parents as somewhat narrow-minded about the prospect of a dairymaid as a daughter-in-law, we are also asked to see them as typical of their class and generation – and to appreciate the Herculean effort by which Angel's mother, unwilling to attend his wedding but disappointed not to meet his bride, convinces herself that the hard-working Tess must resemble the 'virtuous woman' extolled in Proverbs 31: 'Since she is pure and chaste she would have been refined enough for me' (Chapter 39). By the same token, Hardy injects a certain plausibility into the mystique of the landed aristocracy that propels the Durbeyfield family to disaster: we sense that in pushing their daughter forward,

Figure 1 Thomas Hardy (c. 1914) (By permission of the Dorset County Museum)

Tess's hapless parents are merely acting upon a motive that most of the population nurses in secrecy. But it is the issue of self-fashioning, far more than that of social positioning, that preoccupies Hardy in his major novels. 'Autodidacticism' is in this connection a regrettably awkward-sounding term, because the phenomenon of teaching oneself, 'bettering' oneself – making a little formal education go a long way, and shifting course according to exigencies – is for Hardy the very crossroads of pleasure and pain, and that which the novel as a literary form enabled him to analyse and explore.

The first section of this Routledge Sourcebook, 'Contexts', sets forth the circumstances of the novel's publication, and locates *Tess* within the sixty-year arc of Hardy's career. It offers documents which reveal Hardy's immediate frustration with the controversy *Tess* provoked, and offers as well as a series of poems that reveal how the characters, dilemmas and themes of the novel continued to haunt his imagination even after the crisis of its publication had cooled. The second section, 'Interpretations', presents an extensive selection of both early and modern criticism on *Tess*, and shows how powerfully the novel has always engaged the passions even of scholarly readers. After a brief review of the most notable film and stage adaptations of *Tess*, a third section, 'Key Passages', presents textual excerpts and commentary derived from all seven of the novel's 'phases', as Hardy termed them. This section is designed to enrich understanding and enjoyment of the novel by highlighting those moments that epitomize its concerns, describing the tendencies of Hardy's style, and demonstrating the many points of contact between any given scene and Hardy's larger novelistic vision.

1

Contexts

Contextual Overview

When Hardy began work on *Tess of the d'Urbervilles* in 1887, he had already published eleven novels, including *Far from the Madding Crowd* (1874), *The Return of the Native* (1878), *The Mayor of Casterbridge* (1886) and *The Woodlanders* (1887). At forty-seven, he was to all appearances occupying the moment of his artistic prime; the *Contemporary Review*, for example, voiced the critical consensus that, as a stylist particularly, Hardy stood 'higher than any contemporary novelist'. (The field would have included such living luminaries as George Meredith, Henry James and Margaret Oliphant.) But despite this hard-earned and gradually accrued reputation, Hardy was only a decade away from abandoning the novel as a medium: by 1897 he would redirect his literary energies to poetry, with which he had begun to experiment in his middle twenties. In one sense, this shift was the natural outgrowth of his financial success as a novelist. Hardy had originally begun writing fiction partly because, unlike poetry, it afforded the possibility of making a living, and the sales of *Tess* (1891) and *Jude the Obscure* (1895), the best of his career, were such that he was able to think in renewed practical terms about a return to verse. In another sense, however, this new career trajectory was born precipitately, and in great bitterness. Amidst the often positive reception of these two late novels was a loud strain of moralistic attack that Hardy could neither forgive nor forget. As he said of this tide of criticism that began with *Tess* and crested with *Jude*, 'the experience completely cured me of further interest in novel-writing'. (An additional novel, *The Well-Beloved*, was published in 1897, but had been written previously.) The following documents show, first, how the personally frustrating experience of *Tess*'s early reception was channelled by Hardy into a wide-ranging cultural critique; and, second, how several of his recurrent concerns as a novelist, particularly as seen in *Tess*, translate into the parallel universe of his poetry. Finally, a third section of Contemporary Documents provides a sampling of other writers' magazine articles from the 1860s and 1870s, dealing with topics directly relevant to *Tess*.

Hardy leapt to the defence of his artistic goals in *Tess* almost before the ink was dry. His polemical essay 'Candour in English Fiction', a direct response to rejections of the *Tess* manuscript by three 'family' magazines, appeared in the journal *New Review* in January 1890 – even as Hardy was undertaking the revisions that would finally allow for *Tess*'s serial publication, in the magazine *The Graphic*, beginning in July 1891. Though a full appreciation of the process of revision can be gained only by consulting J.T. Laird's monograph *The Shaping of Tess of the D'Urbervilles*,[1] in concert with the textual-historical commentary provided by Mary Jacobus (see **p. 72**), the essential nature of Hardy's revisions is easily grasped. The biggest change was the excision – altogether – of the plot threads that arguably motivate the entire tragedy: the sequence beginning with the night of the Chaseborough Dance, including Alec's rape or seduction of Tess in the forest, and extending to the birth, baptism and death of the child Sorrow. In the *Graphic* version, there is no rape; there is no child; there is no baptism. In place of this multi-chapter sequence is a brief passage (**p. 25**) describing how Tess, after living at Trantridge for some weeks, agrees reluctantly to marry Alec, only to discover that the ceremony itself was fraudulent and without legal standing. It is this betrayal, not any sexual activity in the forest, that in the truncated magazine version causes Tess to return to her family at Marlott.

Obviously this change threatened the coherence and artistic integrity of the novel in the most basic of ways, and Hardy was quick to try to repair the damage, first by immediately publishing much of the excised sequence (omitting the name 'Tess') in two discrete short stories called 'Saturday Night in Arcady' and 'The Midnight Baptism', and then by restoring many of the original plot elements when the first freestanding edition of the novel was published late in 1891. But his bitterness is evident in 'Candour in English Fiction' (see **p. 20**), written at the height of the crisis. Hardy assumes the role of a literary historian taking the broadest possible view of the issue ('Things move in cycles; dormant principles renew themselves, and exhausted principles are thrust by'), but then moves quickly to a hectoring, editorial persona, bent on exposing the law of supply and demand in the literary marketplace ('the object of the magazine and circulating library is . . . to suit themselves to what is called household reading'). From this perspective, he tags the reading public's 'prudery' as dictating 'that certain picked commandments of the ten shall be preserved intact – to wit, the first, third, and seventh; that the ninth shall be infringed but gingerly; the sixth only as much as necessary'. (Here Hardy refers, in the first group, to the commandments forbidding the worship of false gods, the usage of the Lord's name in vain and adultery, and in the second, to those forbidding false witness and murder.) If the essay moves somewhat unevenly between grand pronouncements and localized complaints, however, several of its points do find more level ground as Hardyean axioms, relevant not only to *Tess* but to his entire novelistic canon. In this third mode, Hardy more calmly – and forcefully – insists that, in so far as fiction strives to offer a 'true view' of contemporary life, it should be 'mainly impassive in its tone and tragic in its developments'; also that 'great and profound novels' must necessarily contain 'episode[s] deemed questionable by prudes'; and, crucially for *Tess*, that the 'honest portrayal' of life 'must be largely concerned with . . . the relations of the sexes'.

'Candour in English Fiction' does not quite constitute a valedictory to novel-writing, but, when Hardy later gave his reasons for turning to poetry, he used similar terms to attack bourgeois narrow-mindedness: 'Perhaps', he said, 'I can express more fully in verse emotions which run counter to the inert crystallized

---

1   J.T. Laird, *The Shaping of Tess of the D'Urbervilles* (Oxford: Clarendon Press, 1975), esp. 149–85.

opinion – hard as rock – which the vast body of men have vested themselves in supporting'.[2] Here, the 'emotions' Hardy wishes to express may not necessarily be his own, and might more accurately be thought of as emotionally fraught *situations*, treated with the same balance of 'impassivity' and pathos he cultivated in his fiction, but in a pared-down lyric format that makes the reconstruction of communal codes and traditions – Hardy's old specialty – almost entirely the task of the reader. Thus, while all of the poems chosen for this volume bear thematic relevance to *Tess* (and all but one of this group were composed after the novel was published), they do so upon an intriguingly broad spectrum. 'The Ruined Maid' (**p. 31**), composed some twenty-five years before *Tess*, is a useful point of departure. Its originality lies in its wry humour, and yet it remains a 'social issue' poem, reminding us that, even if this young woman had made the best of a bad situation, the shortage of legitimate work for women is still a pervasive problem. Hardy's later poems do not neglect such issues, but tend to make us think not so much about problems to be solved as about stasis and change in the human condition.

'We Field-Women' (**p. 29**), 'Tess's Lament' (**p. 27**), and 'The Well-Beloved' (**p. 29**) engage the situations and characters of *Tess* more or less directly: we have the familiar signposts of a comfortless Flintcomb-Ash, a fondly remembered dairy and a ghost-ridden Kingsbere, superadded to storylines of love and work, hope and despair. It is important, however, to see these poems not as miniatures of the novel but as self-contained artistic productions. Even 'Tess's Lament', which invites comparisons to the original, diverges from it by dwelling upon Tess's own articulations – plural – of grief and guilt. In using simple, phrasal reiterations as a lyric bridge between the former plenitude of Tess's life and its current emptiness, the poem does something that the novel, oddly, has not the leisure to do. Backed by *Tess*'s plot, yet also freed from it, the 'lament' has the quality, and clearly for Hardy the allure, of a road not taken. 'We Field-Women' is likewise an exploratory, rather than a literal revisitation, as it blends the voices of Tess's co-workers – and perhaps, tantalizingly, of Tess herself – into a choral swell powerful enough to carry them back to the sunlit meadows of the dairy. 'The Well-Beloved' delivers a yet greater sense of variability, amplifying certain gothic-romance elements of *Tess* and presenting a male speaker who is at once like and unlike Angel Clare in his particular ratio of blindness and insight. The main point about these poems is not so much that Hardy is actively rewriting *Tess* as that he is placing its elements in new combinations and frameworks – and that he is doing so, presumably, because they continue to interest him in a human context above and beyond that of the novel.

The other poems included here serve to show Hardy's continuing fascination with the interplay of personal and historical patterns. In several stories of thwarted or ephemeral passion – 'At a Hasty Wedding' (**p. 32**), 'The Turnip-Hoer' (**p. 33**), and 'A Hurried Meeting' (**p. 32**) – it is a fundamental *inequality*, whether of emotional intensity or class status (or both), that lends each situation such humiliating heartbreak for the people involved. Again, Hardy seems deliberately to be courting a number of possible permutations of the *Tess* story. 'At a Hasty Wedding' does so by foregrounding cyclical time and causing it to dominate,

---

2 Michael Millgate (ed.) *The Life and Work of Thomas Hardy* (London: Macmillan, 1984), p. 302.

rather than to complement, the romance. And in 'The Turnip-Hoer' and 'A Hurried Meeting', Hardy inverts the gender-class situation of *Tess* with sad misalliances of naïve working-class men and thoughtless gentlewomen – in the latter case, actually rendering the loss of an illegitimate child far more painful to the father than to the mother. Indeed, it is reasonable to say that, regardless of how we choose to categorize these ironic inversions, what shines through in the poems is a keen sense of dismay, or disbelief: how can this have happened, so ruthlessly in despite of human plans and preferences?

Hardy presses this farther in a third set of poems which nearly erase people from the picture, casting the drama upward to the realm of elemental and cosmic forces. Fittingly, plot seems beside the point in these poems; their main energies are devoted to reflective dialogues, flat statements, unanswerable questions. Both 'Doom and She' (**p. 36**) and 'The Lacking-Sense' (**p. 37**) discuss the haphazard depredations of a 'mighty pair', a sightless female 'world-weaver' representing earthly creation and an emotionless male principle representing time or destiny. In 'Winter in Durnover Field' (**p. 35**), we return to the surface of the earth, but not with any sense of homecoming: three birds occupy a sere and empty landscape like that of Flintcomb-Ash, and simply name, in turn, the things they cannot find. All of these dialogues are strongly reminiscent of medieval morality plays: their profundity and dark humour spring precisely – and, for our modern sensibility, ironically – from the very breadth of their abstraction.

Readers new to Hardy's poetry may find in it a refreshing sense of distance and detachment, relative to the dense layerings of his prose fiction; the unhappiness is still there, but is mediated, perhaps mitigated, by the economies of lyric verse. As Ezra Pound wrote (inflating the numbers somewhat) in 1937, 'Now *there* is a clarity. There *is* the harvest of having written 20 novels first'.[3] This tribute from one of the giants of literary modernism should remind us of Hardy's moderate sympathies with that movement, which, especially in the context of the First World War, sought new artistic techniques to address a growing sense of moral, cultural and psychic disintegration. Hardy's mentality did become more 'modern', more sardonic and less idealizing, in the last thirty years of his life; yet he is not usually considered a 'modernist' poet, because his experiments with poetic form tend to fall within the purview of the English lyric tradition. Perhaps a more straightforward explanation for the linearity and 'cleanness' of so many of his nine hundred poems lies in Hardy's motivation to find order and meaning in the turbulence of his own emotional life. Many of his poems on love and its discontents can be linked to his difficult forty-year marriage to Emma Gifford (one marked by persistent frictions over class status and intellectual interests); his embarkation, after her death in 1912, upon what one critic has called a 'great emotional reawakening';[4] his remarriage in 1914, at the age of 74, to the much younger Florence Dugdale; and more generally, especially in his later years, to the several romantic friendships he pursued with other well-read and artistically talented women. To make these connections is not to render the poems *merely* autobiographical, but rather to corroborate the deep significance of *Tess*-like

3   D.D. Paige (ed.) *The Letters of Ezra Pound, 1907–1941* (London: Faber and Faber, 1951), p. 386.
4   Alan Manford, 'Introduction', in Thomas Hardy, *A Pair of Blue Eyes* (Oxford: Oxford University Press, 1985), p. xii.

narratives for Hardy as a person. One might even argue that it is Hardy's urge to express longing, frustration and vulnerability on a personal (though not always overtly autobiographical) level that makes the universalizing statements in his poetry strangely touching, and more than merely bleak.

Similarly, when we consider *Tess of the d'Urbervilles* as a novel in which questions of history, geography and class are almost as emotion-laden as those involving the fate of the charismatic heroine, it can be useful to think in fairly direct terms about how Hardy may have been affected by contemporary treatments of such topics in the popular press. Following the selection of Hardy's poetry is a series of magazine-article excerpts on matters important to the novel: the mystery and disputed origin of Stonehenge, which is discussed by Tess and Angel as they rest briefly in their flight from the law; the emigration of English farmers to colonial Brazil, a movement in which Angel briefly takes part; and the living conditions of field-labourers such as Tess herself, amidst the agricultural decline that was taking place in late nineteenth-century Britain. Striking, in each of these essays from the 1860s and 1870s, is the discernible commitment of each writer – sometimes fervid, sometimes understated – to engage the reader through sensory and imagistic, as well as emotional appeals. It is well to remember that as a publishing novelist Hardy, too, was often first addressing a magazine readership, even as he resisted the intellectual and social conservatism of that audience as anticipated, or perhaps in some cases constructed, by cautious editors.

Chronology

1840
- Hardy's birth, five months after the marriage of his parents, in village of Higher Bockhampton, Dorset, England; his father is a mason and builder

1848
- After fighting health problems in his early childhood, Hardy attends local school; its limited curriculum is evidently not to his mother's liking

1849
- Begins studying at Dorchester British School, three miles from Bockhampton, where he is first exposed to Latin and French

1853
- Hardy follows Isaac Last, the master of the Dorchester school, to Last's new commercial academy, which emphasizes practical aspects of mathematics and language study

1856
- Apprenticed to John Hicks, a Dorchester architect. Meets Horace Moule, one of seven sons of an important local minister and theologian, who becomes Hardy's most important friend and male mentor; Moule serves as a model for Hardy's ambitions of intellectual self-improvement; Moule would commit suicide in 1873

1860
- Hardy completes apprenticeship with Hicks, and becomes his paid assistant

1862
- Travels to London; finds employment as draughtsman with the architectural firm of Arthur Blomfield, which specializes in work on churches. Remains there for several years, educating himself in poetry and art, but also becoming frustrated with the reality of class distinctions. During this time he is romantically involved and possibly engaged to Eliza Nicholls

1863
• Wins architectural prizes, but also begins considering writing as a money-making venture

1865
• The probable date when Hardy begins writing poems, with some unsuccessful attempts at magazine publication; some sources suggest he began earlier

1866
• Apparently abandons ambitions of attending university, or of a career in the church; relationship with Eliza Nicholls also ends

1867
• Returns to Dorset from London; resumes work for John Hicks, with whom he had apprenticed. Begins first novel, *The Poor Man and the Lady*, which is rejected by several publishers and never printed

1869
• After death of Hicks, moves to Weymouth to work for architect G.R. Crickmay. Begins work on first published novel, *Desperate Remedies*, which eventually appears in 1871 after Hardy assumes the financial risks of its publication

1870–1
• While on a work assignment for Crickmay in Cornwall, meets Emma Gifford; leaves Crickmay's employ in summer of 1870, but returns the following year

1872
• Second novel, *Under the Greenwood Tree*, published, also after difficulties securing a willing publisher; Hardy effectively turns to writing full-time, though he also completes work on school design for the firm of Roger Smith.

1873
• Publication of third novel, *A Pair of Blue Eyes*; suicide of Horace Moule in Cambridge

1874
• Hardy's most successful novel to date, *Far from the Madding Crowd*, is published; his career becomes to arc decisively upward; Hardy and Emma Gifford marry, having overcome resistance from her father

1875–83
• Hardy and Emma move back and forth several times between London and Dorset

1878
• *The Return of the Native* published

1880
- In London borough of Tooting, a health crisis confines Hardy to bed for nearly six months

1885
- Max Gate, Hardy's self-designed home on the outskirts of Dorchester, completed; it will remain Hardy's residence until his death

1886
- Publication of *The Mayor of Casterbridge*

1887
- Publication of *The Woodlanders*; Hardy and Emma travel in France and Italy; Hardy begins *Tess of the d'Urbervilles*

1891
- Publication of *Tess of the d'Urbervilles*

1893
- Meets Florence Henniker, with whom he has long romantic friendship; she dies in 1923

1895
- Publication of *Jude the Obscure*, his final novel, which meets with many harsh reviews protesting its fatalism and 'immorality', especially regarding marriage (*The Well-Beloved*, novel that would appear in volume form in 1897, had been written earlier)

1896
- Hardy begins intensive writing of poetry

1898
- *Wessex Poems*, Hardy's first volume of poetry, is published; continuation of gradual alienation between himself and Emma

1901
- Second volume of poetry, *Poems of the Past and Present*, achieves favourable critical response

1904–8
- *The Dynasts*, Hardy's epic drama in blank verse, published in three instalments; other volumes of poetry would be published in 1909, 1914, 1917, 1922, and 1925; a final posthumous volume would appear in 1928

1905
- First meets Florence Dugdale

1912
- Death of Emma, reflected in many important poems Hardy writes over subsequent months; Macmillan publishes the collected 'Wessex Edition' of his works, for which he had undertaken careful revisions

1914
- Hardy marries the much younger Florence Dugdale

1917
- He and Florence Dugdale Hardy begin work on his memoirs, published after his death (and under her name only) as *The Life of Thomas Hardy*

1928
- Hardy's death; his ashes buried in Westminster Abbey, his heart buried with Emma at Stinsford in Dorset

Figure 2 **Max Gate, the house Hardy designed for himself (By permission of the Dorset County Museum)**

Contemporary Documents

Thomas Hardy, 'Candour in English Fiction', *New Review* (January 1890), pp. 15–21, in *Thomas Hardy's Personal Writings*, ed. Harold Orel (London: Macmillan, 1966), pp. 125–33

As discussed above (**pp. 11–13**), the concerns of this essay, published in the journal *New Review* as part of a three-author 'symposium' on the question of novelistic candour and censorship, are inextricably connected with Hardy's frustrations in getting *Tess* accepted for serial publication in 'family' magazines. The magisterial tone he adopts may well have provoked Mowbray Morris, who had rejected the *Tess* manuscript for *Macmillan's Magazine*, to comment snidely on Hardy's 'grandiose views of the mission of the novelist' in his review of the published novel (**p. 61**).

Though the critical essay genre was never a primary interest of Hardy's, two additional essays should be briefly cited in relation to *Tess*. 'The Science of Fiction', also published in the *New Review* (April 1891), offers a less emotional view of the practical limitations of 'realism' in fiction. 'The Dorsetshire Labourer', published in *Longman's Magazine* in 1883, is largely devoted to exploding the stereotype of 'Hodge' – an ignorant rustic labourer undifferentiated from his equally ignorant peers – and it does so in a manner that directly anticipates Angel Clare's reflections on the Hodge stereotype in *Tess*.

Even imagination is the slave of stolid circumstance; and the unending flow of inventiveness which finds expression in the literature of Fiction is no exception to the general law. It is conditioned by its surroundings like a river-stream. The varying character and strength of literary creation at different times may, indeed, at first sight seem to be the symptoms of some inherent, arbitrary, and mysterious variation; but if it were possible to compute, as in mechanics, the units of power or faculty, revealed and unrevealed, that exist in the world at stated intervals, an approximately even supply would probably be disclosed. At least there is no valid reason for a contrary supposition. Yet of the inequality in its realizations there can be no question; and the discrepancy would seem to lie in contingencies which, at one period, doom high expression to dumbness and encourage the lower forms, and at another call forth the best in expression and silence triviality.

That something of this is true has indeed been pretty generally admitted in relation to art-products of various other kinds. But when observers and critics remark, as they often do remark, that the great bulk of English fiction of the present day is characterized by its lack of sincerity, they usually omit to trace this serious defect to external, or even eccentric, causes. They connect it with an assumption that the attributes of insight, conceptive power, imaginative emotion, are distinctly weaker nowadays than at particular epochs of earlier date. This may or may not be the case to some degree; but, on considering the conditions under which our popular fiction is produced, imaginative deterioration can hardly be deemed the sole or even the chief explanation why such an undue proportion of this sort of literature is in England a literature of quackery.

By a sincere school of Fiction we may understand a Fiction that expresses truly the views of life prevalent in its time, by means of a selected chain of action best suited for their exhibition. What are the prevalent views of life just now is a question upon which it is not necessary to enter further than to suggest that the most natural method of presenting them, the method most in accordance with the views themselves, seems to be by a procedure mainly impassive in its tone and tragic in its developments.

Things move in cycles; dormant principles renew themselves, and exhausted principles are thrust by. There is a revival of the artistic instincts towards great dramatic motives – setting forth that 'collision between the individual and the general' – formerly worked out with such force by the Periclean and Elizabethan dramatists,[1] to name no other. More than this, the periodicity which marks the course of taste in civilized countries does not take the form of a true cycle of repetition, but what Comte,[2] in speaking of general progress, happily character-izes as 'a looped orbit': not a movement of revolution but – to use the current word – evolution. Hence, in perceiving that taste is arriving anew at the point of high tragedy, writers are conscious that its revived presentation demands enrich-ment by further truths – in other words, original treatment: treatment which seeks to show Nature's unconsciousness not of essential laws, but of those laws framed merely as social expedients by humanity, without a basis in the heart of things; treatment which expresses the triumph of the crowd over the hero, of the commonplace majority over the exceptional few.

But originality makes scores of failures for one final success, precisely because its essence is to acknowledge no immediate precursor or guide. It is probably to these inevitable conditions of further acquisition that may be attributed some developments of naturalism in French novelists of the present day, and certain crude results from meritorious attempts in the same direction by intellectual adventurers here and there among our own authors.

Anyhow, conscientious fiction alone it is which can excite a reflective and abid-ing interest in the minds of thoughtful readers of mature age, who are weary of

---

1 By 'Periclean' dramatists, Hardy refers to Greek playwrights of the fifth century BC such as Aeschylus, Sophocles and Euripides; by 'Elizabethan' dramatists he means late sixteenth-century British playwrights such as Christopher Marlowe and William Shakespeare.
2 Auguste Comte (1798–1857), French philosopher.

puerile inventions and famishing for accuracy; who consider that, in representations of the world, the passions ought to be proportioned as in the world itself.
This is the interest which was excited in the minds of the Athenians by their
immortal tragedies, and in the minds of Londoners at the first performance of the
finer plays of three hundred years ago. They reflected life, revealed life, criticized
life. Life being a physiological fact, its honest portrayal must be largely concerned
with, for one thing, the relations of the sexes, and the substitution for such
catastrophes as favour the false colouring best expressed by the regulation finish
that 'they married and were happy ever after,' of catastrophes based upon
sexual relations as it is. To this expansion English society opposes a well-nigh
insuperable bar.

The popular vehicles for the introduction of a novel to the public have grown to
be, from one cause and another, the magazine and the circulating library; and the
object of the magazine and circulating library is not upward advance but lateral
advance; to suit themselves to what is called household reading, which means, or
is made to mean, the reading either of the majority in a household or of the
household collectively. The number of adults, even in a large household, being
normally two, and these being the members which, as a rule, have least time on
their hands to bestow on current literature, the taste of the majority can hardly be,
and seldom is, tempered by the ripe judgement which desires fidelity. However,
the immature members of a household often keep an open mind, and they might,
and no doubt would, take sincere fiction with the rest but for another condition,
almost generally co-existent: which is that adults who would desire true views for
their own reading insist, for a plausible but questionable reason, upon false views
for the reading of their young people.

As a consequence, the magazine in particular and the circulating library in
general do not foster the growth of the novel which reflects and reveals life. They
directly tend to exterminate it by monopolizing all literary space. Cause and effect
were never more clearly conjoined, though commentators upon the result, both
French and English, seem seldom if ever to trace their connection. A sincere and
comprehensive sequence of the ruling passions, however moral in its ultimate
bearings, must not be put on paper as the foundation of imaginative works, which
have to claim notice through the above-named channels, though it is extensively
welcomed in the form of newspaper reports. That the magazine and library have
arrogated to themselves the dispensation of fiction is not the fault of the authors,
but of circumstances over which they, as representatives of Grub Street,[3] have no
control.

What this practically amounts to is that the patrons of literature – no longer
Peers with a taste – acting under the censorship of prudery, rigorously exclude
from the pages they regulate subjects that have been made, by general approval of
the best judges, the bases of the finest imaginative compositions since literature
rose to the dignity of an art. The crash of broken commandments is as necessary
an accompaniment to the catastrophe of a tragedy as the noise of drum and
cymbals to a triumphal march. But the crash of broken commandments shall not

---

3   An area of London stereotypically associated with journalists and commercial writing, often with
    negative connotations.

be heard; or, if at all, but gently, like the roaring of Bottom[4] – gently as any sucking dove, or as 'twere any nightingale, lest we should fright the ladies out of their wits. More precisely, an arbitrary proclamation has gone forth that certain picked commandments of the ten shall be preserved intact – to wit, the first, third, and seventh; that the ninth shall be infringed but gingerly; the sixth only as much as necessary, and the remainder alone as much as you please, in a genteel manner.

It is in the self-consciousness engendered by interference with spontaneity, and in aims at a compromise to square with circumstances, that the real secret lies of the charlatanry pervading so much of English fiction. It may be urged that abundance of great and profound novels might be written which should require no compromising, contain not an episode deemed questionable by prudes. This I venture to doubt. In a ramification of the profounder passions the treatment of which makes the great style, something 'unsuitable' is sure to arise; and then comes the struggle with the literary conscience. The opening scenes of the would-be great story may, in a rash moment, have been printed in some popular magazine before the remainder is written; as it advances month by month the situations develop, and the writer asks himself, what will his characters do next? What would probably happen to them, given such beginnings? On his life and conscience, though he had not foreseen the thing, only one event could possibly happen, and that therefore he should narrate, as he calls himself a faithful artist. But, though pointing a fine moral, it is just one of those issues which are not to be mentioned in respectable magazines and select libraries. The dilemma then confronts him, he must either whip and scourge those characters into doing something contrary to their natures, to produce the spurious effect of their being in harmony with social forms and ordinances, or, by leaving them alone to act as they will, he must bring down the thunders of respectability upon his head, not to say ruin his editor, his publisher, and himself.

What he often does, indeed can scarcely help doing in such a strait, is, belie his literary conscience, do despite to his best imaginative instincts by arranging a dénouement which he knows to be indescribably unreal and meretricious, but dear to the Grundyist[5] and subscriber. If the true artist ever weeps it probably is then, when he first discovers the fearful price that he has to pay for the privilege of writing in the English language – no less a price than the complete extinction, in the mind of every mature and penetrating reader, of sympathetic belief in his personages.

To say that few of the old dramatic masterpieces, if newly published as a novel (the form which, experts tell us, they would have taken in modern conditions), would be tolerated in English magazines and libraries is a ludicrous understatement. Fancy a brazen young Shakespeare of our time – Othello, Hamlet, or Antony and Cleopatra never having yet appeared – sending up one of those creations in narrative form to the editor of a London magazine, with the author's compliments, and his hope that the story will be found acceptable to the editor's pages; suppose him, further, to have the temerity to ask for the candid remarks of

---

4   The weaver and actor in Shakespeare's *A Midsummer Night's Dream* who is magically bestowed with an ass's head and who, thus costumed, frightens and repels the fairy queen Titania.
5   After 'Mrs Grundy', an unseen exponent of conventional morality in the play *Speed the Plough* (1798), by Tom Morton.

the accomplished editor upon his manuscript. One can imagine the answer that young William would get for his mad supposition of such fitness from any one of the gentlemen who so correctly conduct that branch of the periodical Press.[6]

Why the ancient classic and old English tragedy can be regarded thus deeply, both by young people in their teens and by old people in their moralities, and the modern novel cannot be so regarded; why the honest and uncompromising delineation which makes the old stories and dramas lessons in life must make of the modern novel, following humbly on the same lines, a lesson in iniquity, is to some thinkers a mystery inadequately accounted for by the difference between old and new.

Whether minors should read unvarnished fiction based on the deeper passions, should listen to the eternal verities in the form of narrative, is of somewhat a different question from whether the novel ought to be exclusively addressed to those minors. The first consideration is one which must be passed over here; but it will be conceded by most friends of literature that all fiction should not be shackled by conventions concerning budding womanhood, which may be altogether false. It behooves us then to inquire how best to circumvent the present lording of nonage over maturity, and permit the explicit novel to be more generally written.

That the existing magazine and book-lending system will admit of any great modification is scarcely likely. As far as the magazine is concerned it has long been obvious that as a vehicle for fiction dealing with human feeling on a comprehensive scale it is tottering to its fall; and it will probably in the course of time take up openly the position that it already covertly occupies, that of a purveyor of tales for the youth of both sexes, as it assumes that tales for those rather numerous members of society ought to be written.

There remain three courses by which the adult may find deliverance. The first would be a system of publication under which books could be bought and not borrowed, when they would naturally resolve themselves into classes instead of being, as now, made to wear a common livery in style and subject, enforced by their supposed necessities in addressing indiscriminately a general audience.

But it is scarcely likely to be convenient to either authors or publishers that the periodical form of publication for the candid story should be entirely forbidden, and in retaining the old system thus far, yet ensuring that the emancipated serial novel should meet the eyes of those for whom it is intended, the plan of publication

---

6 [Hardy's note] It is, indeed, curious to consider what great works of the past the notions of the present day would aim to exclude from circulation, if not from publication, if they were issued as new fiction. In addition to those mentioned, think of the King Œdipus of Sophocles, the Agamemnon of Æschylus, Goethe's Faust and Wilhelm Meister, the Prometheus of Æschylus, Milton's Paradise Lost. The 'unpleasant subjects' of the two first-named compositions, the 'unsuitableness' of the next two, would be deemed equalled only by the profanity of the last two; for Milton, as it is hardly necessary to remind the reader, handles as his puppets the Christian divinities and fiends quite as freely as the Pagan divinities were handled by the Greek and Latin imaginative authors. Were the objections of the scrupulous limited to prurient treatment of the relations of the sexes, or to any view of vice calculated to undermine the essential principles of social order, all honest lovers of literature would be in accord with them. All really true literature directly or indirectly sounds as its refrain the words in the Agamemnon: 'Chant Ælinon, Ælinon! But may the good prevail.' But the writer may print the not of his broken commandment in capitals of flame; it makes no difference. A question which should be wholly a question of treatment is confusedly regarded as a question of subject.

as a feuilleton[7] in newspapers read mainly by adults might be more generally followed, as in France. In default of this, or coexistent with it, there might be adopted what, upon the whole, would perhaps find more favour than any with those who have artistic interests at heart, and that is, magazines for adults; exclusively for adults, if necessary. As an offshoot there might be at least one magazine for the middle-aged and old.

There is no foretelling; but this (since the magazine form of publication is so firmly rooted) is at least a promising remedy, if English prudery be really, as we hope, only a parental anxiety. There should be no mistaking the matter, no half measures. La dignité de la pensée, in the words of Pascal,[8] might then grow to be recognized in the treatment of fiction as in other things, and untrammelled adult opinion on conduct and theology might be axiomatically assumed and dramatically appealed to. Nothing in such literature should for a moment exhibit lax views of that purity of life upon which the well-being of society depends; but the position of man and woman in nature, and the position of belief in the minds of man and woman – things which everybody is thinking but nobody is saying – might be taken up and treated frankly.

Thomas Hardy, excerpt from serialized version of *Tess of the d'Urbervilles* (1891), in J.T. Laird, *The Shaping of* Tess of the D'Urbervilles (Oxford: Clarendon Press, 1975), p. 151

As described above (pp. 11–12), Hardy radically altered the nature of Alec's 'betrayal' of Tess in order to secure serial publication in the weekly *The Graphic* in 1891. By producing an alternative ending to what we now call Chapter 9, and eliminating entirely what we now call Chapters 10 and 11, Hardy excised the whole series of events involving the night of the Chaseborough dance. Having thus removed the rape and the child Sorrow from the plot, he was forced to produce a new motive for Tess's return home – a motive that would still function plausibly later in the novel as a guilty secret Tess would hide from Angel. The lines below represent Hardy's unsatisfactory solution to this dilemma. When the novel was published as a complete edition in late 1891, the excised plot elements were restored.

'Well! – my dear Tess!' exclaimed her surprised mother, jumping up and kissing the girl. 'How be ye? I didn't see you till you was in upon me! Have you come home to be married?'

'No, I have not come for that, mother.'

'Then for a holiday?'

'Yes – for a holiday; for a long holiday,' said Tess.

---

7   A French term denoting an article, literary sketch or serial instalment appearing in a special section of a newspaper, often at the bottom of a page. The term may also be applied to the section itself.

8   'The dignity of the thought', from the French mathmatician, theologian and philosopher Blaise Pascal (1623–62); the author of *Les Pensées* (1670), a justification of Christianity. Angel Clare quotes Pascal in *Tess*; see Key Passages p. 141 (*Tess* Chapter 18).

Her mother eyed her narrowly. 'Come, you have not told me all,' she said.

Then Tess told. 'He made love to me, as you said he would do; and he asked me to marry him, also just as you declared he would. I never have liked him; but at last I agreed, knowing you'd be angry if I didn't. He said it must be private, even from you, on account of his mother; and by special licence; and foolish I agreed to that likewise, to get rid of his pestering. I drove with him to Melchester, and there in a private room I went through the form of marriage with him as before a registrar. A few weeks after, I found out that it was not the registrar's house we had gone to, as I had supposed, but the house of a friend of his, who had played the part of the registrar. I then came away from Trantridge instantly, though he wished me to stay; and here I am.'

Thomas Hardy, Selection of Poems

Hardy's first volume of poetry, *Wessex Poems*, appeared in 1898, followed by *Poems of the Past and the Present* (1901), *Time's Laughingstocks* (1909), *Satires of Circumstance* (1914), *Moments of Vision* (1917), *Late Lyrics and Earlier* (1922), *Human Shows* (1925), and *Winter Words* (posthumous, 1928). His epic verse-drama *The Dynasts*, set in the Napoleonic period (1793–1815), was published in three instalments between 1904 and 1908.

The nine hundred poems Hardy wrote employ many styles, tones and levels of diction; their formats also range from balladic and narrative pieces to short impressionistic sketches, to sombre philosophical meditations. While some of his volumes of poetry were organized around internal thematic groupings (such as 'War Poems' and 'Poems of Pilgrimage' in *Poems of the Past and the Present*), it was not unusual for poems of jarringly disparate styles to appear beside one another. Hardy was unapologetic about such discontinuities, writing in the introduction to *Past and Present* that his poems represented:

a series of feelings and fancies written down in widely differing moods and circumstances, and at various dates; it will probably be found, therefore, to possess little cohesion of thought or harmony of colouring. I do not greatly regret this. Unadjusted impressions have their value, and the road to a true philosophy of life seems to lie in humbly recording diverse readings of its phenomena as they are forced upon us by chance and change.[1]

When Hardy first began publishing poetry, he was viewed as a novelist dabbling in another genre, but as the years went by and his commitment to poetry became fully apparent, his manifold strengths as a writer of verse became more widely acknowledged. He is now considered by many critics to be the earliest of the modernists in English poetry, and perhaps the most accomplished of any English writer in terms of his dual achievements in poetry and the novel.

It has been argued that there is no clear pattern of chronological development in Hardy's verse. Whether or not this is true, the selection below is

1   Qtd Samuel Hynes, ed. *The Complete Poetical Works of Thomas Hardy*, vol. 1 (Oxford: Clarendon Press, 1982), p. 113.

organized thematically rather than chronologically. The first group is made up of poems that employ characters and settings from *Tess*; the second, beginning with 'The Ruined Maid', is comprised of poems that reconfigure some of socio-sexual conflicts of the novel, specifically those involving illegitimacy and the dangerous intersection of sexual desire and social class; and the third group, beginning with 'Winter in Durnover Field', consists of poems that pursue some of the broad thematic issues (fate, chance, time, the indifference of nature) that underlie not only *Tess* but the entirety of Hardy's novelistic *corpus*.

Most of these poems were first published in the volume *Poems of the Past and the Present* (1901); the exceptions are 'The Turnip-Hoer' and 'A Hurried Meeting', first published in *Human Shows* (1925), and 'We Field-Women', first published in *Winter Words* (1928). The specific texts below are drawn from a variety of editions of Hardy's poetry: 'Tess's Lament', 'The Ruined Maid', 'At a Hasty Wedding', 'Winter in Durnover Field', 'Doom and She', and 'The Lacking Sense' are drawn from *Wessex Poems and Other Verses: Poems of the Past and the Present* (London: Macmillan, 1912). The text of 'The Well-Beloved' is from *The Collected Poems of Thomas Hardy* (London: Macmillan, 1919). Texts of 'The Turnip-Hoer', 'A Hurried Meeting', and 'We Field-Women' are from the first editions of their original volumes, noted above.

Tess's Lament

I

I would that folk forgot me quite,
    Forgot me quite!
I would that I could shrink from sight,
    And no more see the sun.
Would it were time to say farewell,
To claim my nook, to need my knell,
Time for them all to stand and tell
    O' my day's work as done.

II

Ah! dairy where I lived so long,
    I lived so long;
Where I would rise up stanch[2] and strong,
    And lie down hopefully.
'Twas there within the chimney-seat
He watched me to the clock's slow beat –
Loved me, and learnt to call me Sweet,
    And whispered words to me.

2 Quenched or satisfied.

III

And now he's gone; and now he's gone; . . .
    And now he's gone!
The flowers we potted p'rhaps are thrown
    To rot upon the farm.
And where we had our supper-fire
May now grow nettle, dock, and briar,
And all the place be mould and mire
    So cozy once and warm.

IV

And it was I who did it all,
    Who did it all;
'Twas I who made the blow to fall
    On him who thought no guile.
Well, it is finished – past, and he
Has left me to my misery,
And I must take my Cross on me
    For wronging him awhile.

V

How gay we looked that day we wed,
    That day we wed!
'May joy be with ye!' all o'm said
    A standing by the durn.[3]
I wonder what they say o's now,
And if they know my lot; and how
She feels who milks my favourite cow,
    And takes my place at churn!

VI

It wears me out to think of it,
    To think of it;
I cannot bear my fate as writ,
    I'd have my life unbe;
Would turn my memory to a blot,
Make every relic of me rot,
My doings be as they were not,
    And leave no trace of me!

---

3   A doorpost or wooden door frame.

We Field-Women

How it rained
When we worked at Flintcomb-Ash,
And could not stand upon the hill
Trimming swedes for the slicing-mill.
The wet washed through us – plash, plash, plash:
How it rained!

How it snowed
When we crossed from Flintcomb-Ash
To the Great Barn for drawing reed,
Since we could nowise chop a swede. –
Flakes in each doorway and casement-sash:
How it snowed!

How it shone
When we went from Flintcomb-Ash
To start at dairywork once more
In the laughing meads, with cows threescore,
And pails, and songs, and love – too rash:
How it shone!

The Well-Beloved

I wayed by star and planet shine
    Towards the dear one's home
At Kingsbere,[4] there to make her mine
    When the next sun upclomb.

I edged the ancient hill and wood
    Beside the Ikling Way,
Nigh where the Pagan temple[5] stood
    In the world's earlier day.

And as I quick and quicker walked
    On gravel and on green,
I sang to sky, and tree, or talked
    Of her I called my queen.

– 'O faultless is her dainty form,
    And luminous her mind;
She is the God-created norm
    Of perfect womankind!'

A shape whereon one star-blink gleamed
    Glode[6] softly by my side,
A woman's; and her motion seemed
    The motion of my bride.

4   In *Tess*, Kingsbere is the ancient family seat of the d'Urbervilles.
5   A stone circle like that of Stonehenge or Avebury.
6   Glided.

And yet methought she'd drawn erstwhile
    Adown the ancient leaze,[7]
Where once were pile and peristyle[8]
    For men's idolatries.

– 'O maiden lithe and lone, what may
    Thy name and lineage be,
Who so resemblest by this ray
    My darling? – Art thou she?'

The Shape: 'Thy bride remains within
    Her father's grange and grove.'
– 'Thou speakest rightly,' I broke in,
    'Thou art not she I love.'

– 'Nay: though thy bride remains inside
    Her father's walls,' said she,
'The one most dear is with thee here,
    For thou dost love but me.'

Then I: 'But she, my only choice,
    Is now at Kingsbere Grove?'
Again her soft mysterious voice:
    'I am thy only Love.'

Thus still she vouched, and still I said,
    'O sprite, that cannot be!' . . .
It was as if my bosom bled,
    So much she troubled me.

The sprite resumed: 'Thou hast transferred
    To her dull form awhile
My beauty, fame, and deed, and word,
    My gestures and my smile.

'O fatuous man, this truth infer,
    Brides are not what they seem;
Thou lovest what thou dreamest her;
    I am thy very dream!'

– 'O then,' I answered miserably,
Speaking as scarce I knew,
'My loved one, I must wed with thee
    If what thou say'st be true!'

She, proudly, thinning in the gloom:
    'Though, since troth-plight[9] began,
I've ever stood as bride to groom,
    I wed no mortal man!'

---

7 An archaic term for a meadow or plain.
8 A building or courtyard enclosed by columns.
9 The act of making a pledge to marry.

Thereat she vanished by the Cross
   That, entering Kingsbere town,
The two long lanes form, near the fosse[10]
   Below the faneless Down.[11]

– When I arrived and met my bride,
   Her look was pinched and thin,
As if her soul had shrunk and died,
   And left a waste within.

The Ruined Maid

'O 'Melia, my dear, this does everything crown!
Who could have supposed I should meet you in Town?
And whence such fair garments, such prosperi-ty?' –
'O didn't you know I'd been ruined?' said she.

– 'You left us in tatters, without shoes or socks,
Tired of digging potatoes, and spudding up docks;[12]
And now you've gay bracelets and bright feathers three!' –
'Yes: that's how we dress when we're ruined,' said she.

– 'At home in the barton[13] you said "thee" and "thou",
And "thik oon", and "theäs oon", and "t'other"; but now
Your talking quite fits 'ee for high compa-ny!' –
'A polish is gained with one's ruin,' said she.

– 'Your hands were like paws then, your face blue and bleak,
But now I'm bewitched by your delicate cheek,
And your little gloves fit as on any la-dy!' –
'We never do work when we're ruined,' said she.

– 'You used to call home-life a hag-ridden dream,
And you'd sigh, and you'd sock; but at present you seem
To know not of megrims[14] or melancho-ly!' –
'True. One's pretty lively when ruined,' said she.

– 'I wish I had feathers, a fine sweeping gown,
And a delicate face, and could strut about Town!' –
'My dear – a raw country girl, such as you be,
Cannot quite expect that. You ain't ruined,' said she.

---

10 A ditch or trench.
11 A flat expanse of land unmarked by a 'fane'; that is, unmarked by an alter or a place for worship.
12 Weeds, dug with a sharp tool called a spud.
13 Farm.
14 Migraine headaches or, more generally, fits of depression or moodiness.

At a Hasty Wedding (Triolet)[15]

If hours be years the twain are blest,
For now they solace swift desire
By bonds of every bond the best,
If hours be years. The twain are blest
Do eastern stars slope never west,
Nor pallid ashes follow fire:
If hours be years the twain are blest,
For now they solace swift desire.

A Hurried Meeting

It is August moonlight in the tall plantation,
Whose elms, by aged squirrels' footsteps worn,
 Outscreen the noon, and eve, and morn.
On the facing slope a faint irradiation
 From a mansion's marble front is borne,
  Mute in its woodland wreathing.
 Up here the night-jar[16] whirrs forlorn,
And the trees seem to withhold their softest breathing.

To the moonshade slips a woman in muslin vesture:
Her naked neck the goassamer-web besmears,
 And she sweeps it away with a hasty gesture.
Again it touches her forehead, her neck, her ears,
 Her fingers, the backs of her hands.
  She sweeps it away again
  Impatiently, and then
She takes no notice; and listens, and sighs, and stands.

The night-hawk stops. A man shows in the obscure:
 They meet, and passively kiss,
And he says: 'Well, I've come quickly. About this –
  Is it really so? You are sure?'
 'I am sure. In February it will be.
 That such a thing should come to me!
We should have known. We should have left off meeting.
Love is a terrible thing: a sweet allure
  That ends in heart-outeating!'

 'But what shall we do, my Love, and how?'
 'You need not call me by that name now.'
Then he more coldly: 'What is your suggestion?'
 'I've told my mother, and she sees a way,
Since of our marriage there can be no question.

---

15 A eight-line poem (or stanza), rhyming *abaaabab*, in which the fourth and seventh lines are the same as the first, and the eighth line is the same as the second. See also 'Winter in Durnover Field' (p. 35).
16 A nocturnal bird, sometimes called a goatsucker.

We are crossing South – near about New Year's Day
   The event will happen there.
It is the only thing that we can dare
   To keep them unaware!'
    'Well, you can marry me.'
She shook her head. 'No: that can never be.

   'Twill be brought home as hers. She's forty-one,
When many a woman's bearing is not done,
   And well might have a son. –
We should have left off specious self-deceiving:
   I feared that such might come,
   And knowledge struck me numb.
Love is a terrible thing: witching when first begun,
   To end in grieving, grieving!'

And with one kiss again the couple parted:
Inferior clearly he; she haughty-hearted.
He watched her down the slope to return to her place,
The marble mansion of her ancient race,
And saw her brush the gossamers from her face
As she emerged from shade to the moonlight ray.
    And when she had gone away
   The night-jar seemed to imp,[17] and say,
    'You should have taken warning:
Love is a terrible thing: sweet for a space,
   And then all mourning, mourning!'

The Turnip-Hoer

   Of tides that toss the souls of men
Some are foreseen, and weathered warefully;
More burst at flood, none witting why or when,
   And are called Destiny.

   – Years past there was a turnip-hoer,
Who loved his wife and child, and worked amain
In the turnip-time from dawn till day outwore
   And night bedimmed the plain.

   The thronging plants of blueish green
Would fall in lanes before his skilful blade,
Which, as by sleight, would deftly slip between
   Those spared and those low-laid.

17 Enlarge.

'Twas afternoon: he hoed his best,
Unlifting head or eye, when, through the fence,
He heard a gallop dropping from the crest
    Of the hill above him, whence,

Descending at a crashing pace,
An open carriage came, horsed by a pair:
A lady sat therein, with lilywhite face
    And wildly windblown hair.

The man sprang over, and horse and horse
Faced in the highway as the pair ondrew;
Like Terminus[18] stood he there, and barred their course.
    And almost ere he knew

The lady was limp within his arms,
And, half-unconscious, clutched his hair and beard;
And so he held her, till from neighbouring farms
    Came hinds,[19] and soon appeared

Footman and coachman on the way: –
The steeds were guided back, now breath-bespent,
And the hoer was rewarded with good pay: –
    So passed the accident.

'She was the Duchess of Southernshire,
They tell me,' said the second hoe, next day:
'She's come a-visiting not far from here;
    This week will end her stay.'

The hoer's wife that evening set
Her hand to a crusted stew in the three-legged pot,
And he sat looking on in silence; yet
    The cooking saw he not,

But a woman, with her arms around him,
Glove-handed, clasping his neck and clutching his blouse,
And ere he went to bed that night he found him
    Outside a manor-house.

A page there smoking answered him:
'Her Grace's room is where you see that light;
By now she's up there slipping off her trim:
    The Dook's is on the right.'

She was, indeed, just saying through the door,
'That dauntless fellow saved me from collapse:
I'd not much with me, or 'd have given him more:
    'Twas not enough, perhaps!'

---

18 Roman deity who governed boundaries.
19 Farm workers or labourers.

Up till she left, before he slept,
He walked, though tired, to where her window shined,
And mused till it went dark; but close he kept
   All that was in his mind.

'What is it, Ike?' inquired his wife;
'You are not so nice now as you used to be.
What have I done? You seem quite tired of life!'
   'Nothing at all,' said he.

In the next shire this lady of rank,
So 'twas made known, would open a bazaar:
He took his money from the savings-bank
   To go there, for 'twas far.

And reached her stall, and sighted, clad
In her ripe beauty and the goodliest guise,
His Vision of late. He straight spent all he had,
   But not once caught her eyes.

Next week he heard, with heart of clay,
That London held her for three months or so:
Fearing to tell his wife he went for a day,
   Pawning his watch to go;

And scanned the Square of her abode,
And timed her moves, as well as he could guess,
That he might glimpse her; till afoot by road
   He came home penniless . . .

– The Duke in Wessex once again,
Glanced at the Wessex paper, where he read
Of a man, late taken to drink, killed by a train
   At a crossing, so it said.

'Why – he who saved your life, I think?'
– 'O no,' said she. 'It cannot be the same:
He was sweet-breath'd, without a taint of drink;
   Yet it is like his name.'

Winter in Durnover Field (Triolet)[20]

SCENE. – *A wide stretch of fallow ground recently sown with wheat,
and frozen to iron hardness. Three large birds walking about thereon,
and wistfully eyeing the surface. Wind keen from north-east: sky a
dull grey.*

---

20 A eight-line poem (or stanza), rhyming *abaaabab*, in which the fourth and seventh lines are the
   same as the first, and the eighth line is the same as the second. See also 'At a Hasty Wedding' (p. 32).

Rook. – Throughout the field I find no grain;
      The cruel frost encrusts the cornland!
Starling. – Aye: patient pecking now is vain
      Throughout the field, I find . . .
Rook. –   No grain!
Pigeon. – Nor will be, comrade, till it rain,
      Or genial thawings loose the lorn land
      Throughout the field.
Rook. –   I find no grain:
      The cruel frost encrusts the cornland!

Doom and She

I

There dwells a mighty pair –
Slow, statuesque, intense –
Amid the vague Immense:
None can their chronicle declare,
    Nor why they be, nor whence.

II

Mother of all things made,
Matchless in artistry,
Unlit with sight is she. –
And though her ever well-obeyed
    Vacant of feeling he.

III

The Matron mildly asks –
A throb in every word –
'Our clay-made creatures, lord,
How fare they in their mortal tasks
    Upon Earth's bounded bord?

IV

'The fate of those I bear,
Dear lord, pray turn and view,
And notify me true;
Shapings that eyelessly I dare
    Maybe I would undo.

V

'Sometimes from lairs of life
Methinks I catch a groan,
Or multitudinous moan,
As though I had schemed a world of strife,
    Working by touch alone.'

VI

'World-weaver!' he replies,
     'I scan all thy domain;
     But since nor joy nor pain
It lies in me to recognize,
     Thy questionings are vain.

VII

'World-weaver! what *is* Grief?
     And what are Right, and Wrong,
     And Feeling, that belong
To creatures all who owe thee fief?
     Why is Weak worse than Strong?' . . .

VIII

– Unanswered, curious, meek,
     She broods in sad surmise . . .
     – Some say they have heard her sighs
On Alpine height or Polar peak
     When the night tempests rise.

The Lacking Sense

SCENE. – *A sad-coloured landscape, Waddon Vale*

I

'O Time, whence comes the Mother's moody look amid her labours,
     As of one who all unwittingly has wounded where she loves?
Why weaves she not her world-webs to according lutes and tabors,[21]
     With nevermore this too remorseful air upon her face,
          As of angel fallen from grace?'

II

– 'Her look is but her story: construe not its symbols keenly:
     In her wonderworks yea surely has she wounded where she loves.
The sense of ills misdealt for blisses blanks the mien most queenly,
     Self-smitings kill self-joys; and everywhere beneath the sun
          Such deeds her hands have done.'

---

21 Two musical instruments (one stringed, the other a drum), each associated with ancient times.

III

– 'And how explains thy Ancient Mind her crimes upon her creatures,
　　These fallings from her fair beginnings, woundings where she loves,
Into her would-be perfect motions, modes, effects, and features
　　Admitting cramps, black humours, wan decay, and baleful blights,
　　Distress into delights?'

IV

– 'Ah! knowest thou not her secret yet, her vainly veiled deficience,
　　Whence it comes that all unwittingly she wounds the lives she loves?
That sightless are those orbs of hers? – which bar to her omniscience
　　Brings those fearful unfulfilments, that red ravage through her zones
　　Whereat all creation groans.

V

'She whispers it in each pathetic strenuous slow endeavour,
　　When in mothering she unwittingly sets wounds on what she loves;
Yet her primal doom pursues her, faultful, fatal is she ever;
　　Though so deft and nigh to vision is her facile finger-touch
　　That the seers marvel much.

VI

'Deal, then, her groping skill no scorn, no note of malediction;
　　Not long on thee will press the hand that hurts the lives it loves;
And while she dares dead-reckoning on, in darkness of affliction,
　　Assist her where thy creaturely dependence can or may,
　　For thou art of her clay.'

Richard Jeffries, 'The Labourer's Daily Life', *Fraser's Magazine,* n.s. 10
(November 1874), pp. 654–5, 663

Richard Jeffries (1848–87), a writer of diverse interests, was best known for his essays on agricultural life. In these numerous pieces, published in *Fraser's Magazine, The Pall Mall Gazette, Longman's Magazine* and many others, he aimed at a tone of reportorial impartiality, striving for objective accounts of rural conditions – yet also, as seen below, appealing to the emotions through shared ideas of beauty and hardship. In the aggregate his essays reflect his view that the lives of the farmer and labourer were becoming more difficult, despite supposed advances in agricultural technology and educational opportunity. Raised in Wiltshire, essentially the area of 'mid-Wessex' in Hardy's conception, Jeffries was strongly identified with this region. One of his essays, 'The Wiltshire Labourer' (1883), was published in *Longman's* as a follow-up to an essay by Hardy, 'The Dorsetshire Labourer', which the magazine had published a few months earlier. Jeffries is also known for his autobiography, *The Story of My Heart* (1883), which is less a chronological record than a rapturous account of his revelatory awakening to the fullness of Nature's presence.

The essays represented here are mainly informational, addressing social customs and practices that are relevant to Hardy's portrayals in *Tess*. It should be noted that in the first excerpt, the terms 'farmer' and 'labourer' are not interchangeable. A farmer works his own plot of ground, a plot either owned or, more likely, rented. A labourer works on a for-hire basis, much in the way that Tess does after she leaves Talbothays dairy. The second excerpt provides background for the harvest scenes in Chapter 14 which immediately precede the famous 'midnight baptism' episode (see Key Passages, p. 136).

Many labourers can trace their descent from farmers or well-to-do people, and it is not uncommon to find here and there a man who believes he is entitled to large property in Chancery,[1] or elsewhere, as the heir. They are very fond of talking of these things, and naturally take a pride in feeling themselves a little superior in point of ancestry to the mass of labourers. [. . .]

[. . .] [The agricultural classes] work and live and have their being in grooves. So long as they can continue in that groove, and go steadily forward, without much thought or trouble beyond that of patience and perseverance, all goes well; but if any sudden jolt should throw them out of this rut they seem incapable of regaining it. They say, 'I have lost my way; I shall never get it again.' They sit down and regret the past, granting all their errors with the greatest candour; but the efforts they make to regain their position are feeble in the extreme.

So our typical unfortunate farmer folds his hands, and in point of fact slumbers away the rest of his existence, content with the fire-side, and a roof over his head, and a jug of beer to drink. He does not know French [. . .] but he puts the famous maxim in practice, and, satisfied with to-day, says in his heart, *Après nous le Déluge.*[2] No one disturbs him; his landlord has a certain respect and pity for him – respect, perhaps, for an old family that has tilled his land for a century, but which he now sees is slowly but irretrievably passing away. So the decayed farmer dozes out his existence.

[. . .] The summer is the labourer's good season. Then he can make money and enjoy himself. In the summer three or four men will often join together and leave their native parish for a ramble. They walk off perhaps some forty or fifty miles, take a job mowing or harvesting, and after a change of scenery and associates return in the later part of the autumn, full of the things they have seen, and eager to relate them to the groups at the cross-roads or the ale-house. The winter is under the best circumstances a hard time for the labourer. It is not altogether that coals are dear[3] and firewood growing scarcer year by year, but every condition of his daily life has a harshness about it. In the summer the warm sunshine cast a glamour over the rude walls, the decaying thatch, and the ivy-covered window.

---

1   The branch of the English legal system in which wills and inheritances were litigated.
2   'After us, the Flood'. This remark is usually understood as an expression of the speaker's lack of concern for what will happen after he or she dies.
3   Costly.

The blue smoke rose curling beside the tall elm-tree. The hedge parting his garden from the road was green and thick, the garden itself full of trees, and flowers of more or less beauty. Mud floors are not so bad in the summer; holes in the thatch do not matter so much; an ill-fitting window-sash gives no concern. But with the cold blasts and ceaseless rain of winter all this is changed. The hedge next the road is usually only elder, and this, once the leaves are off, is the thinnest, most miserable of shelters. The rain comes through the hole in the thatch (we are speaking of the large class of poor cottages), the mud floor is damp, and perhaps sticky. If the floor is of uneven stones, these grow damp and slimy. The cold wind comes through the ill-fitting sash, and drives with terrible force under the door. Very often the floor is one step lower than the ground outside, and consequently there is a constant tendency in rainy weather for the water to run or soak in. The elm tree overhead, that appeared so picturesque in summer, is now a curse, for the great drops that fall perpetually from it upon the thatch and on the pathway in front of the door.

Richard Jeffries, 'Field-Faring Women', *Fraser's Magazine*, n.s. 12 (September 1875), pp. 382–5

Very few agricultural women have a medical man present at their confinement;[1] they usually entrust themselves to the care of some village nurse, who has a reputation for skill in such matters, but no scientifically acquired knowledge, – who proceeds by rule of thumb. The doctor [. . .] is not called in till after the delivery. The poor woman will frequently come downstairs on the fourth day; and it is to this disregard of proper precautions that the distortions of figure and many of the illnesses of poor agricultural women are attributable. Nothing but the severe training they have gone through from childhood upwards – the exposure to all kinds of weather – the life in the open air, the physical strength induced by labour, can enable them to support the strain upon the frame caused by so quickly endeavouring to resume their household duties. It is probably this reserve of strength which enables them to recover from so serious a matter so quickly. Certainly it is that very few die from confinement; and yet, from the point of view of the middle classes of society, almost every precaution and every luxury by them deemed necessary is omitted. [. . .]

[. . .] In the soft, warm, summer-time, when the Midsummer hum of the myriads of insects in the air sheds a drowsy harmony over the tree-tops, the field-faring woman goes out to haymaking, and leaves her baby in the shade by the hedge-side. A wooden sheepcage,[2] turned upside down and filled with new-made hay, forms not at all a despicable cradle; and here the little thing lies on its back and inhales the fresh pure air, and feels the warmth of the genial sun, cheered from time to time by visits from its busy mother. Perhaps this is the only true poetry of the hayfield, so much talked of and praised. [. . .] The Arcadian[3] innocence of the hayfield, sung by the poets, is the most barefaced fiction; for those times are the

---

1 The period of childbirth.
2 A small rectangular box used for capturing or confining sheep.
3 Referring to the Greek region of Arcadia, and connoting rustic peace, purity and contentment.

rural saturnalia,[4] and the broadest and coarsest of jokes and insinuations are freely circulated; nor does it always stop at language only, provided the master is out of sight. Matrons and young girls alike come in for an equal share of this rude treatment, and are quite a match for the men in the force of compliment. [. . .] It is not that the hayfield itself originates this coarseness, but this is almost the only time of the year when the labouring classes work together in large numbers. A great deal of farm-work is comparatively solitary; in harvest droves of people are collected together, and the inherent vulgarity comes out more strongly. At the wheat-harvest the women go reaping, and exceedingly hard they work at it. There is no harder work under the sun than reaping, if it is well followed up. From earliest dawn to latest night they swing the sickles, staying with their husbands, and brother, and friends till the moon silvers the yellow corn.

Anon., 'The Virgin Forest [of Brazil]', *Bentley's Miscellany*, 55 (May 1864), pp. 479–81

This account opens by describing Brazil in colonial terms; it is avowedly Eurocentric in outlook, and suggests something of the mentality of the wealthy English planter, landowner, or tourist who saw the country as a primitive civilization awaiting European models of economic progress. As such, it can be seen as articulating a perspective that Angel Clare would encounter in trying to establish himself there as a farmer or plantation owner. Primarily, of course, Hardy ironizes such rhetoric by portraying Angel's Brazilian adventure (described in Chapters 41 and 49), like that of many a deluded English settler, as an appalling disaster. Yet the enthusiasm of this anonymous writer has other resonances with *Tess*: consider the comparison of the Brazilian rainforest with druidical groves, and the suggestion that confronting the forest's immensity may lead to spiritual cleansing or epiphany.

For the traveller the virgin forest is divided into three belts: that of the inns, that of the plantations, and that of the uninhabited primeval forest. The first is the smallest, and ends at a short distance from the large seaboard towns and the provincial capitals. It cannot be travelled through with any great amount of pleasure – at least not by the European, who never grows accustomed to the smells produced in the inns by salt fish, spirits, and negroes, and the myriads of insects.

It is capital travelling in the zone of the plantations. If the visitor has but one letter of introduction to a planter, he is recommended by him to another, and everywhere he meets with the most friendly reception. You travel by short stages from plantation to plantation, see something new every day, and hardly anywhere feel a privation of European comforts. If, however, led astray by the demon of curiosity, you venture into the forests of the interior, you must take leave of all reminiscences of civilization. Even the footpaths soon disappear, and you must either go up the rivers in an Indian canoe, or cut a road with a bowie-knife through the impenetrable scrub and thorn-bushes. At night you take shelter in a deserted hut, or hastily make a refuge of branches. [. . .]

---

4   A period of licentiousness and sexual revelry.

If a visit to the virgin forest is to terminate well, a suitable season must be selected. In the south of Brazil, the months from May to October are the most favourable. This period is an eternal spring, such as is seen on the finest days in Provence and Italy. The cold nights and fresh mornings make up for the sultry heat of the day. So soon as the sky returns to its austral path, the atmosphere becomes oppressive, and the sky incandescent. The continuous rains that fall till April and evaporate in the hot sunbeams cover the soil with a dense veil of mist. In this moisture the smallest parasitical plants attain an unheard-of development. After resting for two or three days at a plantation and looking up your boots again, you find them covered with a perfect vegetation of whitish mould.

[. . .] The first impression of entering a virgin forest is composed of amazement and superstitious terror. You think involuntarily of the mysterious shades of the Druidic groves, where the Gauls performed their sanguinary sacrifices. Here the tribes of the desert have contended for centuries. The primeval witnesses of these savage wars of extermination could tell many a dramatic story. Under this bush, with its perfumed flowers, the snake conceals itself; at the foot of this stump, the jaguar and the caiman watch for their prey. If the traveller does not heed the danger, and defies the green wall that rises before him, he at once finds himself entangled in an inextricable net of grasses, plants, and boughs. His hands are caught, his feet seek in vain a support, sharp thorns lacerate his flesh, lianas lash his face, and the gloom heightens his embarrassment. In an instant he is covered by myriads of eggs, caterpillars, insects, and parasites of every description, which penetrate his clothes and bore into his flesh. But when he has grown accustomed to the desert, and his body can endure tropical fatigues and privations, everything becomes smooth before him. His foot grows firm, his eye pierces the leaf-work, his senses acquire a supernatural force, the terrible sanctuary opens its gates to him. The marvels of civilization appear to him as paltry in comparison with this boundless nature, which gives him liberty as a companion, the desert for a home, and infinity as a horizon. Thus he steps fearlessly into the previously inaccessible network. Difficulties seem to disappear, dangers to retreat, and the traveller might almost say that the forest has declared itself his protector, and received him into its family.

James Fergusson, 'Stonehenge', *Quarterly Review*, 108 (July 1860), pp. 202–3, 212

Fergusson (1808–86) was one of the leading nineteenth-century theorists on the origins of Stonehenge and other ancient structures; his books include *Rude Stone Monuments in All Countries: Their Ages and Uses* (London: John Murray, 1872). Although Stonehenge is now thought to date from somewhere between 4000 BC and 2000 BC, Fergusson believed it was not this old and not the work of pre-Roman Druids; rather, he hypothesizes, it 'was erected by Aurelius Ambrosius, who reigned from about 464 to 508 AD,[1] and who raised it as a memorial

---

1   The legendary champion of the British race, supposed to have led the Britons in their fifth-century wars against Saxon invaders from northern Europe.

to those who fell in the Saxon war' (p. 212); in *Rude Stone Monuments* he suggests that it may date from even later. Fergusson viewed most earlier theorists on such structures as 'speculative dreamers' (Preface, *Rude Stone Monuments*) who were insufficiently versed in architectural and scientific practicalities. Even so, in the following account he acknowledges that the visceral wonderment provoked by Stonehenge is so powerful that 'man's agency' in its construction is easily forgotten. (When this piece appeared in the *Quarterly*, Fergusson was not credited, but he later claimed authorship.) When Hardy composed the scene in which Tess and Angel speculate on the origins of Stonehenge, then, he was not introducing a subject utterly new to the reading public, but rather one whose existing associations he could manipulate and redirect for the final crisis of his novel.

It would indeed be difficult to find a building more likely to invite speculation than Stonehenge. There is a grandeur even in its situation which adds immensely to its interest, standing as it does in the centre of a vast open plain, where till very recently no sign of husbandry[2] was to be seen, nor any dwelling or marks of occupation by living man. Every part of the plain is dotted with little groups of barrows marking the monuments of chiefs who had no means of recording their deeds or even their names, but trusted to the rude mound of earth and the pious memories of those acts they seemed so anxious to perpetuate. When viewed from a distance the vastness of the open tract in which Stonehenge stands takes considerably from its impressiveness, but when the observer gets close to its great monolithic masses the solitary situation lends it a grandeur which scarcely any other building of its class can be said to possess. [. . .] [I]ts diameter is greater than the width of the portico of the Parthenon at Athens, the outer circle of stones being 108 feet, or almost exactly the internal diameter of the dome of St. Paul's. [. . .] The Stonehenge blocks have been rudely chiselled and squared into the required shape, but the exposure to the weather during fourteen centuries has so eaten away the softer parts, and the lichens have so rounded off the sharper edges, that there is perhaps no monument in contemplating which we are more inclined to forget man's agency, and in the chaos of ruin in which it now exists to fancy we are looking on some freak of nature which had fashioned these gigantic masses, and heaped them together in such unfamiliar forms and such strange confusion.

2   The keeping of animals.

2

Interpretations

Critical History

An early review of *Tess of the d'Urbervilles* posed the challenge, 'Why should a novelist embroil himself in moral technicalities?' – and, for the ensuing century and more, Hardy's lushest, yet most torturous work has generated a maelstrom of critical discussion and controversy. As daunting as this mass of criticism may appear, however, it is given shape by two powerful tendencies of interpretation. On one side has been an impulse to focus upon Tess herself – as a character and an imaginative construct – and to do so with an intensity that sometimes suggests a slippage into viewing her as a 'real' or historical person. But equally strong has been a tendency to shift attention away from the particularities of her representation, and toward the larger Hardyean themes of thwarted desire, unalterable destiny and Britain's dubious progress from agrarian to industrial modes of living – and thus, by extension, to the status of the novel within yet broader contexts of social and literary history.

One might ordinarily be tempted to say that these are warring or mutually exclusive tendencies in literary criticism; and indeed, they have often led discussants of *Tess* in quite different directions. But more striking, in this body of work, is the extent to which individual critics seem compelled, while pursuing one approach, to account for the other. It often seems, in other words, as if critical readers of this novel are just as deeply invested as Hardy was himself in the linkage between Tess Durbeyfield the fictional character and *Tess of the d'Urbervilles* the novelistic whole. And this is to say a great deal. The biographer Michael Millgate noted in 1971 that 'Nothing is more remarkable in the novel than the extraordinary passion with which Tess is described and justified' (see **p. 168**); and a friend of Hardy's commented that the writer spoke of Tess 'as if she were someone real whom he had known and liked tremendously'.[1] A question obtrudes itself, then: how do we as readers feel about Hardy's strength of feeling? Or, more sharply, how are Hardy's aspirations as a literary artist, and as a social critic, complicated – perhaps compromised – by that undercurrent of emotion? While early critics saw Hardy's intense authorial sympathy as having tempted him towards meretricious claims for Tess's 'purity', modern commentators have

---

1 Florence Emily Hardy, *The Life of Thomas Hardy, 1840–1828* (London: St Martin's, 1962), p. 429.

tended to take a longer view of the case, as seen in John Bayley's observation that Hardy's 'erotic image of Tess is fixed and overmastering, and it also represents [. . .] the culmination of [his] [. . .] daydreams on a womanly image' (p. 75). The movement here, from late-Victorian evaluations of Tess's morality to late twentieth-century considerations of Thomas Hardy's conscious or unconscious desires, could well be said to write small the revolutions in critical theory that have occurred over the last century, in which the idea that an author can control the production and reception of a literary text has been increasingly challenged. But for the moment, a simpler point suffices. To say that this novel is 'about' Tess is potentially to say a number of very different things, and, while Hardy's drive to justify her has met with a variety of responses, both celebratory and hostile, the existence of that drive has never been in dispute. The aim of this Critical History, then, is to emphasize negotiation and dialogue, rather than rigid divisions, among various approaches to the novel.

We may begin with the proposition that early critiques of *Tess* are often more subtle than meets the eye of the modern reader. Victorian reviewers did indeed tend to advance the idea of Tess as a real person without the questions and qualifications we would pose today. And, also unlike most critics from the middle twentieth century onward, most of these early readers were operating within an interpretive model that presumed the inextricability of aesthetic and moral concerns. Thus, Hardy's portrayal of Tess was simultaneously checked against standards of believability (was her portrayal consistent with demographic expectations of labouring-class life?) and standards of conduct (was Tess really 'pure'?, was her behaviour defensible?). This type of inquiry may seem simplistic within a modern framework, but within the framework of late-Victorian novelistic realism it was a high-stakes enterprise admitting of much internal complexity. Indeed, for Victorian critics the didactic tenor of a novel was all-important to its artistic valuation.

Accordingly, much early criticism on *Tess* is devoted to proving that novelistic 'nature' – that is, realism – abhors a moral vacuum. Richard Holt Hutton, for example, though careful to locate his reservations within Hardy's own argumentative and artistic framework, concludes, 'we cannot for a moment admit that even on his own portraiture of the circumstances of the case, Tess acted as a pure woman should have acted under such a stress of temptation and peril. Though pure in instinct, she was not faithful to her pure instinct' (see p. 58). Margaret Oliphant negotiates the intersection of morality and characterological consistency in slightly different terms, accepting for the most part the viability of Tess's depiction, but arguing that, when it breaks down, it does so not simply as a localized failure of craft but as a manifestation of the failure of Hardy's entire cosmology:

> The character of Tess up to her last downfall [. . .] is consistent enough, and we do not object to the defiant blazon of a Pure Woman, notwithstanding the early stain. But a Pure Woman is not betrayed into fine living and fine clothes as the mistress of her seducer by any stress of poverty or misery; and Tess was a skilled labourer, for whom it is very rare that nothing can be found to do. [. . .] We do not for a moment believe that Tess would have done it. Her creator has forced the *rôle* upon her, as he thinks (or says) that the God whom he does not believe in, does. (p. 60)

One can detect here some rapid modulations in the nature of the commentary, as Oliphant moves from logistical quibbling ('Tess was a skilled labourer . . .') to philosophical debate, but there is nothing unusual for the times in her blend of aesthetic and moral judgements. The criticism of the 1890s reflected a cultural milieu in which Christianity was still the assumed norm, notwithstanding the famous 'crises of faith' expressed in earlier decades by, among others, the esteemed Victorian poets Alfred Tennyson and Matthew Arnold. Hardy's subtle manoeuvres regarding Christian doctrine – as in *Tess*'s 'midnight baptism' episode – were, as he knew, almost certain to be read as provocations, and it was in no way surprising that many critics took up the gauntlet. '[W]hat are the higher things to which this poor creature eventually rises?', asked Mowbray Morris in his indignant summary of Tess's career. 'She rises through seduction to adultery, murder, and the gallows' (**p. 62**). Yet even among critics who viewed the novel as morally and theologically suspect, there was wide acknowledgement of its dramatic power, and, perhaps more to Hardy's satisfaction, there was evidence elsewhere of a deeper sympathy with his social agenda. This latter strain of criticism is represented below by Clementina Black, an early champion of the rights of working women, who argued that the novel's essence 'lies in the perception that a woman's moral worth is measurable not by any one deed, but by the whole aim and tendency of her life and nature' (see **pp. 56–7**). Hardy could not have said it better himself.

In criticism dating from the middle to the late twentieth century, the moral evaluation of Tess's behaviour has come increasingly to be seen as extraneous to the broader-scale evaluation of what Hardy's novel communicates and achieves. Merryn Williams, for example, observes that the 'revolutionary implications' of Hardy's protest against the sexual double standard 'have become almost stale for us' (**p. 100**). Irving Howe makes a similar point, though from a more unabashedly appreciative stance, when he argues that the didactic concerns of the Victorian critics are utterly overwhelmed by the triumph of Tess's conception: 'Nothing finally matters in the novel nearly so much as Tess herself', Howe writes, 'not the other characters, not the philosophic underlay, not the social setting. In her violation, neglect and endurance, Tess comes to seem Hardy's most radical claim for the redemptive power of suffering; she stands, both in the economy of the book and as a figure rising beyond its pages and into common memory, for the unconditional authority of feeling' (**p. 64**). Likewise, Tony Tanner (**pp. 83–5**) and Ian Gregor (**pp. 101–4**) regard the novel as offering a grand reconcilement of individual suffering and aesthetic transcendence. But if narrow critiques of Tess's particular actions have largely disappeared, modern critics have continued to examine the details of her characterization, as if to plumb the implications of Hardy's own narrative pronouncement in the novel: 'She was not an existence, an experience, a passion, a structure of sensations, to anybody but herself.' Therefore, while the Modern Criticism subsection, below, classifies 'The Character of Tess' as an issue distinct from 'Hardy's Philosophical Views', 'Tess and Sexuality', and 'Nature and Society', the present summary attempts to show how fertile a ground the 'character' issue itself has proved for a variety of critical schools and approaches to the novel. Given a logical sequence of questions that any interested reader might ask about Tess's characterization, one finds that the most satisfying answers come from a blend of voices. We outline here, first, how aesthetic or 'formal' concerns with Tess's characterization have fanned out to concerns with gender and class; second, how class-based approaches rooted in Marxist theory, or in a 'materialist' view of character-in-culture, have illuminated the specifics of Tess's ties to history, labour and landscape; third, how Tess's ties with 'nature', in turn, can take us to a literary-historical focus on Hardy as a wielder of ideas and a manipulator of narrative form; and, finally, how the narrative experience of *Tess*, an experience that embroils the reader in vicarious desire and victimization, has proved important to the feminist and gender-based inquiries that have galvanized Hardy scholarship over the past three decades – notably, by questioning Hardy's willingness to portray the beautiful Tess as a fully subjective, self-aware human being.

A major concern for modern critics has been the specificity, or rather the vagueness, with which Tess is described. Despite the fact that she is constantly before us, her attributes are usually presented by way of a dimly translucent, not a fully transparent lens, so that what we might term her identity – something different, perhaps, from what the Victorians so confidently divined as the drift of her actions – is itself associated with opacity, blurriness and amorphousness. The landscapes in which Tess moves are often covered in mist or shadow; she is consistently placed in physical surroundings that exude enchantment, mystery or dim confusion. Given that such phenomena are too pervasive to be accidental – that they in fact amplify Hardy's established tendencies as a novelist – recent critics have tried to discern how they *function*, both for Hardy and for the reader, in the construction of the narrative. Janet Freeman identifies the *topos* of blindness as central to Hardy's project, noting that 'Failures to see Tess rightly are everywhere in the novel [. . .] the opportunity to look at her is offered again and again, to one pair of eyes after another, as if it were a test, a measure of value' (pp. 76–7). Kristin Brady, operating more within the reader's perspective, observes that Tess's 'real thoughts and feelings are rarely presented', and that 'the reader can have a firm sense of Tess's suffering and her role as victim, but a somewhat confused sense of her own participation in her fate' (p. 89). Both arguments bear on Tess's status as a woman, and Penny Boumelha radicalizes the issue by suggesting that Hardy has made of the character a blank space for the imposition of male, or authorial fantasies – that where we search for Tess herself as a volitional being, one who actively or decisively makes choices, there is in fact nothingness, as attested partly by Hardy's causing her to be 'asleep, or in reverie, at almost every crucial turn of the plot'. For Bayley, Williams and others, Tess's tantalizing ambiguity is more centrally a matter of class and social position: her sensibilities mark her alternately as a '*grand dame*' and as a lowly 'haggler's daughter', says Bayley (p. 75); and Millgate suggests that, even as the power of Tess's personality 'makes it impossible to accommodate her within any of the conventional categories suggested by the rude facts of her situation and story: the helpless female victim of stage melodrama, the betrayed maiden of the popular moral tract, the seduced country girl of innumerable ballads', it remains true that 'if none of these categories proves adequate to contain Tess, none of them is wholly rejected' (p. 68). These discussions, both individually and in the aggregate, suggest a strange but constructive critical paradox, whereby it becomes equally important to specify Hardy's fascination with Tess, and to emphasize the slippage and spread of her story as exceeding his, and the reader's, literal comprehension.

So while all of these critics (see also Penelope Vigar and Peter Widdowson, below) focus on the novel's pendulum swings between concrete detail and obscuring distance, their disagreements over the significance of this movement help to frame several important questions for us. What is the basis of our attachment to Tess? Is it grounded in her fictional persona, in her status as a victim, or in our imaginative drive to reconstruct the details that Hardy shrouds in fog and mist? Should we view the cryptic nature of Tess's characterization as a weakness of the novel, or as one of its greatest strengths? These questions are made all the more tricky by our persistent sense that Hardy has anticipated them – that he has, in fact, built them into the experience of reading the novel.

This is never more clear, perhaps, than in the title's ironic naming of Tess as '*of the d'Urbervilles*' – a phrase that brings with it a host of thematic, historical and philosophical concerns, surrounding and building upon the figuration of Tess herself. Indeed, it may be argued that the 'd'Urberville' construct is the more direct route to Hardyean social critique, as it shows simultaneously the illusory power and the easy corruptibility of an ancient institution. A number of critics have pursued this theme by applying terms derived from Marxist theory, terms that have helped social historians to characterize England's late medieval transition from a feudal (land-based) to a fiscal (trade-based) economy, as well as the more localized, town-by-town shifts from agrarianism to industrialism that Hardy witnessed during his lifetime. A Marx-derived, 'materialist' view of class and history can help us to understand the contemporary *urgency* behind Hardy's detailed provisions of context for his characters. Regarding the nefarious Alec, for example, Ian Gregor comments that '[his] world, the world of the Stoke-D'Urbervilles, is inseparable from nineteenth-century *laissez-faire* capitalism, [where] what is wanted can be bought' (p. 102); and Bruce Johnson more specifically ties this ironic juxtaposition to Hardy's mental mapping of Wessex: 'It is no accident that the modern country estate of the bastardized Stokes-d'Urbervilles lies adjacent to the contrastingly "primeval" Chase' (p. 104). But this is not to say that Hardy is always on the side of the pre-capitalist past. If the novel often laments the incursions of modernity upon a more innocent pastoral world, it also critiques, as Merryn Williams points out, the feudal nostalgia exhibited by Tess's parents, and thus can be said to illustrate 'the destructive role-played by [. . .] false consciousness in the lives of ordinary people' (p. 100). While Tess is a vastly more modern individual than either of her parents (there are effectively two hundred years between herself and her mother, Hardy tells us in Chapter 3), she is not quite modern enough: at precisely the wrong moments, she reverts to superstition, folklore and conventional mores. Exhibiting both a strong commitment to trad-itional values and an intuitive desire for progress and independence, Tess embodies a broader moment of cultural transition. Gregor notes that, as the novel unfolds, the 'wider world [forces] itself in upon Tess, and the last phases are to be dominated not by the individual consciousness and its correlative, landscape, but by money, changing methods of work, migration of families [. . .] Hardy intro-duces in a sustained and explicit way the agricultural and economic crisis that has overtaken Wessex, and turned families like the Durbeyfields, into migratory "labour" ' (p. 102). With others, Gregor locates *Tess*'s most jaundiced view of modernity in the powerful threshing scene at Flintcomb-Ash farm (Key Passages, p. 165), where a new, pitiless industrial technology blots out human identity.

The Flintcomb-Ash scene is widely viewed as one of the novel's triumphs, an example of Hardy's almost unparalleled ability to make landscape absolutely essential to human consciousness, even as it is absolutely indifferent to human affairs. There is perhaps no other English novelist who can write so beautifully and yet so unsentimentally about landscape. Even the early detractors of *Tess* found it possible to praise Hardy's strong evocations of rural life, especially as seen in the pastoral interlude at Talbothays dairy. Not only do the contrastive scenes at Talbothays and Flintcomb-Ash provide an encapsulation of the novel's overall movement, but they also prove twice over that Hardy is at the height of his own creative powers when foregrounding the mysterious agency of the natural world. We are inevitably led to wonder if his view of 'Nature' is more closely allied to Flintcomb-Ash or to Talbothays – or whether, in some broader scheme of things, the two environments have more in common than meets the eye. And there are immense stakes involved in the novel's definition of 'Nature'. For the social realm, Tanner and others have considered how that definition presumes definitions of morality and purity. Hardy's writing everywhere suggests that, as Tanner puts it, 'The fetish of chastity is a ludicrous aberration in a world which teems and spills with such promiscuous and far-flung fertility every year' (p. 84). For the novel's more philosophic dimension, critics such as F. B. Pinion have noted that Hardy's accounts of nature often imply an entire cosmology, as when Tess compares the remote world of the planets to the family apple tree, and her younger brother, taking up the analogy, asks if they live on a 'splendid' world or a 'blighted' one. Tess's unhesitating answer – 'A blighted one' – neatly expresses the Hardyean worldview. Tess herself has been variously seen as a 'Child of Nature' or, alternatively, a kind of pagan or druidical figure who embodies natural (as opposed to Christian) religion. But these associations also provoke debate: does her identification with Nature affirm her 'purity' or, does it, as David Lodge argues, suggest a kind of amorality, a 'wild, exuberant anarchic life [. . .] that extends far beneath the surface of conventional pastoral prettiness and innocence which that phrase denotes to Angel' (p. 98)? Tanner, for his part, cautions against assuming that the novel treats 'nature' and 'society' as simple binaries: 'if the book was an attempt to show an innocent girl who is destroyed by society though justified by Nature, Hardy could certainly have left the opposition as direct and as simple as that. Social laws hang Tess; and Nature admits no such laws. But it is an important part of the book that we feel Nature itself turning against Tess, so that we register something approaching a sadism of *both* the man-made *and* the natural directed against her' (p. 84).

This returns us to the problem of characterizing Thomas Hardy's particular set of beliefs and intentions as they are played out in *Tess*. Here it should be noted, for first-time readers of Hardy, that what might appear as a literary-critical eagerness to diagram huge circles of potential meaning is actually very much in the spirit of the novelist himself, and an activity that, more often than not, engages Hardy's own terms. Bruce Johnson, for example, notes Hardy's interest in the 'tragic struggle of intrinsically natural man or woman to survive in a world where society has confusingly changed Nature's ambiguous rules of survival'. Johnson's argument also takes up a thread in the commentary of Pinion, who cites evolutionary theory in connection with Hardy's bleak view of universal causation: 'The Darwinian internecine struggle for existence in nature, and the tragic lot of people [. . .] confirmed his belief that the Cause of Things is blind or indifferent, and that life goes on automatically' (p. 86). Gregor is similarly studious of Hardy's beliefs, though he emerges with a different locus of the tragedy in his close reading of the novel's four final sentences, which famously begin, ' "Justice" was done, and the President of the Immortals, in Aeschylean phrase, had ended his sport with Tess.' Insisting on the buildup of tension and even contradiction that the last four sentences successively create, Gregor argues that together they 'constitute a human truth, by catching in varying lights our condition, flux followed by reflux, the fall by the rally' (p. 103). By emphasizing the element of cyclic change in Hardy's closing words, Gregor suggests that the novel's much-decried pessimism has been oversimplified and exaggerated.

The critical consensus has more generally accorded with Tanner's view that '*both* the man-made *and* the natural' are pitted against Tess – as, arguably, is Hardy the omniscient narrator. Attentive readers will notice the way that bad luck, bad timing and chains of improbable coincidence are the proximate causes of her downfall; so, for that matter, will inattentive readers, since Hardy continually reminds us of the labyrinthine pathways of fate, and of all that might have been if a different trail had been taken. This narrative habit is established at the very outset, in the vicar's impulsive mention of the d'Urberville heritage – and in his equally consequential failure to mention that the present 'd'Urbervilles' have simply purchased the name. That Hardy was well aware of the thematic ramifications of such accidents is made clear in Mary Jacobus's account of his revisions to the novel (pp. 72–5). Dorothy Van Ghent articulates the risk Hardy undertook with this strategy: that he may strike readers as 'too much the puppeteer working wires or strings to make events conform to his "pessimistic" and "fatalistic" ideas'. But what emerges from all of this, in her view, is an encompassing philosophical coherence: on the earth as Hardy conceives it, 'coincidence and accident constitute order, the prime terrestrial order, for they too are "the given," impenetrable by human *ratio*, accountable only as mystery' (p. 82). Here it should be noted that the section below on Further Reading lists a number of other very helpful accounts of the intersections of Hardyean textual and philosophical concerns, including, for example, those of Arnold Kettle, Peter Widdowson and J. Hillis Miller.

Still, there is another side to Hardy's pessimism that, for readers and critics alike, has had less to do with philosophy than with feeling. There are several passages in the novel that are simply excruciating to read, as Hardy causes us to experience, ever-so-slowly, Tess's undoing. It is not so much the crises of her suffering that he dwells upon; rather, he prolongs the antecedents to her various disasters, so that we see them coming far in advance and are forced to read along in a state of writhing helplessness. As one critic has said, '[Hardy] is fond of turning the screw, sometimes to the point at which it is hard to acquit him of a certain morbid self-indulgence'.[2] Here we might think again of Tanner's remark that 'we register something approaching a sadism', in the way that human and natural forces seem arrayed against Tess. James Kincaid makes an even more provocative claim, suggesting that not only are these sadistic dynamics crucial to the texture of the novel,

---

2   Arnold Kettle, 'Introduction' *to Tess of the d'Urbervilles* (New York: Harper and Row, 1966), in Albert J. LaValley (ed.) *Twentieth Century Interpretations of* Tess of the d'Urbervilles (Englewood Cliffs, NJ: Prentice-Hall, 1969), p. 25.

but that we ourselves, as readers, are (perhaps unconsciously) titillated by them (**pp. 92–3**). Boumelha identifies a similar kind of violence in the narrative, but locates it in the identifiable maleness of the narrator, whose 'erotic fantasies of penetration and engulfment enact a pursuit, violation and persecution of Tess in parallel with those she suffers at the hands of her two lovers' (**p. 87**).

Boumelha has proved to be a powerful voice in the substantial accrual of feminist scholarship on *Tess* over the past thirty years, and gender-based approaches to the novel have been instrumental in defining the academy's ongoing sense of urgency about studying and teaching it. This makes sense not only within the larger history of literary criticism but also locally: to ask challenging questions about where Hardy's love for Tess leads – to problematize its blend of personal and narrative desire within a cultural context, rather than simply to acknowledge it as a force of nature – is almost unavoidably to draw upon feminist paradigms. And the richness of the problem is such as to have accommodated many shadings of academic feminism. Some sense of this variety, it is hoped, will be conveyed in the necessarily limited selections made for the present volume. One touchstone of interpretation has been the key issue of female 'embodiment'. Boumelha, most prominently, calls attention to the descriptive refrains upon Tess's hair, eyes, and mouth, and suggests that the male narrator (whom she does not precisely equate with Hardy) yearns to comprehend 'the interiority of her sexuality' (**p. 87**). Freeman takes this idea in a slightly different direction, arguing that, while the other characters are blind to his heroine, 'Hardy's own eye remains trained on "beautiful Tess," following her history with singleminded concentration. This occupation is at once his discipline and his virtue – the form his existence takes inside the novel' (**p. 77**). These and related readings suggest that Hardy's idealization of Tess, and specifically his insistence on her 'purity', may actually limit the novel's capacity to represent her as a full, complex and autonomous person.

In a sense, feminist interpretations of *Tess* have effected a turnabout that even Hardy, the great ironist, could not have anticipated: whereas early critics saw the novel as challenging rigid traditional codes of conduct for women, modern feminist critics have viewed it as shaped by the very ideologies of gender it purports to resist. However, some recent critics have posited a middle ground, whereby the emphasis on Tess's sexuality actually enables Hardy to subvert prevailing notions of gender – and, importantly, 'gendered' subjectivity – in unexpected, counter-intuitive ways. A scene useful to this discussion is found early in the novel, in Hardy's description of Tess as a new mother at work in the fields near Marlott. Describing what happens to a woman 'when she becomes part and parcel of outdoor nature, and is not merely an object set down therein', Hardy says that 'A field-man is a personality afield; a field-woman is a portion of the field; she has somehow lost her own margin, imbibed the essence of her surrounding, and assimilated herself with it'. Whether blithely or regretfully, Hardy seems here in spite of his own protestations to be registering as inevitable what feminists have termed the 'objectification' of women. For Merryn Williams, writing in 1972 from a Marxist-feminist perspective, the statement bespeaks the interlocking forces behind Tess's victimization: 'Tess is doubly vulnerable because she belongs to the working class and because she is a girl. She is liable to be reduced, not only to the status of an unskilled labourer, but also to that of a mere sexual object, in a society which she has no means of resisting' (**p. 99**). But for Adam Gussow (pp. 106–9), employing in 2000 a blend of gender studies and postcolonialism, the scene has a more hopeful resonance with the Australian Aboriginal concept of 'dreamtime', whereby humans achieve an enlightened and empowering unity with their natural (and supernatural) environs. Granting the speculativeness of the connection, Gussow uses it to suggest that Tess's dreamy reversions to physicality may serve not only as self-defence against the forces that oppress her, but also as gateways to a spiritualized consciousness that transcends the 'either-or' question of Hardy's complicity in her oppression. Lisa Sternlieb, also writing in 2000, highlights another feminist problematic in the novel – its presentation of two men, Alec and Angel, as exploiting the sexual servitude of many women – but does so, ultimately, to emphasize Hardy's own grasp of the problem. Through parallels to the Old Testament love-triangle of Jacob, Leah and Rachel, Sternlieb argues, Hardy is able to confront the Victorian 'marriage plot', a fantasy of per-fect pairings, with the grittier social reality of 'redundant women' (p. 95) who, especially in rural communities, must compete against each other for the few unmarried men who have not migrated to the cities. For Hardy, Sternlieb adds, this situation was also reminiscent of evolutionary theory, the ramifications of which he, along with many others of his time, found deeply unsettling.

Even as current commentators are pulling away from the gender-class axis in an effort to locate Tess within more specialized cultural contexts, it is also safe to say that the issue of Hardy's authorial control remains as engaging to critics as ever. This is partly because Hardy was so frank about his emotional involvement in the story: once we know this, we begin to perceive him as a self-conscious presence in the narrative, by some lights as much a created 'character' as is Tess herself. But scholars' continued fascination with the shaping of *Tess* has also to do with Hardy's ambitious intellectualism, a quality that extends beyond the story to his concerns with the professional ethics of writing and publishing. Jacobus, for example, recounts the painful plastic surgeries Hardy performed on the original manuscript in order to get it published, changes that required him to decide just how far he was willing to go in violating the plausibility and balance of the story. For the finished novel, Simon Gatrell invites us to consider 'two Hardys' – the sensitive 'envisioner of Tess', and the more distanced 'gentleman-critic' (p. 78) who comments on her plight – as a route to understanding Hardy's own modes of analysis. And, expand-ing outward to the status of the novel as a work of art, Peter Widdowson (pp. 79–81) relates the visual effects of *Tess* to Hardy's notes on the experimental painting of J.M.W. Turner, suggesting that the linkage indicates a willingness on Hardy's part to question the very nature of artistic 'representation', especially as a vehicle for the truth. These, it should be said, are merely the most overt depictions of Hardy's qualities of mind; nearly all of the critical excerpts provided here attest, in some way, to an intellectual persona unafraid to show itself always at work.

Given that Hardy did work so hard to distinguish himself in *his* field, largely by replacing the university education he lacked with the richer, lifelong education he designed for himself, it is fitting to return once more to his image of the 'lost margin' between Tess and the field in which she works. Hardy's idea of Tess as having 'imbibed the essence of her surrounding' speaks as well to his situation as to hers, and points to the complex mutuality of his concerns with her (imagined) personal welfare, and with the changing face of rural life – and thus, by extension, to the allure of his novel as a site of critical debate and contemplative enjoyment.

Early Critical Reception

From **Clementina Black, *Illustrated London News*, 100** (9 January 1892), p. 50

Black (1855–1922) was a novelist and, more prominently, a political activist who advocated women's involvement in trade unions. She is credited with saying, 'What is wrong is not the work for wages of married women but the under-payment' (*Married Women's Work*, 1915). Her best-known novel, *The Agitator* (1894), is based on her experiences as a labour organizer. Her review of *Tess* reveals a profound sympathy with Hardy's goals and purposes, arguing that both men's and women's morality must be judged through the wholeness of character.

Mr. Hardy's new novel is on many respects the finest work which he has yet produced, and its superiority is largely due to a profound moral earnestness which has not always been conspicuous in his writing. Yet this very earnestness, by leading him to deal with serious moral problems, will assuredly cause this book to be reprobated by numbers of well-intentioned people who have read his previous novels with complacency.[1] [. . .]

Mr. Hardy's story [. . .] is founded on a recognition of the ironic truth which we all know in our hearts, and are all forbidden to say aloud, that the richest kind of womanly nature, the most direct, sincere, and passionate, is the most liable to be caught in that sort of pitfall which social convention stamps as an irretrievable disgrace. It is the unsuspicious and fundamentally pure-minded girl in whom lie the noblest possibilities of womanhood, who is the easiest victim and who has to fight the hardest fight.

[. . .] The true country life of hard toil makes a continual background to the figure of country-born Tess; but the background is not always dark. The wholesome life of the dairy farm, and the wonderful pictures of changing aspects and seasons, the descriptions of three or four solitary walks, remain with us like bits

---

1   In nineteenth-century usage, this term did not connote dangerous self-satisfaction, but rather pleasure or even joy.

of personal experience. Perhaps no other English writer could have given pre-cisely these impressions. Yet these, characteristic as they are, are not the essence of the book. Its essence lies in the perception that a woman's moral worth is measurable not by any one deed, but by the whole aim and tendency of her life and nature. In regard to men the doctrine is no novelty; the writers who have had eyes to see and courage to declare the same truth about women are few indeed; and Mr. Hardy in this novel has shown himself to be one of that brave and clear-sighted minority.

From **Anon.**, *Athenaeum*, **3350** (9 January 1892)

> This early review of *Tess* is mainly positive; prior to the passage reprinted here, it calls Hardy's novel 'not only good, but great' and acclaims 'Tess herself' as 'a credible, sympathetic creature, in the very forefront of his women'. As seen in the excerpt below, however, the reviewer questions the artistic wisdom of Hardy's stand on Tess's sexual victimization. Here, then, is one manifestation of the prevailing discomfort about Tess's 'purity', an issue (this critic argues) that Hardy insists upon too strongly.

But was it needful that Mr. Hardy should challenge criticism upon what is after all a side issue? His business was rather to fashion (as he has done) a being of flesh and blood than to propose the suffering woman's view of a controversy which only the dabbler in sexual ethics can enjoy. Why should a novelist embroil himself in moral technicalities? As it is, one half suspects Mr. Hardy of a desire to argue out the justice of the comparative punishments meted to man and to woman for sexual aberrations. To have fashioned a faultless piece of art built upon the great tragic model were surely sufficient. And, as a matter of fact, the 'argumentation' is confined to the preface and subtitle, which are, to our thinking, needless and a diversion from the main interest, which lies not in Tess, the sinner or sinned against, but in Tess the woman. Mr. Hardy's style is here, as always, suave and supple, although his use of scientific and ecclesiastical terminology grows exces-sive. Nor is it quite befitting that a novelist should sneer at a character with the word 'antinomianism',[1] and employ 'determinism' for his own purposes a page or two later. And a writer who aims so evidently at impartiality had been well advised in restraining a slight animosity (subtly expressed though it be) against certain conventions which some people even yet respect. However, all things taken into account, *Tess of the D'Urbervilles* is well in front of Mr. Hardy's previous work, and is destined, there can be no doubt, to rank high among the achievements of the Victorian novelists.

---

1   The belief that Christians are not constrained to follow the law of God, but are instead free to continue sinning so that God's grace may be continually granted.

From **R. H. Hutton, *Spectator*** (23 January 1892)

> Richard Holt Hutton (1826–97) was for over thirty years one of the co-editors of *The Spectator*, during which time it emerged as among the most influential of the reviewing periodicals. A regular reviewer of Hardy's novels over the years, Hutton had intellectual interests that centred on theology and metaphysics, and he favoured literary texts that, like *Tess*, had theological implications.

We must say that had Tess been what Mr. Hardy calls her, a really pure woman, she could not possibly have hesitated to apply to her father and mother-in-law when she felt, as she did feel, that it was a question of life and death to her fidelity of purpose and her purity of heart whether she obtained their protection or not. On the whole, we deny altogether that Mr. Hardy has made out his case for Tess. She was pure enough in her instincts, considering the circumstances and the class in which she was born. But she had no deep sense of fidelity to those instincts. If she had, she would not have allowed herself time after time to be turned from the plain path of duty, by the fastidiousness of a personal pride which was quite out of proportion to the extremity of her temptations and her perils. It is no doubt true that her husband behaved with even less fidelity to her than she to him. Perhaps that was natural in such a pagan as Mr. Hardy depicts him. But we cannot for a moment admit that even on his own portraiture of the circumstances of the case, Tess acted as a pure woman should have acted under such a stress of temptation and peril. Though pure in instinct, she was not faithful to her pure instinct. We should, indeed, say that Mr. Hardy, instead of illustrating his conviction that there is no Power who guides and guards those who are faithful to their best lights, has only illustrated what every Christian would admit, that if fine natures will not faithfully adhere to such genuine instincts as they have, they may deteriorate, and will deteriorate, in consequence of that faithlessness.

From **Margaret Oliphant, *Blackwood's Magazine*, 151** (March 1892), pp. 464–74

> Among the most wildly productive of all the Victorian writers, Oliphant produced nearly one hundred novels in a career that spanned almost fifty years, including, most famously, the Carlingford Chronicles series published in the 1860s and 1870s. Her immense output resulted from financial need, as she was the main breadwinner for a large and extended family. The many reviews she produced for *Blackwood's Magazine* over the years were a part of a long-term business relationship she had with the Blackwood family publishing house. In this excerpt, Oliphant frequently indulges the sort of moralistic and intellectual smugness that Hardy saw his fiction as combating.

We have a great many objections to make to Tess. The fact that what we must call the naughty chapters have had to be printed surreptitiously, in what we presume ought to be described as elderly Reviews, while the rest has come out in the cheerful young newspaper open to all men, is of itself a tremendous objection to our old-fashioned eyes. [. . .]

Tess of the D'Urbervilles is the history, Mr. Hardy tells us, *par excellence*, of a pure woman, which is his flag or trumpet, so to speak, of defiance upon certain matters, to the ordinary world. It is time enough, however, to come to that after we have done justice to the real pictures which an artist cannot help giving, with qualities of life and truth which are independent of all didactic intentions. Tess is a country girl of an extraordinary elevated and noble kind. Everybody knows what Mr. Hardy's peasants in Wessex are. They are a quaint people, given to somewhat highflown language, and confused and complicated reasoning [. . .] They are sometimes a little grotesque, but their sentiments are usually fine. [. . .] It is a pardonable extravagance to make of Tess a kind of princess in this *milieu*, which is a mistake that even the most experienced make from time to time, since there is scarcely a vicaress or rectoress who has not some such favourite in the parish – some girl with all the instincts of a lady, as the kind patroness will tell you. We doubt much, however, whether having passed the Sixth Standard[1] improves the phraseology in the manner believed by Mr. Hardy; but this is of little importance. Tess is, we are ready to allow, the exceptional creature whom we have all seen, beautiful in the bloom of first youth, capable of all things, as the imaginative spectator feels, and whom it is dreadful to think of as falling eventually into the cheerful comely slattern, with a troop of children, which her mother is. But is it not rather dreadful to the superficial eye to think of any lily-girl turning into the stout matron, which, alas! is the almost inevitable end of British beauty?

Tess is plunged at once into the abyss of evil. We need not follow a story which by this time everybody has read, through all its details. It is amusing, however, to find that such a democrat as Mr. Hardy, finding nothing worth his while in any class above that of the actual sons of the soil, should be so indignant at the trumpery person who has assumed the name of D'Urberville, having no sort of right to it. [. . .]

[. . .] Mr. Hardy, as an exponent of peasant life, feels himself justified in going a little further than the commonest of sense permits. His unfortunate young mother is compelled to look upon her poor baby in a different and original way from all previous sufferers of her kind. She holds it on her lap in the reaping-field, 'and looking into the far distance, dandled it with a gloomy indifference that was almost dislike: then all of a sudden she fell to violently kissing it some dozens of times, as if she would never leave off, the child crying at the vehemence of an onset which strangely combined passionateness with contempt'.

The moralizings which follow when the unfortunate baby dies are equally remarkable. Tess is in despair, not for the loss of her child but chiefly about its salvation. 'Like all village girls, she was well grounded in the Holy Scriptures, and she had carefully studied the histories of Aholah and Aholibah, and knew the inferences to be drawn therefrom'. Mr. Hardy, perhaps not having had Tess's advantages in this way, probably believes that these are historical personages like Ruth and Esther. We do not ourselves know Wessex, which is clearly in every way

---

1   In the standardized curriculum, the sixth standard would be the highest level of primary education.

a most remarkable province, and therefore cannot affirm that village girls there do not study diligently the prophecies of Ezekiel: but we certainly have not in any other quarter of the world encountered any who did. But Tess's studies were more enlarged and remarkable still. 'She thought of the child consigned to the nethermost corner of hell, as its double doom for lack of baptism and lack of legitimacy; saw the *arch-fiend tossing it with his three-pronged fork* like the one they used for heating the oven on baking days; to which picture she added many other quaint and curious details of torment taught the young in this Christian country'. Now, so far as we are aware, except, perhaps, in some quaint piece of medieval divinity still less likely to have fallen under Tess's notice than ours, the arch-fiend with the three-pronged toasting-fork (it is well to be particular), with which she was so familiar as to think that it was like the one used for heating the oven, occurs in certain grim passages of the *Inferno*,[2] but in no more popular reading. We have admitted that we have less faith in the Sixth Standard than Mr. Hardy, but it seems probable that we spoke in ignorance. Has it come to that, that Dante is taught and familiarly studied in our village schools? No wonder in that case that to pass the Sixth Standard should be a high test of a liberal education. [. . .]

[. . .] We have not a word to say against the force and passion of this story. It is far finer in our opinion than anything Mr. Hardy has ever done before. The character of Tess up to her last downfall, with the curious exceptions we have pointed out, is consistent enough, and we do not object to the defiant blazon of a Pure Woman, notwithstanding the early stain. But a Pure Woman is not betrayed into fine living and fine clothes as the mistress of her seducer by any stress of poverty or misery; and Tess was a skilled labourer, for whom it is very rare that nothing can be found to do. Here the elaborate and indignant plea for Vice, that it is really Virtue, breaks down altogether. We do not for a moment believe that Tess would have done it. Her creator has forced the *rôle* upon her, as he thinks (or says) that the God whom he does not believe in, does – which ought to make him a little more humble, since he cannot, it appears, do better himself. But whatever Mr. Hardy says, we repeat that we do not believe him. [. . .] '[T]he rich cashmere dressing-gown of grey white, embroidered in half mourning tints'; 'the walking costume of a well-to-do young lady', with a veil over her black hat and feathers; her 'silk stockings' and 'ivory parasol', – are not the accessories of purity, but the trappings of vice. Tess would have flung them out of the window. She would not have stabbed Mr. Alec D'Urberville, her potential husband, with the carving-knife intended for the cold ham (which, besides, awakens all sorts of questions, as – why did Alec D'Urberville, a strong young man, allow himself to be stabbed? and how did it happen that the lodging-house carving-knife, not usually a very sharp instrument, was capable of such a blow?), but have turned him head and shoulders out of the poorest cottage in which he had insulted her with such a proposition. It is no use making men and women for us, and then forcing them to do the last thing possible to their nature. If Tess did this, then Tess, after all her developments, was at twenty a much inferior creature to the unawakened Tess at sixteen who would not live upon the wages of iniquity; and thus two volumes of

---

2   The first section of the *Divina Commedia* by the Italian poet Dante Alighieri (1265–1321), in which the narrator is led downward through the circles of hell.

analysis and experience are lost, and the end is worse than the beginning – which, after watching Tess through these two volumes, and following the progress of her thoughts much more articulately than she could have done herself, we absolutely decline to believe. Whoever that person was who went straight from the endearments of Alec D'Urberville to those of the Clare Angel or the Angel Clare, whatever the image is called, Mr. Hardy must excuse us for saying pointedly and firmly that she was not Tess; neither was she a Pure Woman. This is the portion of the book which was served up to keen appetites in the Reviews, and we rejoice to think that it was so. Let the cultivated reader keep the nastiness for which it seems he longs. We are delighted to find ourselves on the side of the honest lover of a story who requires no strong stimulation of criminality thrown in against all the possibilities of natural life.

Mr. Hardy's indignant anti-religion becomes occasionally very droll, if not amusing. Against whom is he so angry? Against 'the divinities', who are so immoral – who punish the vices of the fathers on the children? Against God? – who does not ask us whether we wish to be created; who gives us but one chance, etc. But then, if there is no God? Why, in that case, should Mr. Hardy be angry? We know one man of fine mind whom we have always described as being angry with God for not existing. Is this perhaps Mr. Hardy's case? But then he ought not to put the blame of the evils which do exist upon this imaginary Being who does not.

From **Mowbray Morris, 'Culture and Anarchy'**, *Quarterly Review*, 174 (April 1892), pp. 317–26

> Morris was the reader for *Macmillan's Magazine* who had turned down the *Tess* manuscript, and in this anonymous review of the first edition he condemns the novel more directly than he had in his professional communication with Hardy. His opening references to the novel's publication history reflect far greater inside knowledge than he admits to, and Morris's stance relative to Hardy is further complicated by the fact that he had actually accepted Hardy's previous novel, *The Woodlanders*, for serial publication in *Macmillan's* after Hardy agreed to revise certain scenes. The mention of the 'Periclean and Elizabethan dramatists' is a reference to 'Candour in English Fiction' (**pp. 20–5**).
>
> Morris's original letter rejecting *Tess* is reprinted in Michael Millgate, *Thomas Hardy: His Career as a Novelist* (London: Bodley Head, 1971), pp. 284–6.

It is a queer story and seems to have been published in a queer manner. The bulk of it originally made its appearance (with some slight modifications) in an illustrated weekly paper; but some chapters, which Mr. Hardy distinguishes as 'most especially addressed to adult readers' had to be relegated (as 'episodic sketches') to other periodicals whose editors presumably take a more liberal view of their duties towards their neighbours [. . .] [O]ne might have thought that a writer who entertains such grandiose views of the mission of the novelist would see something derogatory in this hole-and-corner form of publication. [. . .] For the first half of his story the reader may indeed conceive it to have been Mr. Hardy's design to show how a woman essentially honest and pure at heart will, through the adverse shocks of fate, eventually rise to higher things. But if this were his original purpose he must have forgotten it before his tale was told, or perhaps the 'true sequence of things' was too strong for him. For what are the higher things to which this poor creature eventually rises? She rises through seduction to adultery, murder, and the gallows. [. . .] The Tess of Mr. Hardy's inner consciousness is as much a creature of fantasy as Titania or Fenella.[1] Some such lass may, for aught we know, have herded pigs or dug potatoes in the mystical hamlet of Auburn,[2] but assuredly she never drew breath in any fields trod by human foot. Yet even when thus gloriously free from sense and the reality of things, Mr. Hardy cannot keep true to his own ideals; *desinit in piscem*, his maid of honour ends in a mermaid's tail.[3] A girl unconsciously raised by the mixture of gentle blood in her veins to a higher level of thought and feeling would never have acted as Tess acted. Deserted by her husband, with all the world, as she conceived, against her, she might have joined her fortunes with some man she could love and respect; she would never

Figure 3 Gertrude Bugler, as Eustacia Vye, in the 1920s Hardy Players production of *The Return of the Native* (By permission of the Dorset County Museum)

1 Characters in Shakespeare's *A Midsummer Night's Dream* (1595–6) and Walter Scott's *Peveril of the Peak* (1823).
2 The town described nostalgically by Oliver Goldsmith in his poem *The Deserted Village* (1770).
3 Part of a Latin expression describing a beautiful woman with a fish's tail, meant to connote incongruity of form.

have gone back at the first opportunity to her seducer, a coarse sensual brute for whom she had never professed to feel anything but dislike and contempt.

Considering the book then, with our necessarily imperfect knowledge, it seems only that Mr. Hardy has told an extremely disagreeable story in an extremely disagreeable manner, which is not rendered less so by his affectation of expounding a great moral law, or by the ridiculous character of some of the scenes into which this affectation plunges the reader. [. . .] Mr. Hardy must have read the dramatists of the Periclean and Elizabethan ages very carelessly, or have strangely forgotten them, if he conceives that there is any analogy between their great handling of great tragic motives and this clumsy sordid tale of boorish brutality and lust. Has the common feeling of humanity against seduction, adultery, and murder no basis in the heart of things? It is the very foundation of human society. [. . .]

Modern Criticism

The Character of Tess

From **Irving Howe, Thomas Hardy** (New York: Macmillan, 1967),
pp. 109–10, 123–5, 130–2

> Representative of the many commentators who view Hardy's heroine as tran-
> scending the novel itself, Howe argues that the subtlety of Tess's characteriza-
> tion overrides the novel's lapses into improbable melodrama. Though Howe
> was a leading American socialist intellectual of the 1940s and 1950s, his account
> of the novel reflects his interest in balancing political and literary-historical
> approaches to criticism. The class implications of Tess's stint as a farm labourer
> are reviewed helpfully, but are ultimately seen as contributing to Hardy's larger
> achievement in rendering Tess as three-dimensional and 'real'. For a comple-
> mentary view of the harsh scenes at Flintcomb-Ash see Pinion (**pp. 85–6**);
> for a feminist reading of Tess's character relative to these scenes see Jacobus
> (**pp. 72–5**).

The book stands at the center of Hardy's achievement, if not as his greatest then
certainly his most characteristic, and those readers or critics who cannot accept its
emotional ripeness must admit that for them Hardy is not a significant novelist.
For in *Tess* he stakes everything on his sensuous apprehension of a young woman's life, a girl who is at once a simple milkmaid and an archetype of feminine
strength. Nothing finally matters in the novel nearly so much as Tess herself: not
the other characters, not the philosophic underlay, not the social setting. In her
violation, neglect and endurance, Tess comes to seem Hardy's most radical claim
for the redemptive power of suffering; she stands, both in the economy of the
book and as a figure rising beyond its pages and into common memory, for the
unconditional authority of feeling.

   Tess is one of the greater examples we have in English literature of how a writer
can take hold of a cultural stereotype and, through the sheer intensity of his
affection, pare and purify it into something that is morally ennobling. Tess derives
from Hardy's involvement with and reaction against the Victorian cult of

chastity, which from the beginning of his career he had known to be corrupted by meanness and hysteria. She falls. She violates the standards and conventions of her day. And yet, in her incomparable vibrancy and lovingness, she comes to represent a spiritualized transcendence of chastity. She dies three times, to live again: – first with Alec D'Urberville, then with Angel Clare, and lastly with Alec again. Absolute victim of her wretched circumstances, she is ultimately beyond their stain. She embodies a feeling for the inviolability of the person, as it brings the absolute of chastity nearer to the warming Christian virtue of charity. Through a dialectic of negation, Tess reaches purity of spirit even as she fails to satisfy the standards of the world. [. . .]

[. . .] Where Hardy's art can be brought into more serious question is in the famous sleepwalking scene. It is a set-piece that bears a relation to Hardy's work somewhat like the death of Little Joe to Dickens's. The incident is affecting, it is bold, it is brilliant in conception. Angel, having learned about Tess's past, refuses to go to bed with her on their wedding night; but during a moment of sleepwalking, when his inhibitions are somewhat at rest, he carries her to a stone coffin and places her there lovingly. This piece of action can be seen as a forceful projection of Angel's psychology, in which love and death are sadly compounded. [. . .] That Tess should then lead the stricken Angel back to the house and that Hardy, plunging deeper and deeper into risk, should remark that Tess walks barefoot in the chill night while Angel is in his woolen socks (he would be!) – all this can be accepted as an expressionist strategy for acting out inner states of feeling.

Yet even if we accept this strategy as a way of coping with those incidents in Hardy's fiction which are as improbable as they are crucial, there remain serious difficulties. Hardy is frequently lacking in tact. Almost obsessively, he needs to pile gratuitous excess on top of initial improbability. The idea of the sleepwalking, as it turns out, is not quite enough for him, and to add still another *frisson* – though, if we respond at all, our nerves are by now sufficiently strained – Angel must be shown carrying Tess across a narrow footbridge threatened by autumnal flood, 'a giddy pathway for even steady heads.' The detail itself hardly matters, but it may be just enough to break the current of conviction. In the large, then, the sleepwalking incident strikes one as a perilous touch of genius; it also suggests that genius can be quite compatible with bad taste.

About the sequence at Flintcomb-Ash, however, there is almost no disagreement. Even those critics and readers who question Hardy's place as a novelist are likely to acknowledge the disciplined power of this section. The writing is harsh and compact, absolutely without self-indulgence; there is frequent metaphoric intensification; every word is directed toward a fierce rendering of the sterility of place and the brutality of labor. Nothing in Zola or Dreiser[1] surpasses these pages for a portrayal of human degradation – a portrayal compassionate through its severe objectivity.

The land is barren and flinty, the very opposite of Talbothays. The atmosphere is hushed, death-like. The weather is cruel, apocalyptic. And Tess has been reduced to an agricultural proletarian, working not for a benevolent dairyman

---

1   French and American naturalist novelists, both known for their harsh depictions of contemporary society.

but for an unseen landowner, under the nervous prodding of a foreman and the shock of the new farm machines. Mechanization, impersonality, alienation, the cash nexus, dehumanization – all these tags of modern thought, so worn and all too often true, are brought to quickened reality in Tess's ordeal at Flintcomb-Ash. What Marx wrote about the working day and the outrage of female labor becomes tangible and immediate. [. . .]

[. . .] And what must never be forgotten in thinking about her, as in reading the book it never can be: she is a woman. For Hardy she embodies the qualities of affection and trust, the powers of survival and suffering, which a woman can bring to the human enterprise. The novel may have a strong element of the pessimistic and the painful, but Tess herself is energy and joy, a life neither foolishly primitive nor feebly sophisticated. Though subjected to endless indignities, assaults and defeats, Tess remains a figure of harmony – between her self and her role, between her nature and her culture. Hardy presents her neither from the outside nor the inside exclusively, neither through event nor analysis alone; she is apprehended in her organic completeness, so that her objectivity and subjectivity become inseparable. [. . .]

[. . .] Only one character is almost as important as Tess, and that is Hardy himself. Through his musing voice, he makes his presence steadily felt. He hovers and watches over Tess, like a stricken father. He is as tender to Tess as Tess is to the world. Tender; and helpless. That the imagined place of Wessex, like the real places we inhabit, proves to be inadequate to a woman like Tess – this, if message there must be, is the message of the book. The clash between sterile denial and vital existence occurs repeatedly, in a wide range of episodes, yet through none of them can Hardy protect his heroine. And that, I think, is the full force of his darkness of vision: how little can be done for Tess.

If we see Hardy's relation to Tess in this way, we can be a good deal more patient with the passages of intermittent philosophizing that dot the book. These passages are not merely inert bits of intellectual flotsam marring a powerful narrative. They are evidence of Hardy's concern, tokens of his bafflement before the agony of the world. At best, if not always, the characters in *Tess* are not illustrations or symbols of a philosophic system; at best, if not always, the philosophic reflections comprise a gesture in response to the experience of the characters. It is Hardy ruminating upon the destruction of youth and hope – and if we thus see Hardy's role in his narrative, we can grasp fully the overwhelming force of the lines from Shakespeare with which he prefaces the book: '. . . *Poor wounded name! My bosom as a bed / Shall lodge thee.*'[2]

From **Michael Millgate, *Thomas Hardy: His Career as a Novelist***
(London: Bodley Head, 1971), pp. 266–9, 276

Millgate's superb biography of Hardy (1982) remains the standard life, and is one of several works by which he has established himself as among the ablest

---

2   *The Two Gentlemen of Verona*, I. ii. 120–1.

and most reliable of Hardy commentators. Here in an earlier work Millgate treats several issues that recur in the criticism: Hardy's emotional attachment to Tess; her status as an idealized, or stereotypical, female figure; and the tension between mythic symbolism and sociological realism in the construction of her story. On these matters see in this section, below, Freeman, Jacobus, Van Ghent, Kincaid and Gregor.

[. . .] [I]t is certainly possible to detect the pressure of a directly personal commitment both in the novel itself – in the reference, for example, to the quality of Tess's voice 'which will never be forgotten by those who knew her' – and in Hardy's own comments about it: 'I am glad you like Tess [he told a correspondent in October 1891] – though I have not been able to put on paper all that she is, or was, to me.'[1] It is hard to know what to make of such remarks. In describing Tess's appearance Hardy seems chiefly to have had in mind the woman he thought the most beautiful in England, the wife of the sculptor Hamo Thornycroft, but it is clear both that his acquaintance with Mrs Thornycroft was of a purely social kind and that his use of her as the inspiration for Tess was an act of idealization.[2]

[. . .] The theme of Tess's victimization is enforced throughout the book in terms of scenes and images wholly integrated into the narrative sequence – the cornered animals in the hayfield, the rats in the corn rick, the dying pheasants overhead – and of Tess's geographical wanderings across the face of Wessex, flying like a hunted animal from one refuge to another almost always less satisfactory and safe.[3] At Flintcomb Ash she is surrounded not only by cruelty and oppression, human and climatic, but by people who know different parts of her past and thus represent to her a conscious or unconscious threat. Even in the idyllic days of Angel's courtship Tess is aware of dangers prowling just beyond the circle of light in which she seems so magically to move, and Hardy goes so far as to introduce implicit comparisons with Christ, especially in the analogies between the scene at Stonehenge and the story of Gethsemane.

Such imagery of victimization forms a central element in what can only be described as Hardy's advocacy of Tess's cause. Elliott Felkin recorded in 1919: 'Hardy said of course in writing one had to keep up the immense illusion. In one's heart of hearts one did not of course *really* think one's heroine was as good and pure as all that, but then one was making out a case for her before the world.'[4]

---

1 [Millgate's note] Hardy to T.K. Macquoid, October 29, 1891, quoted [*A Descriptive Catalogue of the Grolier Club Centenary Exhibition of the Works of Thomas Hardy*], p. 33.

2 [Millgate's note] Thornycroft wrote to his wife, May 8, 1894, to report Gosse's account of meeting Hardy at the Royal Academy private view the previous Friday, when Hardy said that he had just been 'cheered up by seeing the most beautiful woman in England or rather her whom *I* think the most beautiful woman in England, her on whom I thought when I wrote Tess of the d'Urbervilles. "And who was that?" said Gosse – "Why it was Mrs Hamo Thornycroft" said Thomas Hardy. Now is not that a nice little story & true?' (letter in possession of Mrs Elfrida Manning). Cf. [Florence Emily Hardy,] *Early Life* [*of Thomas Hardy*], pp. 288–9, 293.

3 [Millgate's note] Cf. John Holloway, 'Hardy's Major Fiction', repr. in Albert J. Guerard, ed., *Hardy: A Collection of Critical Essays*: Englewood Cliffs, N.J., 1963), p. 60, and Philip Mahone Griffith, 'The Image of the Trapped Animal in Hardy's *Tess of the d'Urbervilles*', *Tulane Studies in English*, 13 (1963), 85–94.

4 [Millgate's note] [Elliott] Felkin, 'Days with Thomas Hardy', p. 33.

Hardy apparently learned to regret the subtitle, *A Pure Woman*, which he had added to the first edition of *Tess*: '*Melius fuerat non scribere*,' he remarked in the 1912 Preface. Yet he continued, 'But there it stands' (xxi). What Hardy regretted was the open declaration of interest, the invitation to controversy, not the interest and advocacy itself. Nothing is more remarkable in the novel than the extraordinary passion with which Tess is described and justified, and the 'pure woman' formulation only serves to make explicit what is everywhere implicit – that Tess's personality makes it impossible to accommodate her within any of the conventional categories suggested by the crude facts of her situation and story: the helpless female victim of stage melodrama, the betrayed maiden of the popular moral tract, the seduced country girl of innumerable ballads and anecdotes of oral tradition – like Hardy's ballad of 'The Bride-Night Fire' or the story of Jack Dollop within the novel itself.[5]

But if none of these categories proves adequate to contain Tess, none of them is wholly rejected. Like the various economic roles she occupies from time to time – milkmaid, field-hand, family bread-winner, kept woman – they contribute to that multiplicity of lightly invoked frames and patterns against which her situation and conduct are successively measured and evaluated, and to that wider range of referents – mythological, biblical, and literary as well as historical and sociological – by which the implications of her story are at once defined and drawn out. . . . Although the account of the Trantridge dance lacks in the novel the title, 'Saturday Night in Arcady', under which it was originally published,[6] the couples at the hay-trusser's dance are still described as 'satyrs clasping nymphs – a multiplicity of Pans whirling a multiplicity of Syrinxes; Lotis attempting to elude Priapus, and always failing'; meanwhile various 'Sileni of the throng' sit on benches and hay-trusses nearby. In the vibrant harvest scene of Chapter 14 Tess's method of binding corn is evoked with a precision which serves not only to describe the actual conditions of work for 'field-women'[7] but also to celebrate Tess herself as the performer of actions at once so ancient, so skilful, so suggestive of natural fecundity – and so precisely suited to her name, said in the standard Victorian work on Christian names to mean 'carrying ears of corn' or 'the reaper'.[8]

5   [Millgate's note] 'The Bride-Night Fire' (formerly 'The Fire at Tranter Sweatley's'), *Wessex Poems*, pp. 94–8. A deletion in the *Tess* MS, f. 117, shows that Hardy originally intended the milker's ballad to have been about a murderer (p. 141) to have been about a maid who went to a wood and came back a maid no more. For the importance of ballads and oral tradition in Hardy, see Donald Davidson, 'The Traditional Basis of Thomas Hardy's Fiction', *Southern Review*, 6 (1940), 162–78, repr. in Guerard, ed., *Hardy: A Collection of Critical Essays*, pp. 10–23.
6   [Millgate's note] *National Observer*, November 14, 1891, [673]–675; see [Richard Little] Purdy, [*Thomas Hardy: A Bibliographical Study*,] pp. 69, 77.
7   [Millgate's note] Cf. Hardy's poem, 'We Field-Women' [. . .]. **See p. 29.**
8   [Millgate's note] [Charlotte M. Yonge], *History of Christian Names* (London, 1863), I, 272. Hardy's copy of a one-volume edition (1884) of this work is in the Colbeck Collection of the University of British Columbia.

From **Penelope Vigar, The Novels of Thomas Hardy: Illusion and Reality** (London: The Athlone Press, 1974), pp. 169–71, 179–80, 186–8

Vigar discusses Hardy's visual effects and his 'pictorialism' – that is, his conception of the novel as a series of pictures or artistic studies. Using a formalist approach that is tempered by the techniques of art history, Vigar argues that these scenes embody the novel's central tension between realism and 'mystery'. So while Tess is often presented as a static figure within a staged tableau, Hardy's careful use of light and shade complicates the sense in which she is rendered as a 'symbol'. In citing Hardy's formulations on painterly effects in narrative, Vigar refers to The Life of Thomas Hardy 1840–1928, by Florence E. Hardy (London, 1962; originally published in two volumes, 1928 and 1930), a memoir ostensibly edited by Hardy's second wife but mainly ghostwritten by Hardy himself. For varying approaches to these issues see also Tanner (**pp. 83–5**) and Widdowson (**pp. 79–81**); for scenes mentioned by Vigar see Key Passages on the 'midnight baptism' (**pp. 136–40**) and Stonehenge (**pp. 182–3**).

In *Tess of the d'Urbervilles*, life is played out predominantly 'as a Mystery'. The depth and intensity of the story derive from the great sensitivity of Hardy's 'abstract imaginings', based on a unique appreciation of the 'meaning' *behind* 'simple optical effects' (*Life*, p. 185). Again, in this novel, the exquisite accuracy of concrete detail is shown to be only the visible manifestation of a larger pattern reflecting the ambiguity and complexity of life itself. With his supreme mastery of this technique in *Tess of the d'Urbervilles*, Hardy achieves most nearly an approximation of the quality which he found in Turner's[1] water-colours – of which he observed, at the time of writing the novel, that 'each is a landscape *plus* a man's soul' (*Life*, p. 216). [. . .]

[. . .] At its best, the 'moral' in the story of Tess's life is enacted in physical terms rather than in a consciously psychological or dogmatic framework. Similarly, Hardy's presentation of Tess as a character is, when analysed, seen to be surprisingly restricted to the surface. As the psychological side of her character is generally shown indirectly or in analogy, so, too, the vividness and density of her physical presence is largely pictorial, the result of a painstaking accumulation of concrete and suggestive detail. [. . .]

[. . .] Numerous other scenes seem to be peculiarly static and representative, and in most of them the figure of Tess herself is given special emotional or thematic emphasis. We have, for example, the portrait of the young girl as she appears to the 'surprised vision' of her fellow-travellers, loaded with the fruit and flowers of Alec d'Urberville's bounty (Ch. vi), or the dramatically stylized picture of the unwed mother baptizing her child:

> Her figure looked singularly tall and imposing as she stood in her long white nightgown, a thick cable of twisted dark hair hanging straight

---

1　English painter Joseph Mallord William Turner (1775–1851).

down her back to her waist. The kindly dimness of the weak candle abstracted from her form and features the little blemishes which sunlight might have revealed – the stubble scratches upon her wrists, and the weariness of her eyes – her high enthusiasm having a transfiguring effect upon the face which had been her undoing, showing it as a thing of immaculate beauty, with a touch of dignity which was almost regal. . . . (Ch. xiv)

To the children she does not appear like 'Sissy' any more, but 'as a being large, towering, and awful – a divine personage with whom they had nothing in common'. There is the same conscious use of artistic structure and lighting in, for instance, the highly symbolic vignette of Tess's confession to Angel [. . .] or in her meeting with Alec amid the bonfires, where her odd attire of black and white gives her 'the effect . . . of a wedding and funeral guest in one' (Ch. L). Each picture calculatedly epitomizes her situation and orientates our emotional response to it. Details of dress, attitude and colour all convey implicitly allegorical overtones which are systematically reinforced by the graphic and appropriate use of setting or landscape – the rich languorous azure of the Vale of Blackmoor; the intense sunlight and sharp stubble of the harvest-field; the desolate brown of the swede-plain, and the frost and rain and snow.

[. . .] In none of these tableaux does Hardy give any hint at the development of Tess's individual thoughts or attitudes. We gain from the picture only a visual, objective impression, so that the 'moral' import comes through to us clearly, with no cross-references. [. . .]

[. . .] At the beginning and end of Tess's story, Hardy deliberately evokes an atmosphere of unreality. Her seduction takes place on a night of luminous mists and moonlight. [. . .] Her arrest at Stonehenge, after the avenging of this first wrong, follows the same model. [. . .] In both cases the starkness and grimness of the situation are highlighted by and contrasted with the specifically ethereal, almost fairy-tale quality of the surrounding dimly beautiful countryside. Hardy expressly shows us each episode as softened by strangeness and beauty, transformed into something which man cannot properly understand. The seduction scene is thus glossed over and yet shown even more poignantly by his insistence on Tess's dreaming, unknowing simplicity, by the implied comparison of her vulnerability with that of the 'gentle roosting birds'. Her final capture at the end of the book is presented in exactly the same way; again, she is shown as a dreaming, half-wild creature, caught in a twilight world whose brutality does not really touch her. The two scenes are obviously intended as being complementary: they represent the beginning and end of Tess's confused and bewildered acquaintance with the hard fact of life. She loses her virginity in the haunts of innocence and antiquity amongst skipping rabbits and ancient druidical oaks, and surrenders her right to life in the sacrificial temple of pagans of antiquity. The natural progression of her life is the movement from sleep to sleep.

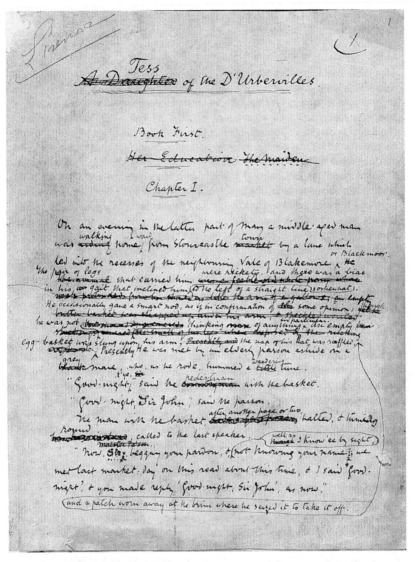

Figure 4 First page of Hardy's *Tess* manuscript (By permission of the
British Library, Add. 38182)

From **Mary Jacobus, 'Tess's Purity',** Essays in Criticism, 26 (1976),
pp. 318–21, 325–7, 334–5

This essay describes Hardy's attempts to revise the novel in order to make it palatable to the family magazines that featured serial publication. While the argument reflects Jacobus's ongoing interests as a prominent feminist critic, it is also extremely useful as a coherent account of Tess's complicated circumstances of production. Jacobus sets out, first, the ironic situation whereby Hardy quietly altered his manuscript in order to forestall moralistic attacks, even as he publicly denounced this anticipated line of criticism in his essay 'Candour in English Fiction' (p. 20). Second, she demonstrates that the attempts to make Tess appear ever more 'blameless' (which violated Hardy's better storytelling instincts) brought problematic changes to other aspects of the novel, by necessitating the 'character-assassination of Alec and Angel' and by further destabilizing the issue of Tess's class identification.

The abbreviations 'P*' and 'P' used by Jacobus denote different manuscript versions, the first indicating Hardy's original manuscript. It should be noted that the full article contains many other interesting details of manuscript revision. For the Margaret Oliphant essay Jacobus cites in the final paragraph of the excerpt see **pp. 58–61.**

'Even imagination is the slave of stolid circumstance': Hardy's lament (in 'Candour in English Fiction') [. . .] is a protest at the tyranny exercised over the novelist by the conditions of magazine publication. Designed for household reading, the family magazines necessarily failed (in Hardy's words) to 'foster the growth of the novel which reflects and reveals life'. In particular, a rigid set of taboos governed the fictional treatment of sexual questions – questions which were increasingly being debated elsewhere at the time, both in the novel itself and in the more progressive journals. [. . .]

[. . .] In the autumn of 1889, three successive rejections of the half-completed Tess had shown Hardy the price he had to pay [. . .] for serial publication. Ironically, the very changes he made to placate 'the Grundyist and subscriber' produced anomalies which the conventional moralists were quick to seize on when the novel finally appeared. Hardy's account in the Life misleadingly suggests that his solution was a cynical and temporary bowdlerization for the purposes of serial publication only.[1] But he also made lasting modifications to his original conception in an attempt to argue a case whose terms were dictated by the conventional moralists themselves. The attempt profoundly shaped the novel we read today, producing alterations in structure, plot, and characterization which undermined his fictional argument as well as strengthening it – or rather, since Hardy himself said of Tess that 'a novel is an impression, not an argument' (1892 Preface), can be claimed to have substantially distorted its final impression.[2]

---

1 [Jacobus's note] See [F.E. Hardy, *The Early Life of Thomas Hardy* (London, 1928)], pp. 290–1.
2 [Jacobus's note] See J.T. Laird [. . .], *The Shaping of Tess of the d'Urbervilles* (Oxford, 1975) [. . .].

The form of Hardy's compromise is implicit in the novel's defiant subtitle, 'A Pure Woman' – added at the last moment, Hardy tells us, as 'the estimate left in a candid mind of the heroine's character – an estimate that nobody would be likely to dispute' (1912 Preface) [. . .] The label caused trouble from the start. To those who accept a Christian definition of purity, it is preposterous, and to those who do not, irrelevant. The difficulty in both cases is the same – that of regarding Tess as somehow immune to the experiences she undergoes. To invoke purity in con- nection with a career that includes not simply seduction, but collapse into kept woman and murderess, taxes the linguistic resources of the most permissive con- ventional moralist. [. . .] On the other hand, to regard Tess as unimplicated is to deny her the right of participation in her own life. Robbed of responsibility, she is deprived of tragic status – reduced throughout to the victim she does indeed become. Worst of all, she is stripped of the sexual autonomy and that capacity for independent being and doing which are among the most remarkable features of Hardy's conception. [. . .]

[. . .] The need to make a special case for his heroine forced Hardy away from the simpler outline and different emphasis of his original conception. [. . .] The original novel was not simply less polemical, but elegiacally explored the recur- rent Hardian theme implied by its original title, 'Too Late, Beloved!' This was to be a lament for unfulfilled love, a tragedy of thwarted potential, focusing on the heroine's appropriation by the wrong man at the wrong time [. . .].

A sustained campaign of rehabilitation makes Tess's so blatant a case of the double standard of sexual morality applied to men and women, and Tess herself so blameless, that the tragedy of the ordinary becomes the tragedy of the exceptional – blackening both man and fate in the process.

[. . .] A necessary consequence of Hardy's campaign to purify Tess is the char- acter-assassination of Alec and Angel. Hardy's remark that, 'but for the world's opinion', her seduction would have been counted 'rather a liberal education to her than otherwise' (f. 136*, p. 135) was always sweeping in view of its result, Sorrow. But it makes more sense in the context of the relationship with Alec as originally envisaged. At this stage Alec had been younger (21 or 22 rather than 23 or 24) and without the later element of fraud. Instead of being a nouveau-riche with a spurious name, he is simply a yeoman-farmer called Hawnferne. Traces of this less hardened character live on in the episode – not present, of course, in the original version – in which Tess goes to claim kin at the Slopes and first meets Alec. We are told that 'a sooty fur represented for the present the dense black moustache that was to be' (ff. 44–5; by the first edition, in 1891, it has grown to 'a well-groomed black moustache with curled points', p. 68); although in training for the role, he is not yet the moustachioed seducer of Victorian melodrama.

Present from the start, however, is the motif of sexual dominance expressed through mechanical power. In the opening pages of the Ur-Tess,[3] Alec has seen Tess at the club-walking and called on her mother; as she drives along in the small hours of the next morning, Tess's last thoughts before dropping off and waking to find Prince impaled by the on-coming mail-coach are of the young man 'whose gig was part of his body' (f. 34*). Alec's gig – here tellingly juxtaposed with the death of

3 'Ur-Tess': the original or earliest Tess.

Prince – is not simply the equivalent of a sports-car, his badge of machismo, wealth, and social status. It is also a symbolic expression of the way in which Tess is to be deprived of control over her own body, whether by Alec himself or by the alien rhythms of the threshing-machine at Flintcombe-Ash, in a scene where sexual and economic oppression are as closely identified as they had been in her seduction.

Besides making the nature of Alec's power over Tess explicit, the gig motif also provides scope for the rough and tumble of a more robustly-conceived situation in their two most important scenes together – the drive to the Slopes and (in the Ur-*Tess*) the night of the seduction itself. It is in these scenes that the effect of Hardy's later modifications to the character of Tess emerges most clearly. The first shows her confused but sturdy in the face of his sexual bullying; above all, it shows her as less conscious. After being forced to clasp his waist during one of the pell-mell down-hill gallops contrived by Alec for the purpose, the original Tess exclaims ' "Safe, thank God !" . . . *with a sigh of relief*'; the later, more aware Tess adds ' "in spite of your folly!" . . . *her face on fire*' (f. 65*, p. 84). In the same way, after her ruse to get out of the gig (letting her hat blow off), she refuses to get up again with ' "No, Sir", she said, *firmly and smiling*' – whereas the later, more sophisticated Tess reveals 'the red and ivory of her mouth *in defiant triumph*' (f. 67*, p. 86). The original relationship is thus both more straightforward and more intimate. Just before the seduction itself, Hardy comments in the manuscript version that 'a familiarity with his presence, which [Alec] had carefully cultivated in [Tess] had removed all her original shyness of him' (f. 92*, pp. 103–4), and we see this familiarity in the earlier version of the scene in which Alec gives her a whistling lesson. Tess purses her lips as he instructs, 'laughing however' (revised to 'laughing *distressfully*, however', f 75*, p. 92), and when she produces a note 'the momentary pleasure of success got the better of her: and she involuntarily smiled in his face *like a child*' (f. 75*, p. 92) – the last phrase being deleted from the revised version. This more naïve and trusting Tess figures in the prelude to her seduction, the orgiastic Trantridge dance. As she looks on, waiting for company on her homeward walk, Alec appears; and we see her confiding her problem to him, declining his offer of a lift warily (' "I am much obliged to 'ee, sir", she answered') but without the formality of the later version – ' "I am much obliged," she answered frigidly' (f. 85*, p. 98) – where she has become the alert repulser of his attentions. [. . .]

[. . .] Mrs. Oliphant wrote indignantly of Tess's collapse, 'If Tess did this, then Tess . . . was at twenty a much inferior creature to the unawakened Tess at sixteen who would not live upon the wages of iniquity'. Exactly; Tess's suffering may deepen her, but it also breaks her. If the wages of sin is death, the wages of virtue – as we see at Flintcombe-Ash – are grinding poverty and back-breaking labour. As Tess puts it succinctly when Angel finds her living with Alec at Sandbourne, ' "He bought me" ' (by 1891, more reticently, ' "He – " ', f. 539, p. 429). Hardy's imaginative allegiance to Tess does not flinch from her subsequent act of murder – carried out with triumphant thoroughness in the earliest manuscript readings. The workman who finds Alec's body reports graphically ' "He has been stabbed – *the carving knife is sticking up in his heart*" ' (toned down to ' "He has been hurt with the carving knife" ', f. 545, p. 434), and Hardy himself underlines Tess's violence with 'The knife had been *driven through the heart* of the victim' (similarly toned down to 'The wound was small, but the point of the knife had touched the heart of the victim', f. 545, p. 343). Later, when Tess tells Angel of the murder, she does so with 'a *triumphant* smile' not 'a pitiful white smile); ' "I have done it *well*" ', she claims, rather than the conventionally helpless ' "I have done it – I don't know how" ' (f. 547, p. 436). Hardy doubtless wished to play down Tess's unbalance for the sake of propriety, but his initial response to this imagined act is more in keeping with the injustice to which Tess has been subjected throughout the book. Here, as elsewhere, Hardy's intuitive commitment was incompletely suppressed by the terms of reference imposed on him.

From **John Bayley, An Essay on Hardy** (Cambridge: Cambridge University Press, 1978), pp. 167, 172, 177–8, 183, 187–9.

> Bayley has recently become known to non-academic audiences for his pub-
> lished reminiscences of his wife, the writer Iris Murdoch. Here, with a lyricism,
> keenness and spontaneity that are characteristic of his long career as a scholar
> of Shakespeare and the novel, Bayley discusses Hardy's 'subjective' attachment
> to Tess, over and against the novelist's desire to cast her as an objective or
> common representative of her class. On the matter of Hardy's erotic attach-
> ment to Tess, Bayley's discussion should be compared to Boumelha's (**p. 87**);
> his discussion of Tess's individuality should be compared with those of Howe
> (**p. 64**), Gatrell (**p. 78**), and Williams (**p. 99**).

[Hardy's] erotic image of Tess is fixed and overmastering; and it also represents, which is perhaps unfair on Angel as a character, the culmination of Hardy's own locality-centred daydreams on a womanly image. [. . .] Hardy's thesis [is] that the milkmaid and the *grande dame* are the same in basic instinct and behaviour. [. . .] [S]he can have the tone of either from moment to moment. A striking instance is after the demise of the baby Sorrow, when she asks the parson to give him Christian burial, as if he had been properly baptized; and with 'the natural feel-ings of a tradesman' whose customers are botching the job themselves, he is disposed to say her own performance of the rite means nothing, but then, relent-ing, finds himself trapped in Tess's logic. Her query – 'another matter – why?' – has the imperiousness of the lady of the manor, but there is an immediate acoustic return to the note of the haggler's daughter when she bursts out with 'I'll never come to your church no more'. [. . .]

[. . .] She is certainly milkmaid personified when it suits Hardy to present her in that light. And this is the paradox, above all, that makes her insubstantial and discontinuous. For she is also one of those about whom he made an entry in his diary on 13 February 1887:

> You may regard a throng of people as containing a certain small minor-
> ity who have sensitive souls; these, and the aspects of these, being what
> is worth observing. So you divide them into the mentally unquickened,
> mechanical, soulless; and the living, throbbing, suffering vital . . .

The triumph involved in Tess's creation, a triumph whose limitations constitute the book's essential form, is the bringing together of such an objective and traditional idea of a milkmaid with the Hardyan intimacy of a 'sensitive soul'. [...]

[...] Thanks to Hardy's method Tess seems to try to fit into life, to try to be 'normal'. The pathos and the pity are in her failure; for the accidents which befall her really seem to arise from her inability to be like other people, and to be the natural consequence of it. That may seem a defect – would she not be more appealing if completely the victim of accident? But a more random victim, otherwise adapted to life, would not attract so many of them. And Hardy here is skilled at giving her the worst of both worlds – the pathos of a common victim, and the pity for a rare and unusual one. As the former, she sings her 'foolish little songs', in the allotment, with hardly a hope that Clare will now ever hear them. As the latter she is a traveller by night, walking the odd twenty miles from Stoke Bare-hills back to Marlott, aware of the sleepers in the cottages she goes by, and their rhythm of repose and labour, in which she is haplessly involved, yet cut off from. The journey by night is Hardy's most moving image, and the one that comes closest to combining an objective idea of Tess with his own imagination of her.

[...] And just as Clare overcomes his physical sense of Tess's difference in their last time together, so Hardy seems to establish in the end the oneness of Tess, although all appearances are against it, although she is seen in such different ways both by others and herself.

He was immensely sensitive to the ways in which a woman does not possess herself but is possessed by others, and the method turns this to account. *His* physical awareness of things was as strong as his sense of disquiet, amounting to incredulity, at the thought of the world they existed in. The image for such a paradox is a feminine one; Tess is the most striking embodiment in literature of the woman realized both as object and as consciousness, to herself and others. [...]

From **Janet Freeman, 'Ways of Looking at Tess',** *Studies in Philology,* 79 (1982), 314–16, 319–20, 322

Drawing implicitly from feminist theories of women's objectification within patriarchal society, Freeman discusses the many ways Tess is seen in the novel – or, more precisely, the many ways in which she is invisible to the men who control her destiny. Failures to perceive Tess as a full human being pervade the novel, Freeman observes, and extend to the denial not only of Tess's personal identity but of her very existence. Within this picture, Hardy's narratorial self-presentation as the one male who *can* see Tess is simultaneously obsessive and necessary: even as Hardy focuses upon her in a protective, paternalistic way, he provides a vivid sense of her existence as an individual. In the process, Freeman argues, Hardy himself is ultimately able to comment on the entire phenomenon of seeing and not seeing Tess. For related observations see Boumelha (**p. 87**) and Widdowson (**p. 79**).

Failures to see Tess rightly are everywhere in the novel [and] the opportunity to look at her is offered again and again, to one pair of eyes after another, as if it were a test, a measure of value. Angel's two brothers, for example, are both short-sighted, though they wear the latest fashion in spectacles (XXV). Blindly, they pass right by Tess, on the day she walked fifteen miles to Emminster Vicarage to ask for help from her father-in-law. [. . .] Overhearing their supercilious conversation about Angel's 'ill-considered marriage' (XLIV), Tess gives up and returns to Flintcomb-Ash. 'No crisis, apparently, had supervened,' Hardy observes (XLIV), yet he calls Tess's decision to leave 'the greatest misfortune of her life' (XLIV). If so, it was surely because of that failure to see her properly. But more is to come: Tess sadly unveils her face as she heads back to Farmer Groby's featureless fields. 'Nobody loves it; nobody sees it,' she says; 'who cares about the looks of a castaway like me!' (XLIV). By that unveiling, however, she makes herself only too visible – for the instantaneous and shocked recognition of Alec d'Urberville, who happens to be preaching nearby. Thus is her fate decided: on whether and how she is seen. Alec d'Urberville finds that the mere sight of her is 'electric,' a terrible threat to his new piety (XLV); Angel Clare found that he had been loving another woman in her 'shape' (XXXV); his brothers look the other way. None of them sees her as she is.

That distinction is reserved for Hardy himself. Repeatedly recording the varieties of blindness and indifference surrounding her, Hardy's own eye remains trained on 'beautiful Tess,' following her history with singleminded concentration. This occupation is at once his discipline and his virtue – the form his existence takes inside the novel. As it is Tess's destiny to be seen, so it is Hardy's destiny to see: he does so unwaveringly, better than anyone else, his presence as observer continually felt. For instance, while the farm women watch Tess suckle her new-born baby during their noon rest (another example of the casual observer, just passively looking), one of them remarks, 'Twas a thousand pities that it should happen to she, of all others.' Hardy is swift to add his own, much more attentive response:

> It was a thousand pities, indeed; it was impossible for even an enemy to feel otherwise on looking at Tess as she sat there, with her flower-like mouth and large tender eyes, neither black nor blue nor gray nor violet; rather all these shades together, and a hundred others, which could be seen if one looked into their irises – shade beyond shade – tint beyond tint – around pupils that had no bottom . . . (XIV)

[. . .] Tess, in kinship with Hardy, is an advocate of the stable, identifiable human individual.

The midnight baptism of her infant, Sorrow, is Tess's most fervent expression of this conviction. By identifying him – giving him a name – she will save him from hell. But she identifies her own self with similar seriousness, when more than once she tells Angel, who tends to confuse her with 'a visionary essence of woman,' to 'call me Tess' (XX), and when she refuses to allow that she herself may not be unique. 'What's the use,' she says to him,

> of learning that I am one of a long row only – finding out that there is set down in some old book somebody just like me, and to know that I shall only act her part; making me sad, that's all. The best is not to remember

that your nature and your past doings have been just like thousands' and thousands', and that your coming life and doings'll be like thousands' and thousands'. (XIX)

She argued the same point to the vicar, after the baby's death. 'Don't for God's sake speak as saint to sinner, but as you yourself to me myself – poor me!' (XIV) And, much later, when his rapture has evaporated, to Angel: 'I thought . . . that you loved me – me, my very self!' (XXXV)

In the end, this form of defense will fail her: 'The woman I have been loving is not you,' Angel says in horror (XXXV), and departs. That denial of Tess's very existence is the most serious crime committed in *Tess of the d'Urbervilles*, and it is committed by a man whose awareness of and respect for Tess as a particular consciousness has been carefully observed and made to seem complete. Angel's experience at the dairy teaches him to perceive uniqueness among the members of Farmer Crick's household, to abandon the notion of a 'typical and unvarying Hodge' (XVIII). He seems aware of the value of Tess's individuality as 'a woman living her precious life – a life which, to herself who endured or enjoyed it, possessed as great a dimension as the life of the mightiest to himself' (XXV). And he loves Tess, or so he thinks, 'for herself . . . her soul, her heart, her substance' (XXVI). This sensitivity makes Angel the perfect mate, 'the right and desired one in all respects' (V). None the less he commits that crime.

[. . .] The murder of Alec d'Urberville is the expression of Tess's violated and denied identity. By means of it, however, she masters her destiny: she succeeds in turning away. Taking the bewildered Angel with her, she willingly leaves the world. Their short happiness – like the life of the infant Sorrow – lasts only a few days. It takes place in a deserted mansion 'whose shuttered windows, like sightless eyeballs, exclude the possibility of watchers' (LVII). Only in secret can this union come to pass, for Tess must not be seen. Again the sun betrays her: 'a stream of morning light through the shutter-chink fell upon the faces of the pair, wrapped in profound slumber' (LVIII) and the old caretaker who peeps in at them turns in the alarm.

From **Simon Gatrell, *Thomas Hardy and the Proper Study of Mankind*** (Charlottesville: University Press of Virginia, 1993), pp. 104–5

The co-editor of the Clarendon Press edition of *Tess*, Gatrell sees the novel as having disparate emotional and intellectual impulses (which he ascribes, rhetorically, to 'two Thomas Hardys'). Though identifying this conflict as central to the novel's shaping, he finally sees it as engendering richness rather than 'contradiction'. The book from which the following excerpt is drawn includes Gatrell's imaginative first-person memoir, titled 'Angel Clare's story', which readers may wish to consult for speculation on Clare's motives and self-understanding.

The double fiction of the writer embodied in the narrative voice of the novel – 'Thomas Hardy' the envisioner of Tess and 'Thomas Hardy' the sometimes bitter and sententious gentleman-critic – offers the reader two hardly separable, inter-twined views of her life and of the other lives that help to shape it, voices that make the fabric of the novel the rich material it is. [. . .]

[. . .] To the creator Hardy Tess is a leopard at a pause, a field mushroom, a pink rose, a sap-filled tree, a wounded pheasant; and more than this. Tess in vital growth is the Froom Valley, Tess in arid emotional starvation is Flintcomb-Ash; Tess receiving the age-old violation her ancestors had dealt is the ancient Chase, Tess suffering the consequences of her violation is Wellbridge Manor; Tess as a kept woman is the splendid but seedy fairy town Sandbourne, Tess as a briefly fulfilled woman is the real fairy palace Bramshurst Court, shut up for years but now momentarily released and filled with love. For this primary Hardy, Tess is a fragment of the natural world, naturally seeking the proper environment for the moments of her life. She is purely and naturally a woman, desiring understanding and satisfaction, meeting male violation of her body and mind, and coping with it, barely, so painful is it; taking in the end a violent remedy out of nature, and finding relief and joy in a momentary union. It is only at the very last that the second Hardy takes over entirely, with more painful results.

To Hardy the gentleman-critic (and I have nothing pejorative in mind in this description – on the contrary, without his voice the novel would be immeasurably the poorer), Tess is an example of the destructive effect of society's pressures and conventions upon a nature naturally pure and unstained; Tess is an issue. He will not allow her to think only as her nature would suggest that she should; he will not allow her to be simply a peasant, existing in a primitive society of harmony with the rest of the world in its pleasure and its pain. Instead Tess has to be educated in the ways of Victorian society, read in English as well as Dorset, conditioned from an early age by the ethical teachings of the church. It is his voice, for instance, that spells out for us the irony in the situation at the end of Chapter XIII. He argues that Tess, wandering in the woods near her home, has been falsely conditioned by English society, as embodied in school and church, to feel herself outcast, by reason of her sexual violation and pregnancy, from the 'purity' of the natural world around her, as well as from that society. In a true view, though, this voice contends, Tess would be seen as thoroughly in harmony with the creatures around her, and (as he suggests in a different place), her experi-ence with Alec d'Urberville in Cranborne Chase would be seen as part of her education rather than as a sin. This is the kind of thing I have in mind when I say that one Thomas Hardy has 'presented' the vision of the other Thomas Hardy.

From **Peter Widdowson, ' "Moments of Vision": Postmodernising**
Tess of the d'Urbervilles; or Tess of the d'Urbervilles **Faithfully**
Presented by Peter Widdowson', in *New Perspectives on Thomas Hardy*,
ed. Charles P.C. Pettit (Houndmills: Macmillan, 1994), pp. 80, 82, 91–2

Widdowson views *Tess* through the critical paradigm of deconstruction, which encourages us to doubt the capacity of any text to deliver stable meaning through the slippery, capricious medium of language. Widdowson suggests that such a position is implied in Hardy's own statements on visuality and narrative, and that these methodological questions posed by Hardy should provoke us, in turn, to question the 'faithful representation' of Tess on several levels. In effect, Widdowson shifts the thematic issue of Tess's 'purity' to a metacritical realm: is 'pure' representation ever possible? This shift, it should be noted, may communicate more about our contemporary processes of reading *Tess* than it does about Hardy's stated interests in painterly technique. In other portions of this essay not reproduced here, Widdowson more directly challenges the humanist-realist tradition in *Tess* criticism. Thus, while he joins Vigar, for example, in citing Hardy's remarks on the painter J.M.W. Turner (in *The Life of Thomas Hardy*), his conclusions are sharply contrasting.

Anyone who has read *Tess of the d'Urbervilles* (and certainly any modern criticism about it) will be in no doubt that the novel is emphatically visual in many of its effects. [. . .] But there is also a great deal of visual imagery in the novel of a rather more self-reflexive sort – a kind of metadiscourse about looking, seeing, perception, representation, imaging. [. . .]

[. . .] It is quite possible to think, therefore, that *Tess of the d'Urbervilles* is actually in some way about seeing and representation. After all, Hardy himself describes it in the preface to the first edition – although we can never really trust that wary old ironist and least self-revealing of writers – as 'an *attempt to give artistic form* to a true sequence of things' (my italics). And he also claims, by way of the novel's hugely contentious subtitle ('appended', he would have us believe in a prefatory postscript of 1912, 'at the last moment' and with no premeditation), that his 'Pure Woman' is '*faithfully presented* by Thomas Hardy' (my italics). Does the phrasing here suggest just how ironically conscious he was of representation as a potent source, precisely, of *mis*representation? Had the image, as we all now know in these post-modern times, already substantively replaced 'the thing itself' for Hardy? Was he already discrediting the notion that there is an ultimate reality, or true essence, outside of history and discourse – such as 'human nature', for example, or even perhaps: *pure woman*? [. . .]

[. . .] [B]y 1886 Hardy is reflecting: 'novel-writing as an art cannot go backward. Having reached the analytic stage it must transcend it by going still further in the same direction. Why not by rendering as visible essences, spectres, etc., the abstract thoughts of the analytic school?' [. . .] What is clear, if nothing else, is that Hardy was being pressed against the limits of conventional realism. The following year, in expressing his admiration for the paintings of 'the much-decried, mad, late-Turner',[1] he rejects 'the original realities – as optical effects, that is' in favour of the 'expression of . . . abstract imaginings' [*Life of Thomas Hardy*, p. 185]. [. . .] [I]t is in a couple of memoranda from 1890 (while he was completing *Tess*) that his most prophetically modernist utterances are made:

> Reflections on Art. Art is a changing of the actual proportions and order
> of things, so as to bring out more forcibly than might otherwise be done

---

1   The English painter Joseph Mallord William Turner (1775–1851), whose landscape paintings became increasingly dominated by swirling fogs, clouds and smoke; amorphous shapes; and the play of light.

that feature in them which appeals most strongly to the idiosyncrasy of the artist.

Art is a disproportioning – (*i.e.* distorting, throwing out of proportion) – of realities, to show more clearly the features that matter in those realities, which, if merely copied or reported inventorially, might possibly be observed, but would more probably be overlooked. Hence 'realism' is not Art. [*Life of Thomas Hardy*, pp. 228–9]

It is here, I think, that the core of Hardy's fictional aesthetic is to be found, and the informing frame of reference for a reading of *Tess*: art is a 'disproportioning' of reality – realism is not art. In other words, 'vision' (abstract imaginings), swinging round its 'moment', makes visible 'essences' (the notion of a 'pure woman', for example). But at the same time, vision 'distorts', 'disproportions', those representations of reality ('copied or reported inventorially') which are the naturalized (mis)representations of Realism, in order to expose essentialist misrepresentation for what it is (how can there, in fact, be 'a pure woman' or 'pure woman'?), and to illuminate another truth which those misrepresentations obscure: that 'reality' is only ever *discourse* – 'seemings', 'imaginings', 'impressions'.

'My art', Hardy wrote in 1886, 'is to intensify the expression of things . . . so that the heart and inner meaning is made vividly visible' [*Life of Thomas Hardy*, p. 177]. Tess, that most 'vividly visible' of novels, may be an example of Hardy 'intensifying the expression' in order to bring into view precisely that 'expression' – the discourses of representation themselves – for scrutiny and demystification in order to exemplify the fact that 'expression' is its own very 'heart and inner meaning', that the 'reality' of an image is the image itself, that its only reality is what it constructs through representation. 'Expression' does not copy 'things as they really are', it forges images in its artifice. Tess may indeed be 'a pure woman', but *only as she is imaged*, only as the 'artificial' construct of representation – and who knows whether this is true or false: except, unless we miss the irony (for Hardy knows full well the claim is nonsense), when she is '*faithfully* presented by Thomas Hardy'.

Hardy's Philosophical Views

From **Dorothy Van Ghent, *The English Novel: Form and Function*** (New York: Holt, Rinehart and Winston, 1953), pp. 203–5

This passage, drawn from a magisterial and often-quoted collection of essays on canonical fiction, confronts the problem of *Tess*'s narrative dependency on random coincidence and bad luck – a problem that Van Ghent and others have found to be fairly typical of Hardy's plots. Defending this 'accidentalism' in *Tess*, Van Ghent maintains that the novel's string of unfortunate events is aesthetically and philosophically coherent. This is so, she argues, not merely because chance is a real part of human experience, but because this novel's 'naturalistic premise' is so thoroughly realized. By highlighting soil, climate and topography as determinants of human experience, Hardy conveys a sense of fundamental 'mystery': to see one's own connection to the earth, in the world of *Tess*, is to glimpse a system of existence and causation one cannot hope to understand. Van Ghent's formalist-inflected sense of how incomprehensibility shapes Tess should be compared with the observations of Pinion (**p. 85**) and Tanner (**p. 83**).

Generally, the narrative system of the book – that is, the system of episodes – is a series of accidents and coincidences (although it is important to note that the really great crises are psychologically motivated: Alec's seduction of Tess, Clare's rejection of her, and the murder). It is accident that Clare does not meet Tess at the May-walking, when she was 'pure' and when he might have begun to court her; coincidence that the mail cart rams Tess's wagon and kills Prince; coincidence that Tess and Clare meet at Talbothays, *after* her 'trouble' rather than before; accident that the letter slips under the rug; coincidence that Clare's parents are not at home when she comes to the vicarage; and so on. Superficially it would seem that this type of event, the accidental and coincidental, is the very least credible of fictional devices, particularly when there is an accumulation of them; and we have all read or heard criticism of Hardy for his excessive reliance upon coincidence in the management of his narratives; if his invention of probabilities and inevitabilities of action does not seem simply poverty-stricken, he appears to be too much the puppeteer working wires or strings to make events conform to his 'pessimistic' and 'fatalistic' ideas. It is not enough to say that there is a certain justification for his large use of the accidental in the fact that 'life is like that' – chance, mishap, accident, events that affect our lives while they remain far beyond our control, are a very large part of experience; but art differs from life precisely by making order out of this disorder, by finding causation in it. In the accidentalism of Hardy's universe we can recognize the profound truth of the darkness in which life is cast, darkness both within the soul and without, only in so far as his accidentalism is *not itself accidental* nor yet an ideology-obsessed puppeteer's manipulation of character and event; which is to say, only in so far as the universe he creates has aesthetic integrity, the flesh and bones and organic development of a concrete world. This is not true always of even the best of Hardy's novels; but it is so generally true of the construction of *Tess* – a novel in which the accidental is perhaps more preponderant than in any other Hardy – that we do not care to finick about incidental lapses. The naturalistic premise of the book – the condition of earth in which life is placed – is the most obvious, fundamental, and inexorable of facts; but because it is the physically 'given,' into which and beyond which there can be no penetration, it exists as mystery; it is thus, even as the basis of all natural manifestation, itself of the quality of the supernatural. On the earth, so conceived, coincidence and accident constitute order, the prime terrestrial order, for they too are 'the given,' impenetrable by human *ratio*, accountable only as mystery. By constructing the *Tess*-universe on the solid ground (one might say even literally on the 'ground') of the earth as Final Cause, mysterious cause of causes, Hardy does not allow us to forget that what is most concrete in experience is also what is most inscrutable, that an overturned clod in a field or the posture of herons standing in a water mead or the shadows of cows thrown against a wall by evening sunlight are as essentially fathomless as the procreative yearning, and this in turn as fathomless as the sheerest accident in event. The accidentalism and coincidentalism in the narrative pattern of the book stand, thus, in perfectly orderly correlation with the grounding mystery of the physically concrete and the natural.

From **Tony Tanner, 'Colour and Movement in Hardy's** *Tess of the d'Urbervilles'*, *Critical Quarterly*, 10 (1968), pp. 223, 225, 231–2, 236–7

In some ways a traditional literary analysis in that it focuses on patterns of imagery and action – a technique reminiscent of mid-twentieth-century formalism in the vein of Van Ghent – Tanner's 1968 essay actually leans more decisively towards the strategies of structuralist and post-structuralist narrative theory that have shaped his work in subsequent decades. This means, in part, that, instead of seeking to illuminate the novel's symbolic or abstract meaning, Tanner strives to literalize the raw potency of Hardy's text, by linking its portrayals of physical and sensory experience with the equally dynamic experience of reading the novel. Thus, the colour red in the novel is not an abstract 'symbol' of blood, Tanner argues; it *is* blood, and is meant to be understood as neither more nor less than the thing itself. It is in such self-sufficient visuals that Tanner locates the reader's apprehension of 'mystery': to 'see' these images is to be reminded instantly of elemental realities for which, as Hardy is well aware, we have ultimately no words. Tanner pursues this thesis through a discussion of the many scenes of difficult walking that serve in themselves as a chronicle of Tess's struggles.

Hardy makes us look at the actual surfaces – the leather, the sleeve, the flesh, the blood. One of the great strengths of Hardy is that he knew, and makes us realize, just how very much the surfaces of things mean.
[. . .] When Alec d'Urberville renews his pressure on Tess, at one point she turns and slashes him across the face with her heavy leather gauntlet. 'A scarlet oozing appeared where her blow had alighted and in a moment the blood began dropping from his mouth upon the straw' [Chapter 47]. [. . .] The man who first made her bleed now stands bleeding from the lips. Blood has blood, and it will have more blood. We need only to see the scene – there, unanalysed, unexplained; a matter of violent movement, sudden compulsions. Hardy spends more time describing the glove than attempting to unravel the hidden thoughts of these starkly confronted human beings. Few other writers can so make us feel that the world is its own meaning – and mystery, requiring no interpretative gloss. Seeing the heavy glove, the sudden blow, the dripping blood, we see all we need to see. [. . .]
[. . .] [T]he most searching of all Hardy's preoccupations [is] walking, travelling, movement of all kinds. Somewhere at the heart of his vision is a profound sense of what we may call the mystery of motion. *Tess of the d'Urbervilles* opens with a man staggering on rickety legs down a road, and it is his daughter we shall see walking throughout the book. Phase the Second opens, once again, simply with an unexplained scene of laboured walking. 'The basket was heavy and the bundle was large, but she lugged them along like a person who did not find her

especial burden in material things. Occasionally she stopped to rest in a mechanical way by some gate or post; and then, giving the baggage another hitch upon her full round arm, went steadily on again.' Such visualized passages carry the meaning of the novel, even down to the material burdens which weigh down that plump, vulnerable flesh: the meaning is both mute and unmistakable. At the start of Phase the Third, again Tess moves: 'she left her home for the second time'. At first the journey seems easy and comfortable in 'a hired trap', but soon she gets out and walks, and her journey again leads her into portents of the life ahead of her. 'The journey over the intervening uplands and lowlands of Egdon, when she reached them, was a more troublesome walk than she had anticipated'. [. . .] Later she walks to Emminster Vicarage on her abortive journey to see Angel's parents. She starts off briskly but by the end she is weary, and there are omens by the way. For instance, from one eminence she looks down at endless little fields, 'so numerous that they look from this height like the meshes of a net' [Chapter 44]. And again she passes a stone cross, Cross-in-Hand, which stands 'desolate and silent, to mark the site of a miracle, or murder, or both'. [. . .] At the end of this journey there is nobody at home and there follows the incident of Tess losing her walking boots, another physical reminder that the walking gets harder and harder for her. 'Her journey back was rather a meander than a march. It had no sprightliness, no purpose; only a tendency' [Chapter 44]. Her movements do get more leaden throughout, and by the end Hardy confronts us with one of the strangest phenomena of existence – motion without volition. . . . Perhaps the ultimate reduction of Tess, the distillation of her fate, is to be seen when she runs after Angel having murdered Alec. Angel turns round. 'The tape-like surface of the road diminished in his rear as far as he could see, and as he gazed a moving spot intruded on the white vacuity of its perspective'. [. . .] [W]e see Tess as a moving spot on a white vacuity. And this extreme pictorial reduction seems to me to be right at the heart of Hardy's vision.

[. . .] [W]e are tempted to ask, what is Hardy's vision of the *cause* of this tale of suffering. Throughout the book Hardy stresses that Tess is damned, and damns herself, according to man-made laws which are as arbitrary as they are cruel. He goes out of his way to show how Nature seems to disdain, ignore or make mockery of the laws which social beings impose on themselves. The fetish of chastity is a ludicrous aberration in a world which teems and spills with such promiscuous and far-flung fertility every year (not to say a brutal caricature of human justice in that what was damned in the woman was condoned in the man). So, if the book was an attempt to show an innocent girl who is destroyed by society though justified by Nature, Hardy could certainly have left the opposition as direct and as simple as that. Social laws hang Tess; and Nature admits no such laws. But it is an important part of the book that we feel Nature itself turning against Tess, so that we register something approaching a sadism of *both* the man-made *and* the natural directed against her. If she is tortured by the man-made threshing-machine, she is also crushed by the forge of the sun; the cold negating metal in Angel is also to be found in the 'steely stars'; the pangs of guilt which lacerate her are matched by the 'glass splinters' of rain which penetrate her at Flintcomb-Ash. Perhaps to understand this feeling of almost universal opposition which grows throughout the book, we should turn to some of Hardy's own words, when he talks of 'the universal harshness . . . the harshness of the position towards the temperament, of the means towards the aims, of today towards yesterday, of hereafter towards today'. When he meditates on the imminent disappearance of the d'Urberville family he says, 'so does Time ruthlessly destroy his own romances'. This suggests a universe of radical Opposition working to destroy what it works to create, crushing to death what it coaxes into life. [. . .] 'All things are born to be diminished' said Pericles at the time of Sophocles; and Hardy's comparable feeling that all things are tended to be obliterated, reveals a Sophoclean grasp of the bed-rock ironies of existence.

[. . .] And why should it all happen to her? You can say, as some people in the book say fatalistically, 'It was to be'. Or you could go through the book and try to work out how Hardy apportions the blame – a bit on Tess, a bit on society, a bit on religion, a bit on heredity, a bit on the Industrial Revolution, a bit on the men who abuse her, a bit on the sun and the stars, and so on. But Hardy does not work in this way. More than make us judge, Hardy makes us see; and in looking for some explanation of why all this should happen to Tess, our eyes finally settle on that red ribbon marking out the little girl in the white dress, which already foreshadows the red blood stain on the white ceiling. In her beginning is her end. It is the oldest of truths, but it takes a great writer to make us experience it again in all its awesome mystery.

From **F.B. Pinion, Hardy the Writer** (New York: Macmillan, 1990), pp. 92–3

Establishing a middle ground between biographical and genre-based approaches to Tess – that is, between studies of Hardy's personal investment in the book, and of the book's allusive roots in romance and classical tragedy – Pinion presents it specifically as a novel of ideas, at once reflecting Hardy's philosophic development and a much larger span of intellectual history. In the threshing scene at Flintcomb-Ash, Pinion sees an especially well-realized expression of Hardy's sense that the baffling relation of humanity to circumstance can be ascribed only to impersonal, uncaring forces of causation. Pinion's point here is not that the threshing-machine itself emblematizes Hardy's entire philosophy, but that its effect upon Tess (enslaving her, singling her out, rattling her very bones and facilitating the renewed attentions of Alec) epitomizes his subtextual interest in what Pinion terms the 'process of exhaustion', the inexorable erosion of human will over time. In other words, the scene brings home the concrete and personal ramifications of blind universal forces. In this connection Pinion briefly mentions Hardy's Dynasts (1904–8), an epic drama composed mainly in blank verse. There, Hardy images a similar kind of unyielding cosmic engine which he terms the 'Immanent Will'.

There is one scene in which action reflects Hardy's philosophy without comment, and it is his most successful achievement of that kind. This is the account of the wheat-threshing at Flintcomb-Ash. Tess is given the most exhausting task by Groby, the farmer who persecutes her; she has to unbind the sheaves for the 'feeder' of the thresher, and she has no respite, for Groby, having to pay by the hour for the threshing-machinery, is set on using it to the maximum capacity. By the third break during the day, she can hardly walk from the shaking of the machine. When she hears of Alec's arrival, she decides to avoid him by staying on the rick for her dinner; though he is a preacher, and she is officially married, he cannot resist her, and joins her on the stack. When he refers to Angel, who has abandoned her, as 'that mule you call husband', her d'Urberville temper gets the better of her, and she smites him across the cheek with one of her leather gloves, drawing blood. 'Turning up her eyes to him with the hopeless defiance of the sparrow's gaze before its captor twists its neck', she cries, 'Whip me, crush me; you need not mind those people under the rick! I shall not cry out. Once victim, always victim – that's the law!' The zest for life which had caused her to rally and set out for the Valley of the Great Dairies is almost exhausted. [. . .]

The crisis on the wheat stack is the most dramatic pointer to the final exhaustion of, first, Tess's patience when Angel's return makes her think that she has been tricked into spiritual degradation by fate, and, secondly, that renewed will to live after the initial victimization from which all her subsequent suffering springs. This process of exhaustion has its correlative in the gradual wearing-down of Tess's physical energy on the thresher, the 'red tyrant' that has to be served. [. . .] The engine is 'the *primum mobile* of this little world', the world of Tess's suffering. It connotes the Primum Mobile or Prime Mover which had been hypostatized in the pre-Copernican era as the source of life and movement in the universe which it surrounded, this being imagined as a series of concentric revolving spheres, the stars on the outer, earth and man at the centre, as if mankind were the supreme creation in the eyes of God. Hardy, who loved the Church of England, especially its music and architecture, and had at one time hoped to be a country curate, with enough leisure to write poetry, had lost his faith in Christian theology. The Darwinian internecine struggle for existence in nature, and the tragic lot of people, individually or internationally, confirmed his belief that the Cause of Things is blind or indifferent, and that life goes on automatically (he twice uses this term with reference to Tess's rally) or by rote. The threshing-scene illustrates a philosophy of the Ultimate which Hardy presented on a large scale in *The Dynasts*:[1]

> Thus does the Great Foresightless mechanize
> In blank entrancement now as evermore. . . .

Nowhere in Hardy are the particular and the universal, the picture and the philosophy, more synoptically and dramatically fused.

---

1   Hardy's epic poem, published in three instalments in 1904, 1906 and 1908.

Tess and Sexuality

From **Penny Boumelha, *Thomas Hardy and Women: Sexual Ideology and Narrative Form*** (Totowa, NJ: Barnes and Noble, 1982), pp. 120, 121, 122, 123, 124, 125, 126, 127, 128

Boumelha's is perhaps the most galvanizing feminist discussion of the novel; it sent shock waves through Hardy scholarship by asserting that Hardy's narrator, if not Hardy himself, enacts a sexual fantasy in the telling of the story. Further, the form of this fantasy is shaped by a violent lust and a desire for absolute possession. More broadly, though, Boumelha also sets forth a fundamental tension between the narrator's impulse to describe Tess objectively and his highly subjective, at times overpowering obsession with her. This tension, Boumelha elaborates, is all the more piquant given that Tess's sexuality itself seems to elude reliable description.

[A]ll the passionate commitment to exhibiting Tess as the subject of her own experience evokes an unusually overt maleness in the narrative voice. The narrator's erotic fantasies of penetration and engulfment enact a pursuit, violation and persecution of Tess in parallel with those she suffers at the hands of her two lovers. Time and again the narrator seeks to enter Tess, through her eyes – 'his [eyes] plumbed the deepness of the ever-varying pupils, with their radiating fibrils of blue, and black, and gray, and violet' [Chapter 27] – through her mouth – 'he saw the red interior of her mouth as if it had been a snake's' [Chapter 27] – and through her flesh – 'as the day wears on its feminine smoothness is scarified by the stubble, and bleeds' [Chapter 14]. The phallic imagery of pricking, piercing and penetration which has repeatedly been noted, serves not only to create an image-chain linking Tess's experiences from the death of Prince to her final penetrative act of retaliation, but also to satisfy the narrator's fascination with the interiority of her sexuality, and his desire to take possession of her. Similarly, the repeated evocations of a recumbent or somnolent Tess awakening to violence, and the continual interweaving of red and white, blood and flesh, sex and death, provide structuring images for the violence Tess suffers, but also repeat that violence. It has even been suggested that the novel takes the form it does in part because the narrator's jealous inability to relinquish his sole possession of her causes both the editing out of her seduction by Alec, and the denial to her of consummated marriage or lasting relationship. [. . .]

[. . .] Tess is asleep, or in reverie, at almost every crucial turn of the plot: at Prince's death, at the time of her seduction by Alec, when the sleep-walking Angel buries his image of her, at his return to find her at the Herons, and when the police take her at Stonehenge. Important moments of speech are absent, too – her wedding-night account of her past life, for example, or the 'merciless polemical syllogism', learnt from Angel, with which she transforms Alec from Evangelical preacher to sexual suitor once more. [. . .]

[. . .] If Tess can be said to have a tragic 'flaw', it is her sexuality, which is, in this novel, her 'nature' as a woman. Her sexuality is above all provocative: she is a temptress to the convert Alec, an Eve to Angel Clare. Such are her sexual attractions that she is obliged to travesty herself into ' "a mommet of a maid" ' in order to protect herself from 'aggressive admiration' [Chapter 42]. Her sexuality is constructed above all through the erotic response of the narrator [. . .].

[. . .] Set against this provocative sexual quality is a lack of calculation, essential if Tess is not to become a posing and self-dramatising *femme fatale* [. . .]. She never declares herself as either virginal or sexually available, and yet her experience is bounded by the power that both these images exercise. Hardy tries to preserve a narrow balance between her awareness of this sexual force (for if she remains wholly unaware, she is merely a passive and stupid victim) and her refusal deliberately to exploit it (for that would involve her too actively as a temptress). The problem becomes acute at the point of her break from Angel:

> Tess's feminine hope – shall we confess it – had been so obstinately recuperative as to revive in her surreptitious visions of a domiciliary intimacy continued long enough to break down his coldness even against his judgement. Though unsophisticated in the usual sense, she was not incomplete; and it would have denoted deficiency of womanhood if she had not instinctively known what an argument lies in propinquity. Nothing else would serve her, she knew, if this failed. It was wrong to hope in what was of the nature of strategy, she said to herself: yet that sort of hope she could not extinguish. [Chapter 36]

The archness of that parenthetical 'shall we confess it' and the elaborately distancing abstract and Latinate vocabulary testify to the difficulty of negotiating this area of a consciousness that must not become too conscious. The shared pronoun ('shall *we* confess it') hovers awkwardly between implying a suddenly female narrator and pulling the implied male reader into a conspiratorial secret (women and their little ways) that remains concealed from Tess. He is obliged to fall back on the old standby of instinct (and, on the next page, intuition) for an explanation of a knowledge that Tess must have, in order not to be deficient in womanhood, and must not have, in order to avoid falling into anything 'of the nature of strategy'. 'Purity' is, in a sense, enforced upon Tess by the difficulty of representing for her a self-aware mode of sexuality.

[. . .] [Tess] is trapped by a sexuality which seems at times almost irrelevant to her own experience and sense of her own identity. She is doomed by her 'exceptional physical nature' [Chapter 36] and by the inevitability of an erotic response from men. That response binds her to male images and fantasies: to the pink cheeks and rustic innocence of Angel's patronising pastoralism, and to the proud indifference that Alec finds so piquantly challenging. Her sexuality, provocative without intent, seems inherently guilty by virtue of the reactions it arouses in others: 'And there was revived in her the wretched sentiment which had often come to her before, that in inhabiting the fleshly tabernacle with which Nature had endowed her she was somehow doing wrong' [Chapter 45]. The echo of *Paradise Lost* in the last sentence of *Tess* has often been remarked, but it is notable that the novel in fact offers a curiously inverted image of Milton's fallen world. The post-lapsarian world of *Tess* is attenuated ('Liza-Lu is only 'half girl, half woman', and both she and Clare seem to have 'shrunk' facially [Chapter 59]) by expulsion from sexuality, and not by the loss of a pre-sexual innocence. In Tess are imaged both a Paradise of sexuality (abundant, fecund, succulent) and the guilt of knowledge that inheres within it.

From **Kristin Brady, 'Tess and Alec: Rape or Seduction?'**, *Thomas Hardy Annual No. 4* (Atlantic Highlands, NJ: Humanities Press, 1986), pp. 129–32, 134–6, 139

> In confronting *Tess*'s mixed messages about how the early relationship of Alec and Tess should be judged, Brady uses character-based questions of blame, purity and volition to advance feminist and gender-studies discussion of the novel. For Brady, much follows from the fact that Tess is shown to have stayed with Alec for several weeks following their initial sexual encounter: this fact, along with Tess's equivocal musings upon it, represents Hardy's broader tendency to interweave moments of moral decision-making or conscious resistance with moments of suspension, reverie or escapist fantasy. John Milton's epic poem *Paradise Lost* (1667) serves Brady as a point of comparison with Hardy's more psychologized blending of 'pride' and passivity in the construction of a female protagonist.

Indeed, Tess's real thoughts and feelings are rarely presented in the novel, except when she suffers the consequences of her actions. Her moral choices seem obscured in ambivalence, while their results are vividly and dramatically portrayed. The effect of these constant jumps in the narration is that the reader can have a firm sense of Tess's suffering and her role as victim, but a somewhat confused sense of her own participation in her fate. The issue of 'purity' is of course crucial here: if Tess's relationship with Alec was based in any sense on her own sexual desire, regardless of whether she 'loved' him or not, then she is not 'pure' in the rigid Victorian sense of that word; if, on the other hand, Tess was simply the passive victim of Alec's sexual aggression, then the question of her own sexuality becomes insignificant. Tess would then be simply a victim of circumstances, not a woman with complex feelings and responses.

[. . .] The central ambivalence in *Tess of the d'Urbervilles* is of course the scene in The Chase, in which the narrator launches into polemics immediately after the description of Alec's discovery of Tess in a sound sleep. The story then leaps into the second phase in the novel, 'Maiden No More' – as if Tess's loss of virginity had taken place on the bare page between the two phases. From the time of the book's publication, the question of whether Tess was raped or seduced has divided critics, and the debate has still not been resolved with perfect clarity. [. . .] An aspect of the confusion, needless to say, lies not just in Hardy's novel but in the inadequacy of the words themselves. 'Rape' suggests physical force alone, while 'seduction' implies merely the pressure of enticement, and neither of the terms comes close to representing precisely how Alec d'Urberville awakened and then exploited the sexual instincts of Tess Durbeyfield. His most effective pressure, for example – both in The Chase and before her second submission to him at the end of the novel – lies in his appeals to her guilt about her responsibilities to her family. By helping them and so requiring gratitude of her, he makes Tess feel all the more compromised in her rebuffs of his sexual advances. If he did exert physical force on her in The Chase, that would have been just one form of his assault on her person.

[. . .] Crucial information is offered, however, in Chapter XII, in which Tess reveals through her conversations with Alec and her mother a number of facts that ought to guide the reader in understanding what the narrator had left unspoken between the phases: that she had stayed with Alec a number of weeks after her loss of virginity, that she had accepted gifts from him, and that she has come to 'loathe and hate' herself for her 'weakness'. She tells Alec, 'My eyes were dazed by you for a little, and that was all'. In response to her mother's disappointment, Tess then rehearses in her mind the sequence of the whole affair, and here, in an unusual departure from his standard tendency to visualize his responses, the narrator presents her thought and memories directly:

> Get Alec d'Urberville in the mind to marry her. He marry *her*! On matrimony he had never said a word. And what if he had? How a convulsive snatching at social salvation might have impelled her to answer him she could not say. But her poor foolish mother little knew her present feelings towards this man. Perhaps it was unusual in the circumstances, unlucky, unaccountable; but there it was; and this, as she had said, was what made her detest herself. She had never wholly cared for him. She did not at all care for him now. She had dreaded him, winced before him, succumbed to adroit advantages he took of her help-lessness; then, temporarily blinded by his ardent manners, had been stirred to confused surrender awhile: had suddenly despised and disliked him, and had run away. That was all.

As far as the scene in The Chase is concerned, there is evidence for both the rape and the seduction arguments in this interior monologue [. . .] but the more important revelation is that the sexual relationship had continued beyond the single encounter in The Chase. [. . .]

[. . .] Common to all the important scenes preceding Tess's night in The Chase is the portrayal of a tension in her between passivity and assertion, between submission and independence, between dream and reality. Present in all of the scenes too is an emphasis on Tess's pride, a sense of self that ultimately leads her to the disastrous descent into Trantridge and the 'fall' in The Chase. Hardy's handling of this tension is not simplistic or moralistic, however: Tess's pride cannot be classified as a vice or a weakness in the way that Eve's can in *Paradise Lost*. Milton's methods, but not his values, survive in Hardy's novel.

Emblematic action appears as early as the club-walking scene, in which Tess Durbeyfield is exclusively chosen by the narrative consciousness even as Angel Clare fails to observe her until it is too late. Though nothing of dramatic import-ance occurs in this scene, it presents many of aspects of Tess that will figure in important ways later on. She is seen both in representative and in individual terms. Her participation in the 'local cerealia', in which she appears like a living symbol carrying white flowers and a peeled willow-wand, links her to ancient fertility rites and so locates her both in the timeless continuum of the nature cycle and in the historical world of Wessex. [. . .]

[. . .] We see Tess both as withdrawn – it is her 'backwardness' that prevents Angel's noticing her before the dance – and as proud. She is mortified by the ludicrous appearance of her father, and responds aggressively to the derisive laughter of her companions: 'Look here; I won't walk another inch with you, if you say jokes about him!' Tess's tone here is defensive as well as aggressive, and the club-walkers curtail their laughter because they see that she is about to lose her composure. But the narrator's language also suggests the potential danger of a loss of control in Tess: 'Perceiving that they had really pained her they said no more, and order again prevailed. Tess's pride would not allow her to turn her head again, to learn what her father's meaning was, if he had any'. The linking of Tess's sense of pride with a potential loss of order (a Miltonic idea) will figure more clearly in later scenes, as will her sensitivity to the laughter and contempt of others.

The series of incidents culminating in the death of Prince can be linked in interesting ways with the scene in The Chase and with the murder of Alec d'Urberville.[1] There is a fatal penetration in all three scenes, and in each Tess is in a state of reverie or sleep – a state of unconsciousness which is linked by mist and halo imagery to the drunkenness of her parents and the Chaseborough revellers. As she drives the cart toward Casterbridge in Chapter 4, Tess lapses into subjective contemplation on her place in the universe:

> The mute procession past her shoulders of trees and hedges became attached to fantastic scenes outside reality, and the occasional heave of the wind became the sigh of some immense sad soul, conterminous with the universe in space, and with history in time.
>
> Then, examining the mesh of events in her life, she seemed to see the vanity of her father's pride; the gentlemanly suitor awaiting personage, laughing at her poverty, and her shrouded knightly ancestry. Everything grew more and more extravagant, and so she no longer knew how time passed. A sudden jerk shook her in her seat, and Tess awoke from the sleep into which she, too, had fallen.

The association of Tess's 'fall' into sleep with that of little Abraham[2] – who also had indulged in grotesque visions – provides both a parallel and a contrast with the deluded dreams of the Durbeyfield parents: all of them are responding to a far from perfect life, but John and Joan Durbeyfield escape reality through their drinking and romantic notions, while their children sink into nightmarish visions of that same reality. [. . .]

[. . .] The Chaseborough dance and its aftermath are the most important emblematic scenes preceding the night in The Chase, and as in the Trantridge scenes, Hardy's language points clearly to the moral action underlying the physical action. Though she never joins this Dionysian dance (as she had eventually joined the more innocent dance of the club-walking), the 'weekly pilgrimages' to Chaseborough still constitute for Tess a kind of rite of passage. Significantly, she

---

1 [Brady's note] See, for example, Lewis B. Horne, 'The Darkening Sun of Tess Durbeyfield', *Texas Studies in Language and Literature*, 13 (1971–2), p. 303.
2 Tess's nine-year-old brother, who is present when the horse Prince is killed.

had first resisted the invitations of her fellow workers to go to Chaseborough, but had eventually begun to join them in their weekend revels after she had been pressured by 'matrons not much older than herself'. The newest revellers, in other words, seek to initiate Tess into the world of sexuality; and though she does not join them in their celebration of the body, she follows them 'again and again' out of an attraction to their 'contagious' 'hilariousness' – an escape from 'her mon-otonous attention to the poultry-farm all the week'. The dance itself is portrayed as another possibility for escape into a dream world: when the couples have been 'suitably matched', 'the ecstasy and the dream [begin], in which emotion [is] the matter of the universe, and matter but an adventitious intrusion likely to hinder you from spinning where you [want] to'. The idea of emotion as 'the matter of the universe' seems a sensual version of Tess's earlier reverie before Prince's death, in which 'the occasional heave of the wind became the sigh of some immense sad soul, conterminous with the universe'; both ideas impose a subjective feeling on to the objective world. But here, as in the earlier scene, dream and matter collide, and the dreamers are restored to harsh reality: as the dancers tumble upon each other 'in a mixed heap', sexual ecstasy gives way to domestic bickering in the impatient complaints of the newly married woman whose husband had caused the accident. A Miltonic parallel is possible here too: the sexual lapse of Adam and Eve was followed quickly by petty recriminations.

From **James Kincaid, ' "You did not come": Absence, Death and Eroticism in Tess'**, in Sex and Death in Victorian Literature, ed. Regina Berreca (Basingstoke: Macmillan, 1990), pp. 14, 17–18, 21

A prominent commentator on constructions of sexuality in Victorian fiction, Kincaid frames the present discussion of Tess by arguing that our modern notion of Victorians as sexually repressed is a 'ludicrou[s] turning of the tables', serving only to promote our self-congratulatory sense of psychic evolution. The excerpt reproduced here suggests that the readerly impulse to label Alec the villain of the piece disguises (perhaps for our own comfort) both that Alec's brand of opportunism is woven into the very descriptive fabric of the novel and that other characters are as deeply implicated as he. Uncovering these facts, Kincaid argues, can prepare us to reflect upon Hardy's anti-dualist strain in the novel – the possibility, for example, that Angel and Alec are not necessarily polar opposites, at least not all the time. Kincaid adds to this analysis the provocative observation that Tess's eroticising of Angel, especially in her tra-versal of the dairy garden to hear him play the harp, is akin to Alec's eroticising of her. (For a related treatment of the garden scene see Lodge, **p. 97**)

The manoeuvres of sadism seem so common in and through *Tess* that the notion of 'perversion' as a peculiar and bizarre practice safely removed from the 'normal' is erased. Formulating images in order to torture seems the normal way of doing business. If we find Tess's career both terrifying and attractive, tragic and titillat-ing, then we are doing no more than dutifully playing the part of the implied reader. [. . .]

Poor Alec Stoke-d'Urberville is made to bear the load of our desperate wish to dissociate ourselves from these sadistic murdering dynamics. He is set up, as all readers have noted with relief, as a sort of moustache-twirling stage villain, presumably without conscience but with a surplus of animal drives. He is, presumably, all genitals and no heart, and can thus focus and drain off our resentment and fear. Tess and most readers position him as a contrast, a black contrast to Angel's whiteness (and her own), to the narrator's grim compassion, and to the reader's stalwart decency. We code Alec as a monster. After all, he likes flash clothes, fast horses, money, and pretty girls. He not only likes pretty girls; he likes to scare them and sleep with them. How unnatural! How unlike us!

Clearly, I am claiming that the series of signals we solidify as 'Alec' function as a loaded and deceptive rhetorical ploy, inviting us to create comforting distance where there is none. It is true that we can see Alec as something of an animated sadism machine; but he differs, if at all, from customary operations only by being somewhat crude, obvious in his devices. He functions on the surface and threatens to give the game away. We are so clearly bombarded in front with his unsubtle mode of operating that we really should be expecting some sneak attack from the rear.

[. . .] But Angel is not the ticket away from that Inferno. He is, in fact, only a form himself, 'not altogether a distinct figure', containing a 'something nebulous' in and about him (Chapter XVIII). Tess, ironically, is beginning to fill him up just as Alec filled her, and she soon, accordingly, finds herself creating erotic sensations mixed inextricably with pain.

Angel sits at an open window strumming on his harp, as Tess wanders in a garden outside (Chapter XIX). Of course it is, as the narrator insists, the commonplace window of an ordinary dairy-man's house; Angel's harp and his musical abilities are frankly 'poor'; the garden is a most prelapsarian[1] Eden, slushing over with cuckoo-spittle, mashed snails, slug-slime, and infested with ripping thistles. But Tess slogs her way through Nature's vomit, responsive only to 'a stark quality like that of nudity' in the air and the lousy music, which hypnotizes her, makes her 'undulate' and get all aflame in her cheeks. One wonders what she would have done had Angel received the benefit of a few lessons. She eroticises a void, what is really 'a typical summer evening' and a not-too-bright and certainly untalented performer. She is playing Alec's game, the only one she knows.

From **William A. Davis, Jr, 'The Rape of Tess: Hardy, English Law, and the Case for Sexual Assault'**, *Nineteenth-Century Literature*, 52 (1997), pp. 224–8

Davis's essay explores the specifically legal ramifications of the question posed by Brady, above ('Rape or Seduction?'). This excerpt details the litigable elements of The Chase episode (Key Passages, **pp. 132–6**), and shows part of Davis's reasoning about why Hardy seemed disinclined to emphasize those

---

1   Prior to Eve's temptation of Adam and the Fall of humankind.

practicalities. Elsewhere in this article, Davis reminds us that Tess's working-class background would have compromised her chances of success in civil and criminal courts, even on the slim chance that she would have known the legal recourses potentially available to her.

A review of Victorian case law shows that the courts held firmly to the idea that a sleeping or unconscious woman was incapable of consenting to a sexual relationship. *R. v. Ryan* (1846), for example, affirmed that 'where a girl is in a state of utter unconsciousness, whether occasioned by the act of the prisoner, or otherwise, a person having connection with her during that time is guilty of a rape.'[1] In *R. v. Mayers* (1872), Richard Mayers, the prisoner, based his defense on the argument that because the prosecutrix (his sister-in-law) did not resist his attempt at connection, he could not be found guilty of attempted rape. Justice Lush countered with an argument more firmly based in logic: 'But if she was asleep it is against her will, and I shall rule that if he had, or attempted to have, connection with the woman while she was asleep he is guilty.'[2] [. . .]

Victorian readers of the 1891 edition of *Tess* read a description of the assault scene containing specific details that would have further established the scene's legal undertones. These details may be traced to Hardy's research, much of which was legal in nature, during the decade leading up to the writing of *Tess*. At some point in the early 1880s – the exact date cannot be determined – Hardy had recorded in his 'Literary Notes III – Facts' commonplace book [. . .] a newspaper report of an assault case from 1826 that contains facts and details very similar to those found in the Chaseborough dance chapter of *Tess* (Chapter 10):

> *Returned soldier* – 'Exeter Assizes.' Wm. Dodd – 35 – assaulting Sarah German. 21st July. Formerly a soldier in East Indies – from which he returned 6 weeks since. Acquired some property in India & has succeeded to some patrimony in this country. Was married the day after the offence, & was apprehended as he & his wife were leaving the Ch[urch]. Sarah G. – pretty girl, apparently innocent & artless, 15. Servant – Got leave from mistress to go to Moreton Hampstead fair – abt. 2 miles distant, her mother living close to the town of M.H., & she was to sleep at mother's, & return to mistress at 7 in morning. At the fair many hours – with another young woman who afterw[ar]d left her. At the Bell Inn there was dancing – went into dancing room – about 2 in morning saw prisoner there – asked her in whisper to go with him. She declined also in whisper. Was coming away – prisoner followed. Made her drink from tumbler of spirits. He came out with her & s[ai]d she sh[oul]d not go to mothers [*sic*] but to her master's. Took her arm by force & led her in that direction . . . Went on[war]d into fields . . . Arrived at mistress's in morning. ('Literary Notes,' pp. 41–42)

---

1   [Davis's note] 'R. v. Ryan' (1846), *Cox's Criminal Law Cases*, 2 (1848), 115.
2   [Davis's note] 'R. v. Mayers' (1872), *Cox's Criminal Law Cases*, 12 (1875), 312.

Possibly Hardy was influenced by his memory of this case when he came to write the dance scene in *Tess*. The parallels between the Assizes case and the novel are clear: each 'innocent' woman attends a fair that continues late into the evening, there is a dancing room at each fair, each woman refuses the offer of an escort home, and each is ultimately led away from the fair by her persecutor. [. . .]

In the 1891 edition of *Tess* Alec gives Tess a draught of a cordial from 'a druggist's bottle' that he 'held . . . to her mouth unawares. Tess sputtered and coughed, and gasping "It will go on my pretty frock!" swallowed as he poured, to prevent the catastrophe she feared' [. . .]. Hardy removed all reference to the cordial ('Spirits' in the manuscript) for the 1892 edition: 'The effect,' write Grindle and Gatrell, 'was more to remove one of the evidences of Alec's premeditated evil intentions than to make Tess any less helpless' ('Introduction,' p. 45).[3] Alec's taking Tess 'unawares' with a drug is not simply an evil intention – it is a criminal act. Halsbury's *The Laws of England* notes that 'if a person by giving a woman liquor makes her intoxicated to such a degree as to be insensible, and then has connection with her, he may be convicted of rape, whether he gave her the liquor to cause insensibility or only to excite her' (IX, 612). [. . .]

Such laws and case rulings suggest that the courts would have interpreted Tess's situation as a case of rape. Why, then, does Hardy keep Tess away from an apparently sympathetic judicial system? (Only in the *Graphic* serial version of the novel do Tess and her mother consider, and then quickly dismiss, prosecution as an answer to the mock marriage arranged by Alec.)[4] To have Tess's status as 'pure' victim following the rape amplified in a court scene would perhaps settle the question of her purity too easily, and Hardy does not want that. Instead, he uses the expansiveness afforded by the novel form (rather than a single scene) to argue for a definition of female purity that includes Tess's sexual nature and her sexual responses to men.

From **Lisa Sternlieb,' "Three Leahs to Get One Rachel":
Redundant Women in *Tess of the d'Urbervilles'*,** *Dickens Studies Annual,* 29 (2000), pp. 352, 354–6, 359, 361

> Beginning with the scene in Chapter 23 in which Angel carries Tess, Marian, Izz and Retty across a flooded lane, Sternlieb argues that Angel's 'off-hand remark' to Tess ('Three Leahs to get one Rachel') provides a key to understanding the novel's interests 'in ancient origins, sexual selection, naïve husbands,

3   Juliet Grindle and Simon Gatrell, 'General Introduction,' in Thomas Hardy, *Tess of the d'Urbervilles*, ed. Grindle and Gatrell (Oxford: Clarendon Press, 1983).

4   [Davis's note] Hardy changed the rape/seduction of the novel to a tamer mock marriage for the *Graphic* serial version of 1891. In the serial version Mrs. Durbeyfield briefly entertains the thought of prosecuting Alec for his clever trick in making Tess think she has gone through the ceremony of marriage before a registrar (who turns out to be a friend of Alec's masquerading as a registrar). [. . .] See my ' "But he can be prosecuted for this": Legal and Sociological Backgrounds of the Mock Marriage in Hardy's Serial *Tess*,' *Colby Library Quarterly*, 25 (1989), 28–41. [For the *Graphic*'s alternative version see Contemporary Documents, **p. 25.**]

unmarriageable women and conveniently replaceable sisters' (p. 352). The excerpt below treats Hardy's experimentation with what Sternlieb calls the 'marriage plot' of Victorian novels. Elsewhere in the essay, she argues that, for Hardy, the 'myth of origin' suggested by the biblical story of Rachel and Leah illuminates 'both the hopefulness and the hopelessness' (p. 352) he felt in light of Charles Darwin's theories of natural selection. She also examines the 'strange domestic arrangement' (p. 354) involving Jacob, Rachel, Leah, Bilhah, Zilpah, and Laban in Genesis 29–31, in which Rachel 'watch[es] her husband father eleven children by other women' and is then remembered by God, bearing Jacob two sons 'before dying' (p. 354).

[Hardy] begins his novel by posing the same question asked in Genesis (29) – What happens when there are not enough men to go around? [. . .] Angel enters the novel as the only man available to partner many women. '. . . what's one among so many!' he asks the members of the dancing club. 'Better than none . . . Now, pick and choose,' replies the boldest young woman [Chapter 2]. Once we accept the improbabilities of Hardy's plot in which Tess continually runs into both Alec and Angel, in which Angel is equally attractive to every woman who meets him, from the dancers, to Mercy Chant, to the dairymaids, to 'Liza Lu, we must notice that Hardy has created a world in which there are essentially two men to accommodate all women. In this agrarian community in which machines have taken their place, men have fled to the cities, leaving the women behind to compete among themselves for the little that is left.

Hardy is making the vexed question of redundant women the very subject of his novel. (The 1851 Census had shown that there were half a million more women than men in Britain. It also revealed that a million women remained unmarried. By 1911 this number rose to nearly one and a half million). In 1862, the well-known journalist, W.R. Greg, advised that single women over the age of thirty be shipped off to the colonies where they would find a surplus of men. [. . .] Hardy is not proposing bigamy or incest as alternatives to Greg's schemes; he is merely exposing the *lie* of the Victorian marriage plot which has always ignored these statistics, which has structured its narratives around the pairing off of all men and women. Tess is punished not simply because Angel chooses unwisely at the Dance, but because in her community the choice of any woman is the rejection of every other. [. . .]

[. . .] It is difficult to think of the work of another Victorian novelist in which the laws of sexual selection are so starkly set forth. The Victorian marriage plot generally shows both men and women negotiating themselves into a partnership. Rather than arguing that Rochester *selects* Jane [in *Jane Eyre*], Hareton [selects] Catherine [in *Wuthering Heights*], or Will [selects] Dorothea [in *Middlemarch*], we think of how these characters independently and mutually learn to come together. Hardy affords his characters in *Tess* no such luxury. His novel is too conscious of the extent to which his men's and women's needs and desires are at odds with each other. When Angel identifies himself with Jacob, he does so with an assured sense of his male advantage. He refers to a cocky Jacob who chooses the woman he wants and must dispense with her sister before getting to her. But if

Angel associates Tess with the young, beloved Rachel, Tess has already identified herself with the older, embittered wife, who waits too long for the fulfilment of her dreams. Asked what she will christen her son the night of his baptism and death, Tess 'had not thought of that. But a name suggested by a phrase in the book of Genesis came into her head as she proceeded with the baptismal service, and now she pronounced it: SORROW' [Chapter 14]. The biblical reference is to Rachel who, on her deathbed names her newborn son Ben-oni (son of sorrow); Jacob calls him Benjamin instead. [. . .]

[. . .] Hardy takes a Darwinian approach to the conclusion of the novel. Four women have been sacrificed so that 'Liza-Lu can be a lover and mother. *Tess of the d'Urbervilles* signals the imminent demise of the Victorian marriage plot. Within a few years George Gissing would write *The Odd Women* which asks even more blatantly than *Tess* – what becomes of the novel when it can neither kill off nor marry off all of its female characters? The Victorian marriage plot often toyed with characters' and readers' desires. Dickens taught Arthur Clennam how to get over Pet Meagles and fall in love with Little Dorrit [in *Little Dorrit*]; George Eliot showed her readers why Daniel Deronda must marry Mirah rather than Gwendolen [in *Daniel Deronda*]. But Hardy has done something quite unprecedented to our narrative desires and expectations. We cannot easily imagine Angel choosing Marian, Izz or Retty, yet we are stunned to see him go off with the non-character, 'Liza-Lu, a woman neither the reader nor Angel has grown to love.

Hardy on Nature and Society

From **David Lodge, *The Language of Fiction: Essays in Criticism and Verbal Analysis of the English Novel*** (New York, 1967), pp. 181–5

Of the critical excerpts reprinted in this volume, this discussion of Tess creeping through the summer garden at Talbothay's dairy is perhaps the most sustained reading of an individual scene. (See Key Passages, **pp. 142–6**.) Lodge argues that Tess's apparent comfort within the wild fecundity of nature is crucial to an understanding of her sensibility, and also reveals the shortcomings of Angel's pastoral idealizations. (Compare Kincaid's briefer reading of this scene, above.) Though best known as the author of satirical novels on academic life, including *Small World* (1984) and *Nice Work* (1988), Lodge is the author of many scholarly books on the novel and narrative theory. This excerpt is from his first book of criticism.

To me the remarkable feature of the paragraph [. . .] is that in it the conventional response (of revulsion) invited by concepts like 'rank', 'offensive smells', 'spittle', 'snails', 'slug-slime', 'blights', 'stains', etc., is insistently checked by an alternative note which runs through the language, a note of celebration of the brimming fertility of the weeds and the keen sensations they afford. This note is conveyed cognitively in words like 'juicy', 'mists', 'blooming', 'dazzling', 'profusion'; but it also seems to invade the very language in which the conventionally noisome features of the garden are described. There is a kind of sensuous relish, enforced by the rhythm and alliteration, in the thickening consonants of 'cuckoo-spittle', 'cracking snails', 'thistle-milk', and 'slug-slime', which is strangely disarming. A linguist would no doubt regard this argument with suspicion; and it is indeed difficult to give a satisfactory account of verbal effects at this depth. But it must be conceded, I think, that if Hardy intended to stress the *unpleasantness* of the garden, he has gone about his task in a curious way.

Even if the reader recoils from the overgrown garden, there is no suggestion that Tess does. She seems at home in it. She moves through the undergrowth 'as stealthily as a cat' – an image which, taken in conjunction with the 'fascinated bird' simile in the preceding paragraph, catches up the whole web of natural imagery and reference applied to Tess throughout the novel. The participles *gathering, cracking, staining*, and *rubbing off*, of which the grammatical subject is Tess, as well as imitating her physical movement, stress the active nature of her relationship with the natural world. [. . .] There are good reasons, therefore, for thinking that in so far as the paragraph has metaphorical implications, it throws light not [. . .] on Clare and what he will do to Tess, but on Tess herself, revealing a facet of her character of which he is significantly ignorant.

This interpretation becomes more attractive as soon as we consider the differences between the characters of Tess and Clare, the nature of their relationship, and the part played in its development by the natural environment.

Talbothays is situated in 'the Valley of the great Dairies, the valley in which milk and butter grew to rankness' (XVI), 'a green trough of sappiness and humidity' (XXVII). [. . .] In this environment humanity is helpless in the grip of its instincts and passions. In Tess, conscience and scruple are inexorably overwhelmed by ' "the appetite for joy" which pervades all creation' (XXX); and 'Amid the oozing fatness and warm ferments of the Froom Vale, at a season when the rush of juices could almost be heard below the hiss of fertilization, it was impossible that the most fanciful love should not grow passionate' (XXIV). There is a relishing of sound in the language of these passages which associates them with the 'weeds' paragraph. [. . .]

The paragraph describing the overgrown garden might be aptly described as an image of 'unconstrained nature'. It reminds us of the wild, exuberant, anarchic life that flourishes on the dark underside, as it were, of the cultivated fertility of the valley. Does it not reveal something similar about Tess – that she is 'a child of Nature' in a sense that extends far beneath the surface of conventional pastoral prettiness and innocence which that phrase denotes to Angel? Let us examine one item in the description in the light of this interpretation:

> . . . rubbing off upon her naked arms sticky blights which, though snow-
> white on the apple-tree trunks, made madder stains on her skin.

There is clearly an antithesis here between *snow-white* and *madder*, which is given a cautionary or ironic note by the *though*: i.e., though the blights looked pretty and pure on the tree trunks, they produced a red stain on Tess's naked arms when she rubbed against them. *Snow-white* has associations with chastity and virginity. Red (the colour of some of the weed-flowers earlier in the passage) is the colour of passion, and of blood (with which Tess is ominously splashed at the death of the horse, Prince – IV). And it is difficult to avoid seeing an [. . .] ambiguity in the word *madder* – no doubt many readers have, like myself, taken it to be the comparative form of *mad* on first reading, not the name of a vegetable dye. Thus, although one cannot paraphrase meanings so delicately hinted, I submit that the force of this connection between Tess and the natural world is to suggest the 'mad' passionate, non-ethical quality of her sensibility.

From **Merryn Williams, *Thomas Hardy and Rural England*** (London: Macmillan, 1972), pp. 90, 93–4, 171–2, 175, 178

> Williams's book is situated near the zenith of academic Marxism, and the passage below remains illuminating today not only for its forthright emphasis on labour and class as encompassing issues, but also for its attentiveness to the small verbal signals and emotive grace-notes which reveal Hardy's own brand of materialist social analysis: for example, his linkage of inmost desires with class identity, and his demystifications of sexual and aristocratic codes of honour. In later criticism Williams has pursued both the socio-economic and the feminist implications of Hardy's work as a novelist. Here, her measured defence of Angel is relevant to the observations of Jacobus (**p. 72**) and Kincaid (**p. 92**).

Tess Durbeyfield, over and above her qualities as a person, is portrayed as a representative of her class and her sex. She is 'a figure which is part of the landscape; a fieldwoman pure and simple' [Chapter 42]. When he is describing the women reapers Hardy explains what this means:

> A field-man is a personality afield; a field-woman is a portion of the field; she has somehow lost her own margin, imbibed the essence of her surrounding, and assimilated herself with it. [Chapter 14]

The method by which the heroine is thus merged and identified both with the landscape in which she works and the other women who work with her reinforces our impression of her as an essentially passive and suffering figure. Tess is doubly vulnerable because she belongs to the working class and because she is a girl. She is liable to be reduced, not only to the status of an unskilled labourer, but also to that of a mere sexual object, in a society which she has no means of resisting. [. . .]

Angel is essentially different from everyone else in the dairy, cut off from the labourers because he is a gentleman, and largely for this reason he is, like Alec, a sexual magnet within his own sphere. This fact is not given overt sexual expression, because Talbothays is gentler than Trantridge and Angel considerably more scrupulous than Alec, but it is nevertheless true that he has 'the honour of all the dairymaids in his keeping'. These girls, all of whom love Angel, have a great importance in the structure of the novel because they represent the class from which Tess emerges. Socially they are in exactly the same position as she is, and their feelings are also very similar – not only their feelings for Angel, but their entire scheme of values. These values are given expression by Marian:

You will think of us when you be his wife, Tess, and of how we told 'ee
that we loved him, and how we tried not to hate you, and did not hate
you, and could not hate you, because you were his choice, and we never
hoped to be chose by him. [Chapter 31]

[. . .] The extreme popularity of *Tess* owes something to the fact that present-
day readers have no trouble in grasping the central point, about 'purity'. [. . .] The
revolutionary implications which were carried by this argument in Hardy's time
have become almost stale for us; so much so that we are tempted by the last two
novels to make Hardy an apologist for a sexual code which would have shocked
him. [. . .]

It is evident that Hardy has no illusions either about the old aristocracy or
about peasant life in the Middle Ages. Particular family fortunes have changed
since the time of the d'Urbervilles; the inhumanity of the relationship between
classes has not. Tess is no princess in rags. [. . .] She is a typical village girl of her
generation (typical in her character, circumstances and destiny) and her ancestry
is also typical in a region where 'many of the present tillers of the soil were once
owners of it'.

What, then, is the reason for Tess's d'Urberville ancestry if it is neither to
emphasize her inherent nobility nor to romanticize the medieval social order?
Almost certainly to illustrate the destructive role played by this kind of false
consciousness in the lives of ordinary people. . . . In the Durbeyfields it takes the
form of monumental delusions of grandeur which, like alcohol, help to prevent
them from facing up to their actual and urgent problems. Joan's description of
their new-found honours helps to show us her confused apprehension of history,
her incurable tendency to shed 'a sort of halo, an occidental glow' over present
arid past:

We've been found to be the greatest gentlefolk in the whole county –
reaching all back long before Oliver Grumble's[1] time – to the days of the
Pagan Turks – with monuments, and vaults, and crests, and 'scutcheons,
and the Lord knows what all.

[. . .] Labour is seen in its most romanticized aspect of Talbothays, where Tess
becomes the conventional 'dazzlingly fair dairymaid' in Angel Clare's eyes. It is
not a false romanticism; Tess like all Hardy's positive characters really fulfils
herself and is happy and skilled at her work. The independent value of this work
is stressed constantly as when the milk is taken to the railway in order to nourish
the people in towns. It makes no unnatural demands on the workers; the community is in 'perhaps the happiest of all positions in the social scale' and each
labourer can freely express his or her own personality – as Angel discovers when
he loses his preconceptions about 'the pitiable dummy known as Hodge'.[2] [. . .]

---

1 Mrs Durbeyfield's term for the seventeenth-century Protestant revolutionary Oliver Cromwell,
   who helped depose King Charles I and threatened the entire institution of the British monarchy.
   Her play (or error) on his name can be seen as connoting ignorance, scorn, or both.
2 A stereotypical term denoting a dull and ignorant peasant labourer; see Key Passage beginning on
   p. 140.

Angel is a very much more complex person and one whom it is easy to mis-understand. Critics of the most diverse kinds have united in abusing him. [. . .] Actually Hardy treated him with much more sympathy than the critics, but he took great pains to emphasize his difference, his sense of distance from the ordin-ary workers at the dairy (symbolized by his eating apart from the rest). In so far as he allows himself to be ruled by snobbish emotions – as when he calls Tess 'an unapprehending peasant woman' – he really is contemptible, but when he is shown struggling to overcome the limitations of his background, to break down his own preconceptions, he is an authentic and sympathetic person. [. . .] The contrast between him and his brothers – 'hall-marked young men, correct to their remotest fibre', one of whom is 'all Church' and the other 'all College' – shows how far he is from being just a middle-class prig. His family worries about him, not just because of his unorthodox opinions but also because of his growing identification with farming people. 'A prig would have said that he had lost culture and a prude that he had become coarse.' At this point he is not a dilettante but genuinely wants to absorb the values of ordinary people, marry among them, become one of themselves.

From **Ian Gregor, *The Great Web: The Form of Hardy's Major Fiction*** (London: Faber and Faber, 1974), pp. 177–9, 192, 196–7, 201–3

Moving against an earlier critical tradition that tended to view 'character' and 'ideas' as opposing forces in Hardy's fiction, Gregor argues for a subtler, syn-thesizing 'rhythm', in *Tess*, whereby internal and external realities are in constant dialogue. In proving this general thesis, Gregor himself makes some remarkable juxtapositions of social contexts with the poetics of specific passages from the novel. His observations on education, class, agrarian labour, and embodiment are resonant with those of more overtly Marxist and feminist critics; see, in this volume, Howe **(p. 64)**, Freeman **(p. 76)**, Boumelha **(p. 87)**, Brady **(p. 89)**, and Williams **(p. 99)**. At the same time, Gregor's analysis of the novel's final paragraph – rendering it, interestingly, somewhat less bleak than meets the eye – shows his allegiance to formalist explication, and places him between Van Ghent **(p. 81)** and Pinion **(p. 85)**, in his brand of commitment to the novel's internal coherence.

I would like to argue, in the account of the novel which follows, that [the] critical debate which, when all qualifications have been made, is polarized around 'character' on one side and 'ideas' on the other, relies, as a condition of its exist-ence, on certain common assumptions about the nature of fiction, assumptions alien to the kind of fiction Hardy wrote. [. . .]

[. . .] In its continuous movement from 'a world' to 'a character', from 'a character' to 'a world', the novel finds its distinctive rhythm.

We can catch this rhythm if we look at two passages relating to Tess. In the first, the narrator describes her in her family home:

Mrs. Durbeyfield habitually spoke the dialect; her daughter, who had passed the Sixth Standard in the National school under a London-trained mistress, spoke two languages; the dialect at home, more or less; ordinary English abroad and to persons of quality ... Between the mother, and her fast-perishing lumber of superstitions, folklore, dialect, and orally transmitted ballads, and the daughter, with her trained National teachings and Standard knowledge under an infinitely Revised Code, there was a gap of two hundred years as ordinarily understood. When they were together the Jacobean and the Victorian ages were juxtaposed.

Some years later, Angel Clare hears 'a fluty voice' which he later learns is that of Tess Durbeyfield talking to Dairyman Crick:

'I don't know about ghosts,' she was saying; 'but I do know that our souls can be made to go outside our bodies when we are alive.'
. . . 'What – really now? And is it so, maidy?' he said. 'A very easy way to feel 'em go,' continued Tess, 'is to lie on the grass at night and look straight up at some big bright star; and, by fixing your mind upon it, you will soon find that you are hundreds and hundreds o' miles away from your body, which you don't seem to want at all.'

[. . .] The first takes us out into the public world, into the world of custom and communication, its crises belong to history. The second affects our own sense of what it is like simply to be, of knowing oneself apart from time and space, its crises are those of the individual psyche. The two are held in tension, and the novel is to explore the intimacy of relationship between them.

[. . .] Alec's world, the world of the Stoke-D'Urbervilles, is inseparable from nineteenth-century *laissez-faire* capitalism, it is the triumph of the individual bourgeois ethic, what is wanted can be bought. So it is now – and really for the first time – that Hardy introduces in a sustained and explicit way the agricultural and economic crisis that that has overtaken Wessex, and turned families like the Durbeyfields, into migratory 'labour'. The wider world is now forcing itself in upon Tess, and the last phases are to be dominated not by the individual consciousness and its correlative, landscape, but by money, changing methods of work, migration of families, 'a fashionable watering place', and the law. Social institutions, economic processes, these are to give a fresh definition to Tess's consciousness, and in its turn, that consciousness is to put such processes under judgement.

[. . .] 'Justice' was done, and the President of the Immortals, in Aeschylean phrase, had ended his sport with Tess. And the d'Urberville knights and dames slept on in their tombs unknowing. The two speechless gazers bent themselves down to the earth, as if in prayer, and remained thus a long time, absolutely motionless: the flag continued to wave silently. As soon as they had strength they arose, joined hands again, and went on.

How often the opening sentence of that paragraph has been quoted in isolation, and made to serve as 'the conclusion' to the novel, whereas Hardy, true to his practice, makes his conclusion multiple in emphasis. The first sentence is a sombre acknowledgement of forces in the world over which we would seem to have little or no control. It is followed by a sentence which shifts from metaphysics to history, proclaiming the serene indifference of the past to the present. These two sentences are followed by two others which indicate contrary possibilities. We see an intimation of human resilience in 'the speechless gazers' who seek in the earth itself, in the conditions of man's terrestrial existence . . . hope and not despair. In the last sentence hope turns into strength, strength to affirm the human bond and to give direction to action, 'they . . . joined hands again, and went on'. It is a sentence which recalls, in its rhythm, the sadness – and the resolution – present in the final lines of *Paradise Lost*:

> They hand in hand with wandring steps and slow,
> Through *Eden* took their solitarie way.

It would be as foolish to isolate Hardy's last sentence and see the final emphasis of the novel to lie there as it would be to isolate the first. For him, it is the four sentences taken together which constitute a human truth, by catching in varying lights our condition, flux followed by reflux, the fall by the rally; it is this sense of continuous movement which suggests that the fiction which records it should be described as 'a series of seemings'.

[. . .] 'All is trouble outside there; inside here content.' Tess's reflection on her brief interlude in the deserted house with Angel comes close to describing, in more general terms, her mood at the end, and it enables her to find within herself the strength to see Angel's life continuing without her. Life has become so precious to her that, paradoxically, she cannot think of confining it to her individual existence, and in her sister she sees an extension of that life, 'She has all the best of me without the bad of me; and if she were to become yours it would almost seem as if death had not divided us. . .' And so in a delicate and gentle way, 'the rally' begins again. The movement of the novel, the flux and reflux, is misread if this final emphasis is not taken. That the pendulum should begin to swing is not an intrusion on the author's part of an unassimilated belief in 'evolutionary meliorism', affixed to a narrative quite alien to that idea, it is implicit within the whole oscillating structure of the novel. It is in fact Hardy's own way of paying tribute to the kind of strength he sees in Tess, a strength which seeks to go beyond the sufferings of one individual: her seeing herself, neither as 'a soul at large', nor as a fly trapped between the blank gaze of earth and heaven, but as a person who can, with full consciousness of purpose and with no self-diminution, give herself to forces outside her and say 'I am ready'. That 'readiness' is built into the hope which Angel and 'Liza-Lu draw from the earth and which in turn gives them their strength. And it is with the phrase 'and went on' that the novel ends.

In establishing a wider context for the reading of the final paragraph of the novel, I have tried to indicate that in its movement, in its shifts of emphasis, it enacts the movement of the whole novel which precedes it. [. . .]

[. . .] What harmonizes the dialectic within the novel, what gives direction to its movement, is not just a reconciliation of contraries within the mind of the author, it is the feeling which encompasses both 'character' and 'idea'. And in Hardy that feeling is an overwhelming compassion, which virtually never fails him.

From **Bruce Johnson, ' "The Perfection of Species" and Hardy's Tess'**, in *Nature and the Victorian Imagination*, ed. U.C. Knoepflmacher and G.B. Tennyson (Berkeley: University of California Press, 1977), pp. 261–2, 271, 273–5

> This essay links *Tess* with Hardy's longstanding interests in geology and anthropology, and particularly his investment in the idea of historical periodicity or layering. The novel's profoundly neutral account of 'nature', in Johnson's view, is mediated through the characters' dual assimilation of pagan and Christian traditions. Johnson's argument leans deliberately toward the presentation of Tess as a kind of pawn or construct, and in this it forms an interesting contrast to the basically characterological approach that informs so much criticism of this novel. Portions of the essay not reprinted here discuss Hardy's avowed interest in evolutionary theory and what Johnson calls his 'rather special understanding of Darwin'.

It is no accident that the modern country estate of the bastardized Stokes-d'Urbervilles lies adjacent to the contrastingly 'primeval' Chase, 'wherein Druidical mistletoe was still found on aged oaks, and where enormous yew trees, not planted by the hand of man, grew as they had grown when they were pollarded for bows' [Chapter 5]. It is characteristically Hardian that the mistletoe is 'Druidical,' for he sees his country folk as the result of a more-or-less steady evolution from Druidical culture, Christianity representing an interference with such evolution. Christianity, in fact, has made the meaning of the Maypole dance inaccessible even to the dancers. Hardy seems to associate the ability to be in touch with primeval, pagan meanings with the ability to be in touch with the emotional, primitive sources of one's own being; the buried geological or archeological, or even paleontological, metaphors of his work really imply an ideal model of consciousness, an awareness of the primeval energies that have shaped even the mind's outward topography. [. . .]

[W]e have met the country zealot who goes around daubing his religious 'texts' on every likely barn or stile; Tess had felt his categorical condemnations to be 'horrible' [Chapter 12], and Hardy now contrasts them with the sun worship of her ancestors:

> The sun, on account of the mist, had a curious sentient, personal look, demanding the masculine pronoun for its adequate expression. His present aspect, coupled with the lack of all human forms in the scene, explained the old-time heliolatries in a moment. One could feel that a saner religion had never prevailed under the sky. The luminary was a golden-haired, beaming, mild-eyed, God-like creature, gazing down in the vigor and intentness of youth upon an earth that was brimming with interest for him. [Chapter 14]

Here Hardy implies that Christianity's capacity for creating guilt is unfortunate and that the old heliolatry had no such intent. [. . .]

In short, any ability in Tess to make contact with earlier, more primitive, though not necessarily unconscious, levels of her mind might have diminished her sense of guilt. Her 'Druidical' past is associated, not primarily with oak forests and mistletoe, but with Stonehenge and the worship of the sun. The final crushing irony of the novel is that as Tess lies on the altar (a pagan come home), the first constable rises just where the sun should have risen. Tess is sacrificed to the restrictions and punishments of modern society rather than to the sun. The sun suggests a higher awareness: an ancient organically evolved consciousness that dynamically retains in the present remnants of the past. [. . .]

[. . .] In Tess the family history is like that of the old landscapes. Far from there being a real conflict in the reader's tripartite identification of Tess as a child of Nature, of the folk culture, and the long d'Urberville inheritance, to Hardy's way of thinking the d'Urberville psychic inheritance was itself subject to great and natural evolutionary forces that make it part of Tess's consciousness as much, and in the same way, as the old landscape are part of Var Vale. [. . .]

[. . .] [The] struggle towards existence or death on the 'tangled bank'[1] occasionally becomes, in Hardy, literally a tragic struggle of intrinsically natural man or woman to survive in a world where society has confusingly changed Nature's ambiguous rules of survival. Thus in Tess we have her real affinities with basic natural processes, her limited but important participation in a rudimentary form of ancient folk culture, her introduction to the byways and perversion of 'modern' society, especially as Alec manifests them (and as they are symbolically rendered in connection with Alec and the 'modern' threshing-machine), and finally a betrayal by an imagined denial of modern society in Angel's Hellenistic[2] Nature worship. [. . .]

[. . .] Tess seems to me at least in part Hardy's answer to the following suppositions: Suppose man had not passed beyond heliolatry or the ill-defined folk culture that is not so far removed from its pagan origins in Stonehenge, and that survives in a debased form, all around Tess. Suppose he had not been victimized by a Christian talent for ideals that generate guilt and remorse and, perhaps even worse, forgiveness as their psychological essence. And suppose, finally, that we are not talking about 'survival' solely in the mindless, brutal way (as the d'Urbervilles survived for so long by human measure), but as a quality that both depends on and furthers the peculiar essence of the species; this in man means survival with some sensitivity and awareness of evolutionary kinship with all life. [. . .]

Tess is a victim of modern society, but most important she is a victim of Angel's denial of her true, truly Darwinian, affinities with Nature. The geological and palaeontological metaphors that Hardy uses firmly establish her ancientness and

---

1   The phrase is from the final passage of Charles Darwin's manifesto of evolutionary theory, *The Origin of Species* (1859); it reads, 'It is interesting to contemplate a tangled bank, clothed with many plants of many kinds, with birds singing on the bushes, with various insects flitting about, and with worms crawling through the damp earth, and to reflect that these elaborately constructed forms, so different from each other, and dependent upon each other in so complex a manner, have all been produced by laws acting around us'.

2   Greek, in this case connoting pagan.

the ideal quality of her consciousness. She really does come home, then, to Stonehenge – a *pagan*, but as the *ideal* pagan, evolved beyond the paganism of her 'noble' and nominally Christian ancestors. She is capable of the 'happiness' of a species so attuned to its total environment (Nature and limited forms of society, in her case) that its essence, whatever it may be, flourishes and rejoices. [. . .] Had Tess not been born into a world where the steam-thresher and Alec and Angel dominate, the ideal pagan might at least have gone home to Stonehenge as a genuine sacrifice to the sun, and thus no victim at all.

From **Adam Gussow, 'Dreaming Holmberry-Lipped Tess: Aboriginal Reverie and Spectatorial Desire in *Tess of the d'Urbervilles*',** *Studies in the Novel*, 32 (2000), pp. 443–4, 446–7, 459–61

This reading of the novel – in which Tess's dreaminess and withdrawals into apparent passivity are presented as positive modes of spiritual sustenance, analogous to the psycho-spiritual life of Australian aboriginal tribes – may initially seem far-fetched. But Gussow's argument is not for the literal equation of Aboriginal 'Dreaming' with Tess's retreats into herself. Rather he proposes that this model is useful is suggesting some alternatives to the usual critical interpretations of Tess's passivity and identification with nature. While acknowledging the power and aptness of feminist readings focusing on male attempts to objectify Tess, he suggests that her 'heathen' inclinations – and ironically, her troublesome heredity – actually do provide her a limited means of shelter; they are, he suggests, a kind of escape into her ancient past, away from the 'wholesale distractions' of Angel and Alec. Gussow's original discussion mentions several of the novel's scenes, beginning with John Durbeyfield's opening drunken reverie, and including Tess's eating of the strawberries, her journey over the hills to Talbothays dairy, her walk in the wild garden at Talbothays and her sufferings at Flintcomb-Ash farm. The excerpt below focuses on the final scene at Stonehenge (Key Passages, p. 182), which Gussow sees as the culminating example of Tess's 'ancestral and spiritual convergence'.

[. . .] Any character sketch of Tess which begins with lips and legs – unwillingly projected sensuality and wide-ranging bipedal mobility – must end by acknowledging a third defining mode: Tess and Dreamer, by night and day. [. . .] 'The incarnate state of Tess's soul,' remarks Mary Jacobus, 'appears to be as close to sleep – to unconsciousness – as is compatible with going about her work.'[1] Feminist readers of *Tess* have generally been quick to mark such dreaminess as invidious, part of an ideological project through which Tess, with her 'mobile peony mouth,' is constructed as an instance of the natural – all skittering instinct and passive acquiescence and free-floating reverie, in contrast to Alec's focused willfulness and Angel's intellectual stringency. This politically retrograde 'natural' Tess is both a sadistically exploited object of male scopic[2] desire and a

---

1   [Gussow's note] Mary Jacobus, quoted in Penny Boumelha, *Thomas Hardy and Women*, p. 121.
2   That is, pertaining to vision, especially intensely focused vision.

continually self-liquidating subject, the 'charm[ing]' field-woman upon whose pulchritudinous[3] form Hardy and his textual surrogates gaze with unseemly voyeuristic hunger.[4] ['T]hose of the other sex,' remarks the narrator of *Tess* in an oft-cited passage,

> were the most interesting of this company of binders, by reason of the charm which is acquired by woman when she becomes part and parcel of outdoor nature, and is not merely an object set down therein as at ordinary times. A field-woman is a personality afield; a field-woman is a portion of the field; she has somehow lost her own margin, imbibed the essence of her surrounding, and assimilated herself with it. [Chapter 14]

Yet such reverie-in-nature – the field-woman's losing of 'her own margin' – may be a form of spirit-work, a legitimate mode of defense, a variety of religious experience struggling against colonial enclosure or male scopic desire. What the narrator refers to as 'Tess's unassisted power of dreaming' [Chapter 43] might remind us, I suggest, of another subject people pressured – like the Durbeyfield tribe (indeed, like Hardy himself)[5] – by the force of a calculating metropolitan gaze, a people with a submerged but passionately embraced prehistory rooted in a primordial event known as 'the Dreaming.' I am referring to the Australian Aborigines – or, rather, the decimated remnants of five-hundred-odd tribes grouped under that name and bound into an informal polity by shared beliefs, rituals, and modes of long-distance communication, the 'songlines' memorably evoked by Bruce Chatwin.[6]

Australia is mentioned explicitly at several points in Hardy's novel – it, like the American West, is one of several frontiers Angel considers making his fortune on – but my argument here is not for Hardy's deliberate mapping of Aboriginal modes of religious beliefs on to the inhabitants of Wessex. It is, instead, for a series of striking parallels between the two communities, arising from what might be termed an Aboriginal collective unconscious, which throw the overarching plot of *Tess* in sharp relief and force us to rethink the nature/culture opposition (Tess-as-Nature's-Body, desired/inscribed/raped by men) on which many readings of the novel have pivoted. What passes for an ideological encoding of the natural in *Tess* – for example, her explicitly remarked continuity with the hills, dales, fields, and photosphere of Wessex – may be seen from an Aboriginal perspective as a sign both of proper acculturation and spiritual attainment, the achieved power of mapping oneself on to and into numinous[7] ancestral terrain. [. . .]

---

3   Having great physical beauty.
4   [Gussow's note] For a critique of the various claims for Tess's passivity, see Rosemarie Morgan, 'Passive Victim?: Tess of the d'Urbervilles,' *The Thomas Hardy Journal* 5 (1989): 28–46.
5   [Gussow's note] See [Julie Grossman, 'Hardy's Tess and "The Photograph": Images to Die for,' *Criticism* 35 (1993)], esp. pp. 617–19, for a discussion of the way in which Hardy's portrait of Tess reflects both his anxiety about being 'an object of public inspection' as a novelist and guilt at having projected that anxiety into his 'guilty' heroine on whom all eyes feast.
6   See Bruce Chatwin's narrative of his travels in the Australian outback, *Songlines* (London: Jonathan Cape, 1987).
7   Spiritual or supernatural.

[. . .] [I]n Aboriginal conceptions [creation was] a time of 'Dreaming' in which a pristine landscape was endowed with geographical features and criss-crossed with songlines. 'Not until the period of *tjukuba* of Dreaming,' recounts James Cowan,

> and the mysterious appearance of Sky Heroes, either from inside the earth itself or from an ill-defined upper region, did the landscape take on a truly cosmic significance and attain to form. At the conclusion of the Dreaming period the Sky Heroes disappeared from the face of the earth, leaving in their place their personalized 'signatures' in the guise of topographic landmarks, contour variations, trees, animals – in fact, all manifestations of life on earth.[8]

An Aborigine makes contact with 'his' Dreaming – with the Sky Heroes responsible for singing his local habitat into being – by setting off on a Dream-Journey; he goes Walkabout, descends into reverie, sings or dances, regains his soul by reestablishing his bond with numinous ancestral territory. [. . .]

[. . .] Literary criticism – the product of a culture premised on an extreme heightening of the visual sense above all others – is uneasy with the sort of language I've just been using, which it tends to dismiss as mystification. Modern regimes of knowledge are regimes of *sight*, after all: the prisoner observed, the disease-carrier labeled, the narrative anatomized. To this extent criticism is bound up with the general Western drift towards spectacularity – a separation of vision from participation [. . .]. I make this point as a way of introducing the figure of Tess, whom, I would argue, criticism has had a far easier time *seeing* than inhabiting. The very notion of 'inhabiting' a character is suspect, an imposition of power effected with the help of hungry, oppressive eyes. 'To realize Tess as consciousness,' insists Boumelha, 'with all that entails of representation and display, inevitably renders her all the more the object of gaze and knowledge for reader and narrator' (p. 120) [See Modern Criticism p. 879]. It is true that we 'know' Tess only through the narrator's eyes, eyes which both report on and take part in her construction as a fetish-object of extraordinary visual charisma. But the Tess so-depicted has another quality – a chameleonic insistence on melting into the landscape, retreating into a reverie – which represents both a negation of the pressure of so many prying eyes and a positive assertion of spiritual identity. Tess uniquely exemplifies the pain inflicted by spectacularity on a soul that knows its own deepest pleasure as a mode of unselfconscious, unconstrained being which is antithetical to spectacle. The real Tess (so to speak) may escape us in those moments of reverie and dissolution if we insist on reading them solely as an annihilation of self, if we refuse to acknowledge the existence and claims of her Dreaming. [. . .]

[. . .] What the ending at Stonehenge offers us, I suggest, is a Tess who has miraculously fought her way back into contact with what turns out to have been her true ancestral songline all along; a Tess whose death, while tragic in the sense of grossly premature, is nevertheless the ritual completion of a spiritual quest that

---

8   James Cowan, *Mysteries of the Dream-Time: The Spiritual Life of Australian Aborigines* (1898; Bridpart: Prism Press, 1992), pp. 25–6.

she has been pursuing, if not always consciously then with fortuitous intuition, since the novel's opening pages. This quest, it should be noted, has nothing to do with Angel Clare; the 'marriage-of-true-minds' plot, by which Tess murders Alec in a spasm of agonized resurgent love for Angel, is merely the mechanism for freeing her to resume a Dream Journey from which *both* men are, albeit in different ways, wholesale distractions.

[. . .] Stonehenge is Tess's Uluru (Ayers Rock),[9] a terrainian[10] point of ancestral and spiritual convergence, Home Base on the cosmological map. Her Dream-Journey has come to an end, which is why sleepiness suddenly overtakes her. ' "I like very much to be here," she murmured. "It is so solemn and lonely – after my great happiness – with nothing but the sky above my face" ' [Chapter 58]. She falls asleep shortly before dawn, when a band of pursuers emerges from the countryside to bring her in. They allow her to sleep on for a few moments before the sun pushes under her eyelids. Those spectacular lips, cause of so much of her grief, are nowhere to be found in these final pages, as though some escape from burdening embodiment has finally been achieved. [. . .] Late Victorian Wessex was not Australia; Tess had been given no rules for 'going back.' Forced to improvise, repeatedly sidetracked by an economy of male desire in which her spectacular good looks were deadly currency, she manages to walk herself to the rightest available death. Her spiritual economy triumphs as the bearer of it is extinguished: a familiar theme in the West's various narratives of colonial expansion and tribal sundown, no cause for celebration, but a small and important victory even so.

---

9 The Aboriginal and English names of a huge sandstone monolith in the heart of the Australian outback. It is a sacred site of the Anangu people.
10 Earthly.

The Work in Performance

That Hardy conceived of *Tess* as a novel suitable for theatrical adaptation and performance is best demonstrated by the plain fact that he wrote such an adaptation himself. His stage version of *Tess* was begun around 1895, but, after initial discussions of possible production scenarios, it lay aside for almost thirty years.[1] Then, in a surprising flurry of activity in what turned out to be the last three years of Hardy's life, it was produced, first locally in Dorchester in late 1824, and then briefly in London's West End in 1825. The play was politely but not enthusiastically received, as Keith Wilson describes in 'Tess on Stage: Dorchester and London';[2] the circumstances surrounding its production have been of interest to scholars primarily because of Hardy's apparent infatuation with the young actress, Gertrude Bugler, who played the role of Tess in the Dorchester production. Fifty years younger than Hardy, who was by this time in his middle eighties, Bugler had acted in other local adaptations of Hardy's novels (see **p. 62**); in a remarkable twist of fate, she was the daughter of a milkmaid named Augusta Way who, as Michael Millgate describes, had 'first suggested the figure of Tess to [Hardy's] imagination'[3] more than thirty years earlier. Thus the romantic infatuation that Hardy had initially had with his own fictional character was recapitulated and brought eerily to life; Hardy's feelings were obvious enough that they caused a great deal of consternation to Florence Dugdale, his second wife.[4]

Wilson is an expert on Hardyean stage adaptations; those interested in versions of *Tess* for other media are directed to Peter Widdowson's 'Thomas Hardy on Radio, TV, and Film', from his *Hardy in History* (1989).[5] Widdowson's discussion occurs within a larger examination of the historical processes that have shaped, and continue to shape, our perception of Hardy and his canon. Though he offers a fascinating overview of BBC radio productions of Hardy, the majority of Widdowson's account focuses on the best-known adaptation of the novel, the 1979 film *Tess* directed by Roman Polanski. Widdowson writes that 'Polanski's

1 See Michael Millgate, *Thomas Hardy: A Biography* (Oxford: Oxford University Press, 1982), pp. 363–4, 375–6, 555–8, 563, 604n, 605n, 617n.
2 In Keith Wilson, *Thomas Hardy on Stage* (New York: St Martin's, 1995), pp. 132–58.
3 Millgate, *Hardy: A Biography*, pp. 293–4; 600n.
4 Millgate, *Hardy: A Biography*, pp. 557–9, 563.
5 Peter Widdowson, *Hardy in History: A Study in Literary Sociology* (London: Routledge, 1989), pp. 93–126.

Tess is someone trying to be her own woman, adrift in a world whose values she cannot relate to, who wants to love and be loved as an existential human subject in a society of exploitation and sham. She is doomed, not so much by history, but by her difference. She is, in late twentieth-century terms, *l'etranger*: the authentic individual whom the world must destroy' (p. 123). Because this film and a 1998 BBC/A&E television production are by far the most readily available adaptations of *Tess*, it is appropriate to offer some additional comments on them.

Polanski's *Tess* (1979) is indeed a stupendously effective rendering of the novel, even given some controversial directorial and casting choices. A young Nastassja Kinski is both dazzling and haunting in the lead role of Tess. Though her physical presence is perhaps too ethereal and fragile in nature – it is hard to pretend, even for a moment, that she is a 'typical country girl' – it allows her successfully to project the aura of transcendent womanliness that the novel urges on us. The film lavishes attention on Kinski's eroticism, especially in the early scene of strawberry-eating, and it gives visual proof to the sexual tensions that the text narrates in circumspect language. And, by contrast, Kinski can transform into a wordless embodiment of pain and suffering. It is certainly possible to quibble with Polanski's depiction of the scene in The Chase, and, more generally, with the way he represents Tess's balance of passivity and assertion, guilt and victimization. But these elements are, of course, at the core of the novel's own purposeful ambiguities. The male leads (Leigh Lawson as Alec, and Peter Firth as Angel) may initially strike viewers as physically miscast, but their performances are excellent.

The film is a visual triumph. Polanski produces both distant and close-up shots that project the beauty and harshness of the unpeopled landscape. Indeed, the physical earth, which Hardy foregrounds in the novel, is also foregrounded here, in all its glorious vitality, emptiness, rawness and implacability. Polanski is

Figure 5 **Nastassja Kinski, in *Tess*, dir. Roman Polanski (1979) (© Renn/Burrill/SFP. Courtesy of the Kobal Collection)**

equally successful at conveying the essential conditions of life in rural Wessex. Though the settings are sometimes beautiful and sometimes desolate, several of the most effective scenes are those where nature is depicted as neither a beneficent God nor an evil enemy, but as a kind of moderate annoyance and relentless fact of country life. The loneliness and tenacity of small rural communities is made palpable. The film is generally, though certainly not entirely, faithful to the plot, and at three hours may be, for some, too long and slowly paced. But the slowness of the film is arguably one of its greatest virtues: it is exquisite at depicting stillness, or languor, or dull suffering, or the painful passing of minutes. Nominated for several Academy Awards, including Best Picture and Director, it won Oscars for Cinematography, Costumes and Art/Set Direction.

There is also a reasonably effective and fairly lavish 1998 BBC/A&E production starring Justine Waddell as Tess. Also three hours in length, this version tries more assiduously to check-off all of the plot events, but this very assiduousness sometimes leads to a sense of hurried compression, and sometimes to problematic distortions. In the final scene, for example, the Hardyean voice-over narrator intones that 'Mankind' – rather than the 'President of the Immortals' – had finished its sport with Tess. Though the abandoning of Hardy's explicit reference to Aeschylus is understandable given the assumption of a popular audience, the substitution of 'Mankind' seems to reflect a basic misunderstanding of, or lack of concern for, Hardy's actual cosmology. Some directorial choices are also open to criticism. The character of Alec, played by Jason Flemyng, is sometimes shown in a strangely sympathetic light; but both Flemyng and Oliver Milburn as Angel give

Figure 6 **Minnie Maddern Fiske as Tess in the 1897 New York stage production, adapted from the novel by Lorimer Stoddard (By permission of the Library of Congress, 91796068)**

fine, complex performances. The film is sometimes heavy-handed in trying to establish a vision of Tess as unique and otherworldly, but as the story unfolds and we see more of Waddell's range, her performance becomes more and more impressive. Though this film is not as grand as Polanski's, its locations are none the less sweeping, beautiful and carefully rendered. It is a worthy and generally compassionate production.

3

Key Passages

Introduction

The following selection of excerpts from *Tess of the d'Urbervilles* offers what might be called a set of stepping-stones for understanding the novel. Some passages are primarily descriptive, and have been chosen both for their value in illustrating Hardy's methods as a writer and for their helpfulness in the exposition of important themes and plotlines. Other passages focus more directly on action, usually through crucial exchanges of dialogue. (Hardy's facility with this mode is itself interesting in light of his efforts to align Tess's story with the conventions of tragic drama.) The introductory notes, shaded in grey, are written so as to orient each passage within the story and, in some cases, relative to adjacent excerpts. These notes usually discuss what is typically 'Hardyean' about the passage; how the passage itself operates as a coherent piece of writing (for example, how its imagery might signal a shift from one mood or perspective to another); how it functions in plot and character development; and, where applicable, how it has played into scholarly discussions of the novel. A concerted effort has been made to cross-reference the specific topics and episodes seen here with the most relevant arguments that appear in this volume's Interpretations section, above.

Two other features of the 'key passages' bear some explanation here. First, brief footnotes mainly address regional dialect, archaic terms and literary allusions which, it is anticipated, many readers may find confusing. At the same time, it needs to be said that Hardy's writing is famously dense in description and allusion, and that his quasi-anthropological view of 'Wessex' (springing from his strong affiliation to the real region of Dorset) is deliberately that of a specialist in arcane social customs and half-forgotten country lore. In other words, there are few readers of Hardy who will catch absolutely all of his references. To feel slightly at sea, slightly overwhelmed by detail, is in some ways simply to join the ranks of Hardy readers over the past century. The best advice is to use the footnotes, but to avoid allowing minor questions of vocabulary to interfere with the upsweep and grandeur of the story. Second, Hardy himself worked hard to provide a sense of structure – and dramatic movement – for *Tess*, by dividing the book's fifty-nine chapters into seven 'Phases'. The titles of these, and their very presence as typographical markers, are important to the reader's unfolding perception of the novel. Poetic and thought-provoking in themselves, the 'Phases' provide a good sense of the tragic arc of the story.

Taken in sequence, the Key Passages may also serve to clarify the plot of *Tess*, but only in a skeletal way. They have not been chosen to condense Hardy's nearly 400-page novel so much as to survey or 'map' it. In fact, the only way to get a truly full picture of *Tess* – including the workings of its plot – is to read the book itself. There are perhaps three major aspects of the novel that are difficult to represent wholly in this, or any, selection of passages:

1. *The cumulative effect of scenes and episodes in context.* This applies not only to Hardy's complex dovetailing of bad omens and painful ironies but also to his profoundly beautiful evocations of quiet happiness. For example, the decision was made to skip a sequence of thirteen chapters from 'Phase the Third' and 'Phase the Fourth', because these chapters work together so symbiotically in showing the progress of a romantic attraction that no one episode (as in real life, perhaps) can stand on its own as representing the whole.

2. *The 'deep background' Hardy provides for people and places.* While several of the excerpts here, especially those concerning the family backgrounds of Tess, Alec and Angel, provide a sense of Hardy's historical impulse, that impulse is also seen in dozens of 'minor' passages throughout the novel, extending, for example, to the names and operations of businesses, the purchase or inheritance of property, the workings of farm machines, the ongoing exchange of gossip, the evolution of local customs and so on. The Wessex of *Tess* and Hardy's other novels is as fully realized a fictive setting as one will ever find, but one must read several of his works before the magnitude of his conceptual achievement becomes apparent.

3. *The thematic importance of work and travel.* The selected passages here, with their necessary attention to key moments in the plot, exclude several scenes devoted to the details of work and farm labour. Hardy devotes much time and attention to specific agricultural processes, and – even more importantly – to the difficult day-to-day lives of individual workers. In Tess's case, there is a whole range of work experiences (from the skilled work she performs at the dairy to the back-breaking regimen she endures at Flintcomb-Ash) that could be made to form a conceptual unit unto themselves. Usually, as with the episode involving the butter-churn at Talbothays, Hardy employs these work-episodes to further the development of his themes and characters, but it must be recognized that, at some level, he was recording these details as an act of historical preservation.

The reading text below is based on Hardy's 1912 'Wessex Edition' of *Tess*, though a few slight adjustments in punctuation have been made for purposes of modern presentation. After the difficulties surrounding *Tess*'s first publication in 1891 (see p. 11), Hardy essentially stabilized the text of the novel for the edition of 1895. Even so, he continued to make minor changes, mostly in punctuation but occasionally in wording, in later editions, including both the Wessex edition and a new impression of that edition that appeared in 1920. John Laird's *The Shaping of Tess of the D'Urbervilles* (Oxford: Clarendon Press, 1975) is the best guide to the text's evolution in the years between 1888 and 1912. Many modern editions of the novel employ the Wessex edition for their basic text. The current Penguin

(2003) and Oxford World's Classics (1998) editions offer the most significant alternatives, but even in these cases the differences are fairly subtle. For more on currently available editions of *Tess*, and their editorial rationales, see Further Reading.

Key Passages

From 'Phase the First: The Maiden'

From Chapter 2: The Village of Marlott, and the May-Day Dance

This early passage, which introduces the Vale of Blackmoor and Tess's village, exhibits the dynamic nature of Hardy's concern with landscape, both as an artistic backdrop and as a force in human life. Beginning with a distant view 'from the summits of the hills', the description telescopes downward to the village of Marlott, eventually fixing on a group of local girls participating in a yearly May-Day dance. Such a progression is typical of Hardy: rarely are we allowed to believe that we can 'know' a place from a single perspective. Accordingly, the passage also moves from a geographic account of the region to a historical one, suggesting that there is variability even among distanced viewpoints. Throughout the passage, human society is seen as gradually altering, but never overcoming, an immemorial landscape; this idea is reflected semi-humorously in the list of Blackmoor localities, whose humble names connote an earthbound, hardscrabble way of life.

The valley's special character as a 'fertile and sheltered' region is highlighted, predicting the characterization of Tess herself as at once vibrantly sexual and tragically naïve. Likewise, the story of the doomed White Hart foreshadows the catastrophic encounter between Tess and Alec in The Chase. And with similar unobtrusiveness, the discussion of the ancient origins of the dance introduces three themes that will be elaborated over the course of the narrative: the continuing influence of the past on the present; the uneasy coexistence of 'pagan' and 'modern' customs; and the tension between 'Ideal and real', which will later be linked to Hardy's presentation of Tess as simultaneously typical of her class and utterly distinctive.

On this last point, it should be noted that while Hardy aspires to a historically distanced, 'objective' account of the sufferings of a person like Tess, he also wishes to observe her closely, intimately, and emotionally. So while the opening of the passage warns against the confusion that comes from proximity and close observation, the end of the passage warns against the opposite, decrying 'the habit of taking long views [that has] reduced emotions to a monotonous

average'. In this phrasing, we see Hardy's desire to tell Tess's story as a sociological parable, but also – if this is not a contradiction – with the passion that it
deserves. The resulting instabilities of tone have prompted a great deal of scholarly discussion; see here, for example, the arguments made by Howe (**p. 64**),
Bayley (**p. 75**), Freeman (**p. 76**), Gatrell (**p. 78**), and Williams (**p. 99**).

The village of Marlott lay amid the north-eastern undulations of the beautiful
Vale of Blakemore or Blackmoor aforesaid, an engirdled and secluded region, for
the most part untrodden as yet by tourist or landscape-painter, though within a
four hours' journey from London.

It is a vale whose acquaintance is best made by viewing it from the summits of
the hills that surround it – except perhaps during the droughts of summer. An
unguided ramble into its recesses in bad weather is apt to engender dissatisfaction
with its narrow, tortuous, and miry ways.

This fertile and sheltered tract of country, in which the fields are never brown
and the springs never dry, is bounded on the south by the bold chalk ridge that
embraces the prominences of Hambledon Hill, Bulbarrow, Nettlecombe-Tout,
Dogbury, High Stoy, and Bubb Down.[1] The traveller from the coast, who, after
plodding northward for a score of miles over calcareous downs[2] and corn-lands,
suddenly reaches the verge of one of these escarpments, is surprised and delighted
to behold, extended like a map beneath him, a country differing absolutely from
that which he has passed through. Behind him the hills are open, the sun blazes
down upon fields so large as to give an unenclosed character to the landscape, the
lanes are white, the hedges low and plashed, the atmosphere colourless. Here, in
the valley, the world seems to be constructed upon a smaller and more delicate
scale; the fields are mere paddocks,[3] so reduced that from this height their hedge-
rows appear a network of dark green threads overspreading the paler green of the
grass. The atmosphere beneath is languorous, and is so tinged with azure that
what artists call the middle distance partakes also of that hue, while the horizon
beyond is of the deepest ultramarine. Arable lands are few and limited; with but
slight exceptions the prospect is a broad rich mass of grass and trees, mantling
minor hills and dales within the major. Such is the Vale of Blackmoor.

The district is of historic, no less than of topographical interest. The Vale was
known in former times as the Forest of White Hart, from a curious legend of King
Henry III's reign,[4] in which the killing by a certain Thomas de la Lynd of a
beautiful white hart[5] which the king had run down and spared, was made the
occasion of a heavy fine. In those days, and till comparatively recent times, the
country was densely wooded. Even now, traces of its earlier condition are to be
found in the old oak copses and irregular belts of timber that yet survive upon its
slopes, and the hollow-trunked trees that shade so many of its pastures.

---

1   Hardy's imaginary place-names, based on actual locales in south-central England.
2   Land impregnanted with calcium deposits.
3   A small enclosure for animals.
4   1216–72.
5   A male deer or stag.

The forests have departed, but some old customs of their shades remain. Many, however, linger only in a metamorphosed or disguised form. The May-Day dance, for instance, was to be discerned on the afternoon under notice, in the guise of the club revel, or 'club-walking', as it was there called.

It was an interesting event to the younger inhabitants of Marlott, though its real interest was not observed by the participators in the ceremony. Its singularity lay less in the retention of a custom of walking in procession and dancing on each anniversary than in the members being solely women. In men's clubs such celebrations were, though expiring, less uncommon: but either the natural shyness of the softer sex, or a sarcastic attitude on the part of male relatives, had denuded such women's clubs as remained (if any other did) of this their glory and consummation. The club of Marlott alone lived to uphold the local Cerealia.[6] It had walked for hundreds of years, if not as benefit-club, as votive[7] sisterhood of some sort; and it walked still.

The banded ones were all dressed in white gowns – a gay survival from Old-Style days, when cheerfulness and May-time were synonyms – days before the habit of taking long views had reduced emotions to a monotonous average. Their first exhibition of themselves was in a processional march of two and two round the parish. Ideal and real clashed slightly as the sun lit up their figures against the green hedges and creeper-laced house-fronts; for, though the whole troop wore white garments, no two whites were alike among them. Some approached pure blanching; some had a bluish pallor; some worn by the older characters (which had possibly lain by folded for many a year) inclined to a cadaverous tint, and to a Georgian style.[8]

In addition to the distinction of a white frock, every woman and girl carried in her right hand a peeled willow wand, and in her left a bunch of white flowers. The peeling of the former, and the selection of the latter, had been an operation of personal care.

From **Chapter 2: An Early Description of Tess**

This brief passage introduces us in a limited way to Tess, and in a more complex way to Hardy's tendencies in describing her. As with his landscape description, counterpoint is the general strategy, though here that technique is used to convey malleability rather than permanence – specifically, the extent to which Tess, at 16, is still unformed and unknowable, even to herself. Thus we see her as both womanly and childish, both uniquely 'fascinating' and an ordinary 'country girl', having some education, but still speaking the dialect of her native valley. Her red mouth – a physical feature that Hardy returns to often in the novel – is here used as another illustration of Tess's emerging, unfixed character: it has 'hardly as yet settled into its definite shape'.

---

6   A festival honouring Ceres, Roman goddess of agriculture.
7   Reflective of a vow or commitment.
8   Generally, the years extending from 1714–1830.

What complicates this picture, we realize later, is that Tess seems to evolve not toward a firmer, more delineated identity, but toward new levels of subjective indefinability. Hardy clearly wishes to emphasize the 'rich' and elusive nature of Tess's being, but some critics have seen him constructing her as a blank screen on to which various idealized images can be projected. Critics who confront aspects of this problem include Boumelha, Freeman, Bayley, Brady and Vigar. The most sweepingly favourable of these interpretations is Howe's: 'Hardy presents her neither from the outside nor the inside exclusively, neither through event nor analysis alone; she is apprehended in her organic completeness, so that her objectivity and subjectivity become inseparable' (p. 66).

Tess Durbeyfield at this time of her life was a mere vessel of emotion untinctured by experience. The dialect was on her tongue to some extent, despite the village school,[1] the characteristic intonation of that dialect for this district being the voicing approximately rendered by the syllable UR, probably as rich an utterance as any to be found in human speech. The pouted-up deep red mouth to which this syllable was native had hardly as yet settled into its definite shape, and her lower lip had a way of thrusting the middle of her top one upward, when they closed together after a word.

Phases of her childhood lurked in her aspect still. As she walked along to-day, for all her bouncing handsome womanliness, you could sometimes see her twelfth year in her cheeks, or her ninth sparkling from her eyes; and even her fifth would flit over the curves of her mouth now and then.

Yet few knew, and still fewer considered this. A small minority, mainly strangers, would look long at her in casually passing by, and grow momentarily fascinated by her freshness, and wonder if they would ever see her again: but to almost everybody she was a fine and picturesque country girl, and no more.

From **Chapter 4: The Death of Prince**

One of many scenes that takes place in poor or uncertain light conditions, this sequence leading to the death of the Durbeyfield family horse is of signal importance for two reasons. The first is that it contains Tess's early statement of what has variously been called Hardy's pessimism or fatalism – her declaration to her younger brother, as they travel under the stars, that they live on a 'blighted' world. This is significant not only because it may be the clearest philosophical statement that she expresses in the entire novel (though it will be echoed, arguably, in her later cry, 'Once a victim, always a victim!') but also because it precedes all of the novel's tragic events. It suggests that, even in her state of relative innocence and inexperience, she is disposed to a kind of fatalism.

1   One of the emphases of the village school would have been the attempted reduction in students' use of their local dialect.

Her consideration of the 'mesh of events of her own life' reads remarkably like the sort of conclusion she might reach much later, but at this early moment the judgement is unexpected and jarring.

The passage also has a decisive role in the plot: the loss of Prince precipitates the financial crisis that the Durbeyfields seek to solve by sending Tess to 'claim kin' with the d'Urbervilles of Trantridge. It should be added, however, that even as the accident catalyses the first phase of Tess's ruination, virtually the entire novel is presented as a chain of (disastrous) cause and effect, beginning with the encounter between the parson and Tess's father that opens it (see Van Ghent in Modern Criticism, p. 81). The end of the passage, in fact, reminds us that, if anyone is to blame for this episode, it is her negligent father. Having failed to deliver the hives himself, he reasserts his familial pride in an extravagantly misplaced manner – 'ris[ing]' to the occasion', Hardy tells us sarcastically, and refusing to sell Prince's body for the small sum offered. The concluding image, of Tess as 'dry and pale', stricken with guilt and yet emotionless, furthers her separation from her sentimental and irrational family. Her self-assessment as 'a murderess' seems cold and unduly harsh, but it is strongly predictive of how the world works, and of what she will become.

Her mother at length agreed to this arrangement. Little Abraham was aroused from his deep sleep in a corner of the same apartment, and made to put on his clothes while still mentally in the other world. Meanwhile Tess had hastily dressed herself; and the twain,[1] lighting a lantern, went out to the stable. The rickety little waggon was already laden, and the girl led out the horse Prince, only a degree less rickety than the vehicle.

The poor creature looked wonderingly round at the night, at the lantern, at their two figures, as if he could not believe that at that hour, when every living thing was intended to be in shelter and at rest, he was called upon to go out and labour. They put a stock of candle-ends into the lantern, hung the latter to the off-side of the load, and directed the horse onward, walking at his shoulder at first during the uphill parts of the way, in order not to overload an animal of so little vigour. To cheer themselves as well as they could, they made an artificial morning with the lantern, some bread and butter, and their own conversation, the real morning being far from come. Abraham, as he more fully awoke (for he had moved in a sort of trance so far), began to talk of the strange shapes assumed by the various dark objects against the sky; of this tree that looked like a raging tiger springing from a lair; of that which resembled a giant's head.

When they had passed the little town of Stourcastle, dumbly somnolent under its thick brown thatch,[2] they reached higher ground. Still higher, on their left, the elevation called Bulbarrow or Bealbarrow, well-nigh the highest in South Wessex, swelled into the sky, engirdled by its earthen trenches. From hereabout the long road was fairly level for some distance onward. They mounted in front of the waggon, and Abraham grew reflective.

1   Two.
2   Roof material, probably straw.

'Tess!' he said in a preparatory tone, after a silence.

'Yes, Abraham.'

'Bain't you glad that we've become gentlefolk?'

'Not particular glad.'

'But you be glad that you 'm going to marry a gentleman?'

'What?' said Tess, lifting her face.

'That our great relation will help 'ee to marry a gentleman.'

'I? Our great relation? We have no such relation. What has put that into your head?'

'I heard 'em talking about it up at Rolliver's when I went to find father. There's a rich lady of our family out at Trantridge, and mother said that if you claimed kin with the lady, she'd put 'ee in the way of marrying a gentleman.'

His sister became abruptly still, and lapsed into a pondering silence. Abraham talked on, rather for the pleasure of utterance than for audition, so that his sister's abstraction was of no account. He leant back against the hives, and with upturned face made observation on the stars, whose cold pulses were beating amid the black hollows above, in serene dissociation from these two wisps of human life. He asked how far away those twinklers were, and whether God was on the other side of them. But ever and anon his childish prattle recurred to what impressed his imagination even more deeply than the wonders of creation. If Tess were made rich by marrying a gentleman, would she have money enough to buy a spy-glass so large that it would draw the stars as near to her as Nettlecombe-Tout?

The renewed subject, which seemed to have impregnated the whole family, filled Tess with impatience.

'Never mind that now!' she exclaimed.

'Did you say the stars were worlds, Tess?'

'Yes.'

'All like ours?'

'I don't know; but I think so. They sometimes seem to be like the apples on our stubbard-tree.[3] Most of them splendid and sound – a few blighted.'

'Which do we live on – a splendid one or a blighted one?'

'A blighted one.'

' 'Tis very unlucky that we didn't pitch on a sound one, when there were so many more of 'em!'

'Yes.'

'Is it like that *really*, Tess?' said Abraham, turning to her much impressed, on reconsideration of this rare information. 'How would it have been if we had pitched on a sound one?'

'Well, father wouldn't have coughed and creeped about as he does, and wouldn't have got too tipsy to go on this journey; and mother wouldn't have been always washing, and never getting finished.'

'And you would have been a rich lady ready-made, and not have had to be made rich by marrying a gentleman?'

'O Aby, don't – don't talk of that any more!'

Left to his reflections Abraham soon grew drowsy. Tess was not skilful in the

---

3   A variety of apple.

management of a horse, but she thought that she could take upon herself the entire conduct of the load for the present, and allow Abraham to go to sleep if he wished to do so. She made him a sort of nest in front of the hives, in such a manner that he could not fall, and, taking the reins into her own hands, jogged on as before.

Prince required but slight attention, lacking energy for superfluous movements of any sort. With no longer a companion to distract her, Tess fell more deeply into reverie than ever, her back leaning against the hives. The mute procession past her shoulders of trees and hedges became attached to fantastic scenes outside reality, and the occasional heave of the wind became the sigh of some immense sad soul, conterminous with the universe in space, and with history in time.

Then, examining the mesh of events in her own life, she seemed to see the vanity of her father's pride; the gentlemanly suitor awaiting herself in her mother's fancy; to see him as a grimacing personage, laughing at her poverty, and her shrouded knightly ancestry. Everything grew more and more extravagant, and she no longer knew how time passed. A sudden jerk shook her in her seat, and Tess awoke from the sleep into which she, too, had fallen.

They were a long way further on than when she had lost consciousness, and the waggon had stopped. A hollow groan, unlike anything she had ever heard in her life, came from the front, followed by a shout of 'Hoi there!'

The lantern hanging at her waggon had gone out, but another was shining in her face – much brighter than her own had been. Something terrible had happened. The harness was entangled with an object which blocked the way.

In consternation Tess jumped down, and discovered the dreadful truth. The groan has proceeded from her father's poor horse Prince. The morning mail-cart, with its two noiseless wheels, speeding along these lanes like an arrow, as it always did, had driven into her slow and unlighted equipage. The pointed shaft of the cart had entered the breast of the unhappy Prince like a sword, and from the wound his life's blood was spouting in a stream, and falling with a hiss into the road.

In her despair Tess sprang forward and put her hand upon the hole, with the only result that she became splashed from face to skirt with the crimson drops. Then she stood helplessly looking on. Prince also stood firm and motionless as long as he could; till he suddenly sank down in a heap.

By this time the mail-cart man had joined her, and began dragging and unharnessing the hot form of Prince. But he was already dead, and, seeing that nothing more could be done immediately, the mail-cart man returned to his own animal, which was uninjured.

'You was on the wrong side,' he said. 'I am bound to go on with the mail-bags, so that the best thing for you to do is bide here with your load. I'll send somebody to help you as soon as I can. It is getting daylight, and you have nothing to fear.'

He mounted and sped on his way; while Tess stood and waited. The atmosphere turned pale, the birds shook themselves in the hedges, arose, and twittered; the lane showed all its white features, and Tess showed hers, still whiter. The huge pool of blood in front of her was already assuming the iridescence of coagulation; and when the sun rose a hundred prismatic hues were reflected from it. Prince lay alongside still and stark; his eyes half open, the hole in his chest looking scarcely large enough to have let out all that had animated him.

' 'Tis all my doing – all mine!' the girl cried, gazing at the spectacle. 'No excuse for me – none. What will mother and father live on now? Aby, Aby!' She shook the child, who had slept soundly through the whole disaster. 'We can't go on with our load – Prince is killed!'

When Abraham realized all, the furrows of fifty years were extemporized on his young face.

'Why, I danced and laughed only yesterday!' she went on to herself. 'To think that I was such a fool!'

' 'Tis because we be on a blighted star, and not a sound one, isn't it, Tess?' murmured Abraham through his tears.

In silence they waited through an interval which seemed endless. At length a sound, and an approaching object, proved to them that the driver of the mail-cart had been as good as his word. A farmer's man from near Stourcastle came up, leading a strong cob. He was harnessed to the waggon of beehives in the place of Prince, and the load taken on towards Casterbridge.

The evening of the same day saw the empty waggon reach again the spot of the accident. Prince had lain there in the ditch since the morning; but the place of the blood-pool was still visible in the middle of the road, though scratched and scraped over by passing vehicles. All that was left of Prince was now hoisted into the waggon he had formerly hauled, and with his hoofs in the air, and his shoes shining in the setting sunlight, he retraced the eight or nine miles to Marlott.

Tess had gone back earlier. How to break the news was more than she could think. It was a relief to her tongue to find from the faces of her parents that they already knew of their loss, though this did not lessen the self-reproach which she continued to heap upon herself for her negligence.

But the very shiftlessness of the household rendered the misfortune a less ter-rifying one to them than it would have been to a striving family, though in the present case it meant ruin, and in the other it would only have meant inconveni-ence. In the Durbeyfield countenances there was nothing of the red wrath that would have burnt upon the girl from parents more ambitious for her welfare. Nobody blamed Tess as she blamed herself.

When it was discovered that the knacker and tanner[4] would give only a very few shillings for Prince's carcase because of his decrepitude, Durbeyfield rose to the occasion.

'No,' said he stoically, 'I won't sell his old body. When we d'Urbervilles was knights in the land, we didn't sell our chargers for cat's meat.[5] Let 'em keep their shillings! He've served me well in his lifetime, and I won't part from him now.'

He worked harder the next day in digging a grave for Prince in the garden than he had worked for months to grow a crop for his family. When the hole was ready, Durbeyfield and his wife tied a rope round the horse and dragged him up the path towards it, the children following in funeral train. Abraham and Liza-Lu sobbed, Hope and Modesty discharged their griefs in loud blares which echoed from the walls; and when Prince was tumbled in they gathered round the grave. The bread-winner had been taken away from them; what would they do?

---

4 Tradesmen who use the body and skin of dead horses.
5 i.e., we have too much pride to settle for something so paltry.

'Is he gone to heaven?' asked Abraham between the sobs.

Then Durbeyfield began to shovel in the earth, and the children cried anew. All except Tess. Her face was dry and pale, as though she regarded herself in the light of a murderess.

From Chapter 5: Discussion of the d'Urberville Lineage; Tess Meets Alec d'Urberville

Hardy's darkly ironic sensibility is never better displayed than in this passage, which contains Tess's famous first encounter with Alec d'Urberville. Alec is clearly portrayed as a villain – 'the moustachioed seducer of Victorian melodrama', Mary Jacobus calls him (p. 73) – and it is impossible not to notice intimations of his predatory sexuality as he guides Tess around the property, pushing artificially ripened strawberries between her lips. (Film adaptations of *Tess* have made much of this scene; see the Work in Performance section above.) But the real darkness of the passage is not in its immediate characterization of Alec, but in the background information about his family. Having previously read of the Durbeyfields' hope that their rich relations will somehow save them from their desperate plight, we are greeted in this chapter with a vision of pervasive fraudulence. The supposed relations are not d'Urbervilles at all, but a family called Stoke who have abandoned the North of England, partly to avoid retribution from clients swindled by old Mr Simon Stoke during his career as a money lender. The cynicism of everything d'Urberville, extending to the purchase of their very name, stands in brutal contrast to the sincerity and vulnerability of Tess as she presents herself to Alec. Hardy, as is his way, relentlessly underscores this contrast. He begins the passage by mentioning that the parson who capriciously informed John Durbeyfield of his grand lineage, just as capriciously failed to mention 'what he knew very well, that the Stoke-d'Urbervilles were no more d'Urbervilles of the true tree then he was himself'. In short, then, Tess's errand – and everything that follows in the novel – is premised on folly and deceit, knowledge of which makes her undoing that much more absurd, savage and painful for the reader. For commentary on the crassness of the Stokes and their relation to modernity see Gregor (p. 101) and Johnson (p. 104).

The characterization of Alec has provoked much discussion. While the general view is that he is a caricatured villain, virtually a flat character, there is some evidence that Hardy attempted to complicate him, especially through his late period of religious conversion. Another perspective is offered by James Kincaid, who argues that, for all his villainy, Alec is a sort of red herring for the reader's own voyeurism regarding Tess (p. 92). Any discussion of Alec's wickedness, however, should be referenced through Jacobus's discussion of the changes Hardy made to the manuscript in an effort to make Tess appear more pure and victimized (pp. 72–5).

Some elements of Tess's characterization should be noted here as well. Once Alec has broken her initial resistance to his advances, she obeys him 'like one in a dream', as he loads her with strawberries and roses. It is another instance – as, immediately before, with the death of Prince – in which Tess is literally or figuratively asleep at the very moment she should be excercising mastery and self-discipline (see Boumelha, **p. 87**). Where Boumelha suggests that Hardy is unwilling or unable to grant Tess full agency, one could also speculate that his decision to have her sleep in this manner is a hedge against having to assign her guilt and responsibility for her situation.

The d'Urbervilles – or Stoke-d'Urbervilles, as they at first called themselves – who owned all this, were a somewhat unusual family to find in such an old-fashioned part of the country. Parson Tringham had spoken truly when he said that our shambling John Durbeyfield was the only really lineal representative of the old d'Urberville family existing in the county, or near it; he might have added, what he knew very well, that the Stoke-d'Urbervilles were no more d'Urbervilles of the true tree than he was himself. Yet it must be admitted that this family formed a very good stock whereon to regraft a name which sadly wanted such renovation.

When old Mr Simon Stoke, latterly deceased, had made his fortune as an honest merchant (some said money lender) in the North, he decided to settle as a county man in the South of England, out of hail of his business district; and in doing this he felt the necessity of recommencing with a name that would not too readily identify him with the smart tradesman of the past, and that would be less commonplace than the original bald stark words. Conning[1] for an hour in the British Museum the pages of works devoted to extinct, half-extinct, obscured, and ruined families appertaining to the quarter of England in which he proposed to settle, he considered that *d'Urberville* looked and sounded as well as any of them: and d'Urberville accordingly was annexed to his own name for himself and his heirs eternally. Yet he was not an extravagant-minded man in this, and in constructing his family tree on the new basis was duly reasonable in framing his inter-marriages and aristocratic links, never inserting a single title above a rank of strict moderation.

Of this work of imagination poor Tess and her parents were naturally in ignorance – much to their discomfiture; indeed, the very possibility of such annexations was unknown to them; who supposed that, though to be well-favoured might be the gift of fortune, a family name came by nature.

Tess still stood hesitating like a bather about to make his plunge, hardly knowing whether to retreat or to persevere, when a figure came forth from the dark triangular door of the tent. It was that of a tall young man, smoking.

He had an almost swarthy complexion, with full lips, badly moulded, though red and smooth, above which was a well-groomed black moustache with curled points, though his age could not be more than three or four-and-twenty. Despite the touches of barbarism in his contours, there was a singular force in the gentleman's face, and in his bold rolling eye.

'Well, my Beauty, what can I do for you?' said he, coming forward. And

---

1 Studying.

perceiving that she stood quite confounded: 'Never mind me. I am Mr d'Urberville. Have you come to see me or my mother?'

This embodiment of a d'Urberville and a namesake differed even more from what Tess had expected than the house and grounds had differed. She had dreamed of an aged and dignified face, the sublimation of all the d'Urberville lineaments, furrowed with incarnate memories representing in hieroglyphic the centuries of her family's and England's history. But she screwed herself up to the work in hand, since she could not get out of it, and answered –

'I came to see your mother, sir.'

'I am afraid you cannot see her – she is an invalid,' replied the present representative of the spurious house; for this was Mr Alec, the only son of the lately deceased gentleman. 'Cannot I answer your purpose? What is the business you wish to see her about?'

'It isn't business – it is – I can hardly say what!'

'Pleasure?'

'Oh no. Why, sir, if I tell you, it will seem –.' Tess's sense of a certain ludicrousness in her errand was now so strong that, notwithstanding her awe of him, and her general discomfort at being here, her rosy lips curved towards a smile, much to the attraction of the swarthy Alexander.

'It is so very foolish,' she stammered; 'I fear can't tell you!'

'Never mind; I like foolish things. Try again, my dear,' said he kindly.

'Mother asked me to come,' Tess continued; 'and, indeed, I was in the mind to do so myself likewise. But I did not think it would be like this. I came, sir, to tell you that we are of the same family as you.'

'Ho! Poor relations?'

'Yes.'

'Stokes?'

'No. D'Urbervilles.'

'Ay, ay; I mean d'Urbervilles.'

'Our names are worn away to Durbeyfield; but we have several proofs that we are d'Urbervilles. Antiquarians hold we are, – and – and we have an old seal, marked with a ramping lion on a shield,[2] and a castle over him. And we have a very old silver spoon, round in the bowl like a little ladle, and marked with the same castle. But it is so worn that mother uses it to stir the pea-soup.'

'A castle argent[3] is certainly my crest,' said he blandly. 'And my arms a lion rampant.'

'And so mother said we ought to make ourselves beknown to you – as we've lost our horse by a bad accident, and are the oldest branch o' the family.'

'Very kind of your mother, I'm sure. And I, for one, don't regret her step.' Alec looked at Tess as he spoke, in a way that made her blush a little. 'And so, my pretty girl, you've come on a friendly visit to us, as relations?'

'I suppose I have,' faltered Tess, looking uncomfortable again.

'Well – there's no harm in it. Where do you live? What are you?'

---

2   The seal is a piece of engraved metal, used as a stamp for authenticating documents; a ramping lion is one that rears on his hind legs.
3   Heraldic term for silver.

She gave him brief particulars; and responding to further inquiries told him that she was intending to go back by the same carrier who had brought her.

'It is a long while before he returns past Trantridge Cross. Supposing we walk round the grounds to pass the time, my pretty Coz?'[4]

Tess wished to abridge her visit as much as possible; but the young man was pressing, and she consented to accompany him. He conducted her about the lawns, and flower-beds, and conservatories; and thence to the fruit-garden and green-houses, where he asked her if she liked strawberries.

'Yes,' said Tess, 'when they come.'

'They are already here.' D'Urberville began gathering specimens of the fruit for her, handing them back to her as he stooped; and, presently, selecting a specially fine product of the 'British Queen' variety, he stood up and held it by the stem to her mouth.

'No – no!' she said quickly, putting her fingers between his hand and her lips. 'I would rather take it in my own hand.'

'Nonsense!' he insisted; and in a slight distress she parted her lips and took it in.

They had spent some time wandering desultorily thus, Tess eating in a half-pleased, half-reluctant state whatever d'Urberville offered her. When she could consume no more of the strawberries he filled her little basket with them; and then the two passed round to the rose trees, whence he gathered blossoms and gave her to put in her bosom. She obeyed like one in a dream, and when she could affix no more he himself tucked a bud or two into her hat, and heaped her basket with others in the prodigality of his bounty. At last, looking at his watch, he said, 'Now, by the time you have had something to eat, it will be time for you to leave, if you want to catch the carrier to Shaston. Come here, and I'll see what grub I can find.'

Stoke-d'Urberville took her back to the lawn and into the tent, where he left her, soon reappearing with a basket of light luncheon, which he put before her himself. It was evidently the gentleman's wish not to be disturbed in this pleasant *tête-à-tête* by the servantry.

'Do you mind my smoking?' he asked.

'Oh, not at all, sir.'

He watched her pretty and unconscious munching through the skeins[5] of smoke that pervaded the tent, and Tess Durbeyfield did not divine, as she innocently looked down at the roses in her bosom, that there behind the blue narcotic haze was potentially the 'tragic mischief' of her drama – one who stood fair to be the blood-red ray in the spectrum of her young life. She had an attribute which amounted to a disadvantage just now; and it was this that caused Alec d'Urberville's eyes to rivet themselves upon her. It was a luxuriance of aspect, a fulness of growth, which made her appear more of a woman than she really was. She had inherited the feature from her mother without the quality it denoted. It had troubled her mind occasionally, till her companions had said that it was a fault which time would cure.

4 Cousin.
5 Tangled strings or coils.

From **Chapter 11: The Journey through The Chase, and Tess's Rape**

This passage describes the disastrous events that occur in the ancient tract of forest known as The Chase, and it includes the material Hardy initially removed from the manuscript so that it would be accepted for serial publication (**see pp. 11–12**). Though I follow many modern critics in classifying the encounter between Alec and Tess as a rape, Kristin Brady calls attention to the episode as 'the central ambivalence' in the novel, and reminds us that 'From the time of the book's publication, the question of whether Tess was raped or seduced has divided critics, and the debate has still not been resolved with perfect clarity' (**p. 89**). In this regard it is important to note that the scene takes place in a 'fog, which . . . disguises everything' for characters and readers alike. Brady discusses this ambiguity in so far as it has implications for the novel's presentation of Tess's 'purity' and autonomy. William Davis, Jr takes the issue outside the text, examining Victorian case law regarding rape and sleeping women (**p. 93**). Mary Jacobus chooses to call the encounter a 'seduction', but also demonstrates how Hardy reworked the manuscript to make Tess appear ever more 'blameless', and Alec more villainous (**p. 72**). And, in a discussion that places the rape within the novel's broader scheme of tragedy and survivalism, Bruce Johnson discusses The Chase as a locus of the pagan (**p. 104**).

The way this scene unfolds is typical of Hardy's narrative technique. First, he ensures that multiple coincidences lead Tess into the dark forest with Alec. Second, he dwells on the variability in Tess's character and behaviour, especially as seen in the self-assertive, even feisty retorts that set her apart from other country girls while only momentarily deflecting Alec's advances. Her flashes of resistance to Alec are important: she is not blind to his stratagems, and she is suspicious of his motives, though one guesses that she never fully imagines what may await her at his hands. Further, it is Tess's awkward relationship with the other labourers that isolates her and makes her vulnerable to Alec's opportunism; here and elsewhere, her distinctiveness seems a dubious gift that exposes her to the workings of Fate. Hardy's concluding remarks about the inexplicableness of her destiny are tantalizing but elusive. He suggests that a recurrence to fatalism is the habit of inexperienced country-folk (who simply say 'It was to be'), and yet he declines – or seems to decline – the opportunity to make an alternative statement himself. It may be, of course, that it is too early for such a statement, but perhaps his position is best viewed as a negative: why these things should have happened to Tess 'many thousand years of analytical philosophy have failed to explain to our sense of order'.

She was inexpressibly weary. She had risen at five o'clock every morning of that week, had been on foot the whole of each day, and on this evening had in addition walked the three miles to Chaseborough, waited three hours for her neighbours without eating or drinking, her impatience to start them preventing either; she had then walked a mile of the way home, and had undergone the excitement of the quarrel, till, with the slow progress of their steed, it was now nearly one o'clock. Only once, however, was she overcome by actual drowsiness. In that moment of oblivion her head sank gently against him.

D'Urberville stopped the horse, withdrew his feet from the stirrups, turned sideways on the saddle, and enclosed her waist with his arm to support her.

This immediately put her on the defensive, and with one of those sudden impulses of reprisal to which she was liable she gave him a little push from her. In his ticklish position he nearly lost his balance and only just avoided rolling over into the road, the horse, though a powerful one, being fortunately the quietest he rode.

'That is devilish unkind!' he said. 'I mean no harm – only to keep you from falling.'

She pondered suspiciously; till, thinking that this might after all be true, she relented, and said quite humbly, 'I beg your pardon, sir.'

'I won't pardon you unless you show some confidence in me. Good God!' he burst out, 'what am I, to be repulsed so by a mere chit[1] like you? For near three mortal months have you trifled with my feelings, eluded me, and snubbed me; and I won't stand it!'

'I'll leave you to-morrow, sir.'

'No, you will not leave me to-morrow! Will you, I ask once more, show your belief in me by letting me clasp you with my arm? Come, between us two and nobody else, now. We know each other well; and you know that I love you, and think you the prettiest girl in the world, which you are. Mayn't I treat you as a lover?'[2]

She drew a quick pettish[3] breath of objection, writhing uneasily on her seat, looked far ahead, and murmured, 'I don't know – I wish – how can I say yes or no when –'

He settled the matter by clasping his arm round her as he desired, and Tess expressed no further negative. Thus they sidled slowly onward till it struck her they had been advancing for an unconscionable time – far longer than was usually occupied by the short journey from Chaseborough, even at this walking pace, and that they were no longer on hard road, but in a mere trackway.

'Why, where be we?' she exclaimed.

'Passing by a wood.'

'A wood – what wood? Surely we are quite out of the road?'

'A bit of The Chase – the oldest wood in England. It is a lovely night, and why should we not prolong our ride a little?'

'How could you be so treacherous!' said Tess, between archness and real dismay, and getting rid of his arm by pulling open his fingers one by one, though at the risk of slipping off herself. 'Just when I've been putting such trust in you, and obliging you to please you, because I thought I had wronged you by that push! Please set me down, and let me walk home.'

'You cannot walk home, darling, even if the air were clear. We are miles away from Trantridge, if I must tell you, and in this growing fog you might wander for hours among these trees.'

'Never mind that,' she coaxed. 'Put me down, I beg you. I don't mind where it is; only let me get down, sir, please!'

---

1   A child or young woman.
2   I.e., one with whom there is some assumed mutuality of romantic affection. This term does not connote the modern sense of sexual intimacy.
3   Petulant; peevish.

'Very well, then, I will – on one condition. Having brought you here to this out-of-the-way place, I feel myself responsible for your safe-conduct home, whatever you may yourself feel about it. As to your getting to Trantridge without assistance, it is quite impossible; for, to tell the truth, dear, owing to this fog, which so disguises everything, I don't quite know where we are myself. Now, if you will promise to wait beside the horse while I walk through the bushes till I come to some road or house, and ascertain exactly our whereabouts, I'll deposit you here willingly. When I come back I'll give you full directions, and if you insist upon walking you may; or you may ride – at your pleasure.'

She accepted these terms, and slid off on the near side, though not till he had stolen a cursory kiss. He sprang down on the other side.

'I suppose I must hold the horse?' said she.

'Oh no; it's not necessary,' replied Alec, patting the panting creature. 'He's had enough of it for to-night.'

He turned the horse's head into the bushes, hitched him on to a bough, and made a sort of couch or nest for her in the deep mass of dead leaves.

'Now, you sit there,' he said. 'The leaves have not got damp as yet. Just give an eye to the horse – it will be quite sufficient.'

He took a few steps away from her, but, returning, said, 'By the bye, Tess, your father has a new cob[4] to-day. Somebody gave it to him.'

'Somebody? You!'

D'Urberville nodded.

'O how very good of you that is!' she exclaimed, with a painful sense of the awkwardness of having to thank him just then.

'And the children have some toys.'

'I didn't know – you ever sent them anything!' she murmured, much moved. 'I almost wish you had not – yes, I almost wish it!'

'Why, dear?'

'It – hampers me so.'

'Tessy – don't you love me ever so little now?'

'I'm grateful,' she reluctantly admitted. 'But I fear I do not –' The sudden vision of his passion for herself as a factor in this result so distressed her that, beginning with one slow tear, and then following with another, she wept outright.

'Don't cry, dear, dear one! Now sit down here, and wait till I come.' She passively sat down amid the leaves he had heaped, and shivered slightly. 'Are you cold?' he asked.

'Not very – a little.'

He touched her with his fingers, which sank into her as into down. 'You have only that puffy muslin dress on – how's that?'

'It's my best summer one. 'Twas very warm when I started, and I didn't know I was going to ride, and that it would be night.'

'Nights grow chilly in September. Let me see.' He pulled off a light overcoat that he had worn, and put it round her tenderly. 'That's it – now you'll feel warmer,' he continued. 'Now, my pretty, rest there; I shall soon be back again.'

---

4 Horse.

Having buttoned the overcoat round her shoulders he plunged into the webs of vapour which by this time formed veils between the trees. She could hear the rustling of the branches as he ascended the adjoining slope, till his movements were no louder than the hopping of a bird, and finally died away. With the setting of the moon the pale light lessened, and Tess became invisible as she fell into reverie upon the leaves where he had left her.

In the meantime Alec d'Urberville had pushed on up the slope to clear his genuine doubt as to the quarter of The Chase they were in. He had, in fact, ridden quite at random for over an hour, taking any turning that came to hand in order to prolong companionship with her, and giving far more attention to Tess's moon-lit person than to any wayside object. A little rest for the jaded animal being desirable, he did not hasten his search for landmarks. A clamber over the hill into the adjoining vale brought him to the fence of a highway whose contours he recognized, which settled the question of their whereabouts. D'Urberville there-upon turned back; but by this time the moon had quite gone down, and partly on account of the fog The Chase was wrapped in thick darkness, although morning was not far off. He was obliged to advance with outstretched hands to avoid contact with the boughs, and discovered that to hit the exact spot from which he had started was at first entirely beyond him. Roaming up and down, round and round, he at length heard a slight movement of the horse close at hand; and the sleeve of his overcoat unexpectedly caught his foot.

'Tess!' said d'Urberville.

There was no answer. The obscurity was now so great that he could see abso-lutely nothing but a pale nebulousness at his feet, which represented the white muslin figure he had left upon the dead leaves. Everything else was blackness alike. D'Urberville stooped; and heard a gentle regular breathing. He knelt and bent lower, till her breath warmed his face, and in a moment his cheek was in contact with hers. She was sleeping soundly, and upon her eyelashes there lingered tears.

Darkness and silence ruled everywhere around. Above them rose the primeval yews and oaks of The Chase, in which there poised gentle roosting birds in their last nap; and about them stole the hopping rabbits and hares. But, might some say, where was Tess's guardian angel? where was the providence of her simple faith? Perhaps, like that other god of whom the ironical Tishbite spoke, he was talking, or he was pursuing, or he was in a journey, or he was sleeping and not to be awaked.[5]

Why it was that upon this beautiful feminine tissue, sensitive as gossamer,[6] and practically blank as snow as yet, there should have been traced such a coarse pattern as it was doomed to receive; why so often the coarse appropriates the finer thus, the wrong man the woman, the wrong woman the man, many thousand years of analytical philosophy have failed to explain to our sense of order. One may, indeed, admit the possibility of a retribution lurking in the present

---

5   In 1 Kings 18.27, Elijah uses this set of images to mock the priests of Ba'al, who are unable to secure a response in an attempted sacrifice to their pagan god. But even though the biblical passage goes on to reveal the triumphant authority of the God of Israel, Hardy's use of Elijah's words here has the effect of equating pagan and biblical traditions as equally ineffectual.

6   Light, delicate or filmy.

catastrophe. Doubtless some of Tess d'Urberville's mailed ancestors[7] rollicking home from a fray[8] had dealt the same measure even more ruthlessly towards peasant girls of their time. But though to visit the sins of the fathers upon the children may be a morality good enough for divinities, it is scorned by average human nature; and it therefore does not mend the matter.

As Tess's own people down in those retreats are never tired of saying among each other in their fatalistic way: 'It was to be.' There lay the pity of it. An immeasurable social chasm was to divide our heroine's personality thereafter from that previous self of hers who stepped from her mother's door to try her fortune at Trantridge poultry-farm.

From 'Phase the Second: Maiden No More'

From Chapter 14: The Midnight Baptism and the Burial of Sorrow

As with the scene in The Chase, this section describing Tess's efforts to con- duct a baptism and burial for her baby was initially suppressed when the novel was serialized in The Graphic; a version of it was published as a short sketch in the Fortnightly Review (1 May 1891).[1] Early critics who questioned the novel's morality seized on this episode for its implicit sanctioning of heterodoxy and, potentially, agnosticism. Structuring the scene as a broad clash between legal- istic theology and human realities, Hardy twice makes this conflict overt, first describing how 'the man and the ecclesiastic fought within [the vicar], and the victory fell to the man', and later having Tess appeal to the vicar: 'Don't for God's sake speak as saint to sinner, but as you yourself to me myself – poor me!' While the characterization of the vicar is gentle, it is implied that he is role- playing as a church functionary much in the way Tess is; just as she officiates over her own homemade service of baptism, he is described as 'endeavour[ing] to graft technical belief on actual scepticism' and as having 'the natural feelings of a tradesman at finding that a job he should have been called for has been unskilfully botched by his customers'.

The scene is also noteworthy for its modulations of narrative voice. Hardy's reference to 'Poor Sorrow's campaign against the world' is presented with an aloofness that, somewhat unexpectedly, shields the reader from any powerful sense of suffering, or, indeed, Sorrow. Yet the next sentence, an equally ironic invocation of the relative ignorance of Tess's siblings, is comparatively painful. So

---

7   Knightly forebears.
8   Battle.

---

1   For a detailed reconstruction of the multiple printed and manuscript versions of *Tess*, including those involving the 'midnight baptism', see J.T. Laird, *The Shaping of* Tess of the D'Urbervilles (Oxford: Clarendon Press, 1975). Laird argues that the sketch that appeared in the *Fortnightly* was more anti-religious than the version that was reincorporated into the novel.

while Hardy's alternation between 'objective' and 'emotional' presentations of Tess has already been noted, we must also register his varieties of irony, including, as here, both the tragic and the dry and semi-humorous. A search for Hardy's 'true' affiliation to any one of these perspectives is likely to end in frustration. Describing the jar of water into which Tess places Sorrow's memorial flowers, he writes, 'What matter was it that on the outside of the jar the eye of mere observation noted the words "Keelwell's Marmalade"? The eye of maternal affection did not see them in its vision of higher things.' Is this a defence of Tess's maternal sincerity? A sardonic comment on the dismalness of the scene? Or an attempt to use ironic detachment as a way of controlling emotion?

Finally, it should be noted this is another scene in which Tess is made temporarily to appear transcendent or superhuman, and it is significant that it occurs outside the idealizing gaze of a male admirer. Penelope Vigar uses the tableau of Tess standing regally in her nightgown as an example of how Hardy shapes readers' emotional responses by the use of pictorial effects (p. 69).

She lit a candle, and went to a second and a third bed under the wall, where she awoke her young sisters and brothers, all of whom occupied the same room. Pulling out the washing-stand so that she could get behind it, she poured some water from a jug, and made them kneel around, putting their hands together with fingers exactly vertical. While the children, scarcely awake, awe-stricken at her manner, their eyes growing larger and larger, remained in this position, she took the baby from her bed – a child's child – so immature as scarce to seem a sufficient personality to endow its producer with the maternal title. Tess then stood erect with the infant on her arm beside the basin, the next sister held the Prayer-Book open before her, as the clerk at church held it before the parson; and thus the girl set about baptizing her child.

Her figure looked singularly tall and imposing as she stood in her long white nightgown, a thick cable of twisted dark hair hanging straight down her back to her waist. The kindly dimness of the weak candle abstracted from her form and features the little blemishes which sunlight might have revealed – the stubble scratches upon her wrists, and the weariness of her eyes – her high enthusiasm having a transfiguring effect upon the face which had been her undoing, showing it as a thing of immaculate beauty, with a touch of dignity which was almost regal.

The little ones kneeling round, their sleepy eyes blinking and red, awaited her preparations full of a suspended wonder which their physical heaviness at that hour would not allow to become active. The most impressed of them said: 'Be you really going to christen him, Tess?'

The girl-mother replied in a grave affirmative.

'What's his name going to be?'

She had not thought of that, but a name suggested by a phrase in the book of Genesis came into her head as she proceeded with the baptismal service, and now she pronounced it:

'SORROW, I baptize thee in the name of the Father, and the Son, and the Holy Ghost.' She sprinkled the water, and there was silence.

'Say "Amen," children.'

The tiny voices piped in obedient response 'Amen!'

Tess went on: 'We receive this child' – and so forth – 'and do sign him with the sign of the Cross.'

Here she dipped her hand into the basin, and fervently drew an immense cross upon the baby with her forefinger, continuing with the customary sentences as to his manfully fighting against sin, the world, and the devil, and being a faithful soldier and servant unto his life's end. She duly went on with the Lord's Prayer, the children lisping it after her in a thin gnat-like wail, till, at the conclusion, raising their voices to clerk's pitch, they again piped into silence, 'Amen!'

Then their sister, with much augmented confidence in the efficacy of the sacrament, poured forth from the bottom of her heart the thanksgiving that follows, uttering it boldly and triumphantly in the stopt-diapason[2] note which her voice acquired when her heart was in her speech, and which will never be forgotten by those who knew her. The ecstasy of faith almost apotheosized[3] her; it set upon her face a glowing irradiation, and brought a red spot into the middle of each cheek; while the miniature candle-flame inverted in her eye-pupils shone like a diamond. The children gazed up at her with more and more reverence, and no longer had a will for questioning. She did not look like Sissy to them now, but as a being large, towering, and awful – a divine personage with whom they had nothing in common.

Poor Sorrow's campaign against sin, the world, and the devil was doomed to be of limited brilliancy – luckily perhaps for himself, considering his beginnings. In the blue of the morning that fragile soldier and servant breathed his last, and when the other children awoke they cried bitterly, and begged Sissy to have another pretty baby.

The calmness which had possessed Tess since the christening remained with her in the infant's loss. In the daylight, indeed, she felt her terrors about his soul to have been somewhat exaggerated; whether well founded or not she had no uneasiness now, reasoning that if Providence would not ratify such an act of approximation she, for one, did not value the kind of heaven lost by the irregularity – either for herself or for her child.

So passed away Sorrow the Undesired – that intrusive creature, that bastard gift of shameless Nature who respects not the social law; a waif to whom eternal Time had been a matter of days merely, who knew not that such things as years and centuries ever were; to whom the cottage interior was the universe, the week's weather climate, new-born babyhood human existence, and the instinct to suck human knowledge.

Tess, who mused on the christening a good deal, wondered if it were doctrinally sufficient to secure a Christian burial for the child. Nobody could tell this but the parson of the parish, and he was a new-comer, and did not know her. She went to his house after dusk, and stood by the gate, but could not summon courage to go

---

2   Connoting a sound of rich fullness and harmony, implying the opening of stops on a church organ.
3   Deified; made godlike.

in. The enterprise would have been abandoned if she had not by accident met him coming homeward as she turned away. In the gloom she did not mind speaking freely.

'I should like to ask you something, sir.'

He expressed his willingness to listen, and she told the story of the baby's illness and the extemporized ordinance.

'And now, sir,' she added earnestly, 'can you tell me this – will it be just the same for him as if you had baptized him?'

Having the natural feelings of a tradesman at finding that a job he should have been called in for had been unskilfully botched by his customers among themselves, he was disposed to say no. Yet the dignity of the girl, the strange tenderness in her voice, combined to affect his nobler impulses – or rather those that he had left in him after ten years of endeavour to graft technical belief on actual scepticism. The man and the ecclesiastic fought within him, and the victory fell to the man.

'My dear girl,' he said, 'it will be just the same.'

'Then will you give him a Christian burial?' she asked quickly.

The Vicar felt himself cornered. Hearing of the baby's illness, he had conscientiously gone to the house after nightfall to perform the rite, and, unaware that the refusal to admit him had come from Tess's father and not from Tess, he could not allow the plea of necessity for its irregular administration.

'Ah – that's another matter,' he said.

'Another matter – why?' asked Tess, rather warmly.

'Well – I would willingly do so if only we two were concerned. But I must not – for certain reasons.'

'Just for once, sir!'

'Really I must not.'

'O sir!' She seized his hand as she spoke.

He withdrew it, shaking his head.

'Then I don't like you!' she burst out, 'and I'll never come to your church no more!'

'Don't talk so rashly.'

'Perhaps it will be just the same to him if you don't? ... Will it be just the same? Don't for God's sake speak as saint to sinner, but as you yourself to me myself – poor me!'

How the Vicar reconciled his answer with the strict notions he supposed himself to hold on these subjects it is beyond a layman's power to tell, though not to excuse. Somewhat moved, he said in this case also –

'It will be just the same.'

So the baby was carried in a small deal box, under an ancient woman's shawl, to the churchyard that night, and buried by lantern-light, at the cost of a shilling and a pint of beer to the sexton, in that shabby corner of God's allotment where He lets the nettles grow, and where all unbaptized infants, notorious drunkards, suicides, and others of the conjecturally damned are laid. In spite of the untoward surroundings, however, Tess bravely made a little cross of two laths[4] and a piece

---

4   Narrow strips of wood.

of string, and having bound it with flowers, she stuck it up at the head of the grave one evening when she could enter the churchyard without being seen, putting at the foot also a bunch of the same flowers in a little jar of water to keep them alive. What matter was it that on the outside of the jar the eye of mere observation noted the words 'Keelwell's Marmalade'? The eye of maternal affection did not see them in its vision of higher things.

From 'Phase the Third: The Rally'

From **Chapter 18: Introduction of Angel Clare**

This passage introduces Angel Clare at Talbothays dairy. Tess, newly employed there as a dairymaid, has already recognized him as the gentleman traveller who passed through Marlott on May-Day (see excerpt from Chapter 2, above). The first sentence of Chapter 18 describes Angel as 'not altogether . . . a distinct figure', a formulation that instantly reminds us of the earliest descriptions of Tess, but we then learn the essentials of his family and educational history: the third son of an Evangelical clergyman, Angel was expected to follow his brothers to Cambridge until his father, who views a University degree strictly as preparation for a career in the church, learned of his deep scepticism toward religion. Having accepted his father's unwillingness to finance his education on secular terms, Angel – ironically, more academically inclined than either of his brothers – has decided to train himself in various aspects of farming, with the hope that this profession will allow him to continue his scholarly interests on the side.

Concerning Hardy's methods of characterization, this sketch is centrally informed by the theme of change: Angel's outlook on rustic labour transforms utterly as he becomes acquainted with the individual dairymen and women, yet they themselves encourage and perpetuate certain lines of class demarcation to which he acquiesces, almost as inevitabilities. Then again, there may be a subtler and deeper, almost spiritual change in him, as the final paragraph here hints – a new receptivity to the natural world, with its cyclic 'moods' and 'tempers'. Significantly, this coda to Angel's history leads directly into an account of his first taking notice of Tess; it will be here that he describes her to himself as 'a fresh and virginal daughter of Nature'.

Early association with country solitudes had bred in him an unconquerable, and almost unreasonable, aversion to modern town life, and shut him out from such success as he might have aspired to by following a mundane calling in the impracticability of the spiritual one. But something had to be done; he had wasted many valuable years; and having an acquaintance who was starting on a thriving life as a Colonial farmer, it occurred to Angel that this might be a lead in the right direction. Farming, either in the Colonies, America, or at home – farming, at any rate, after becoming well qualified for the business by a careful apprenticeship – that was a vocation which would probably afford an independence without the sacrifice of what he valued even more than a competency – intellectual liberty.

So we find Angel Clare at six-and-twenty here at Talbothays as a student of kine,[1] and, as there were no houses near at hand in which he could get a comfortable lodging, a boarder at the dairyman's.

His room was an immense attic which ran the whole length of the dairy-house. It could only be reached by a ladder from the cheese-loft, and had been closed up for a long time till he arrived and selected it as his retreat. Here Clare had plenty of space, and could often be heard by the dairy-folk pacing up and down when the household had gone to rest. A portion was divided off at one end by a curtain, behind which was his bed, the outer part being furnished as a homely sitting-room.

At first he lived up above entirely, reading a good deal, and strumming upon an old harp which he had bought at a sale, saying when in a bitter humour that he might have to get his living by it in the streets some day. But he soon preferred to read human nature by taking his meals downstairs in the general dining-kitchen, with the dairyman and his wife, and the maids and men, who all together formed a lively assembly; for though but few milking hands slept in the house, several joined the family at meals. The longer Clare resided here the less objection had he to his company, and the more did he like to share quarters with them in common.

Much to his surprise he took, indeed, a real delight in their companionship. The conventional farm-folk of his imagination – personified in the newspaper-press by the pitiable dummy known as Hodge[2] – were obliterated after a few days' residence. At close quarters no Hodge was to be seen. At first, it is true, when Clare's intelligence was fresh from a contrasting society, these friends with whom he now hobnobbed seemed a little strange. Sitting down as a level member of the dairyman's household seemed at the outset an undignified proceeding. The ideas, the modes, the surroundings, appeared retrogressive and unmeaning. But with living on there, day after day, the acute sojourner became conscious of a new aspect in the spectacle. Without any objective change whatever, variety had taken the place of monotonousness. His host and his host's household, his men and his maids, as they became intimately known to Clare, began to differentiate themselves as in a chemical process. The thought of Pascal's was brought home to him: 'A mesure qu'on a plus d'esprit, on trouve qu'il y a plus d'hommes originaux. Les gens du commun ne trouvent pas de différence entre les hommes.'[3] The typical and unvarying Hodge ceased to exist. He had been disintegrated into a number of varied fellow-creatures – beings of many minds, beings infinite in difference; some happy, many serene, a few depressed, one here and there bright even to genius, some stupid, others wanton, others austere; some mutely Miltonic, some potentially Cromwellian;[4] into men who had private views of each other, as he had of

1 Cows.
2 A stereotypical term denoting a dull and ignorant peasant labourer.
3 The passage, from the General Preface of Blaise Pascal's *Pensées* (1670), may be translated, 'In proportion as one is more independent-minded, one finds more unique men. Commoners do not see the difference between men.' Clare's reference to this work can be seen as unintentionally ironic, since the *Pensées* was intended as a defence of Christianity, and a rejection of the free-thinking tradition.
4 An allusion to Thomas Gray's immensely popular poem 'Elegy Written in a Country Churchyard' (1751), meant to convey Clare's sense that the labourers at Talbothays not only demonstrate basic differences in temperament and intelligence, but that some among them have untapped reservoirs of genius and power. In concert with his preceding reference to Pascal, the allusion has the curious effect of revealing Clare's reverence for conventional demonstrations of knowledge and intelligence, even as he is in the act of challenging such conventionalities.

his friends; who could applaud or condemn each other, amuse or sadden themselves by the contemplation of each other's foibles or vices; men every one of whom walked in his own individual way the road to dusty death.

Unexpectedly he began to like the outdoor life for its own sake, and for what it brought, apart from its bearing on his own proposed career. Considering his position he became wonderfully free from the chronic melancholy which is taking hold of the civilized races with the decline of belief in a beneficent Power. For the first time of late years he could read as his musings inclined him, without any eye to cramming for a profession, since the few farming handbooks which he deemed it desirable to master occupied him but little time.

He grew away from old associations, and saw something new in life and humanity. Secondarily, he made close acquaintance with phenomena which he had before known but darkly – the seasons in their moods, morning and evening, night and noon, winds in their different tempers, trees, waters and mists, shades and silences, and the voices of inanimate things.

From **Chapter 19: Tess and Angel in the Garden**

Notable for its ravishing description of the evening atmosphere and the luxuriant garden at Talbothays, this remarkable passage develops several of the novel's themes at once, especially those concerning individuality. Tess and Angel are seen groping toward deeper understandings of one another, an effort that is continually burdened by their awareness of class difference. Yet even as they reach out, each is also shown to have an impulse toward the consolidation of the self – even the soul – that has little to do with romance or sex. In Tess's case, this impulse is presented as natural instinct (she moves as a stealthy cat and a 'fascinated bird') and as conscious understanding ('what's the use of learning', she asks, 'that I am one of a long row only – finding out that there is set down in some old book somebody just like me, and to know that I shall only act her part?').

These discussions are focused primarily through depictions of their educations and – though Clare shows himself to be ambivalent about such terms – epistemologies. Tess's learning is non-systematic and anecdotal, but her range of references, from Peter the Great to the Queen of Sheba, extends beyond what we would assume to be typical of her station. But her certainty about the very viability of this knowledge is subject to rapid changes and crises of confidence. Perhaps surprisingly, Angel expresses similar uncertainties. Torn between honouring her native intelligence on its own terms, and assuming she needs a programme of study and reading to improve herself, he is continually haunted by his relationship to conventional modes of thought. The garden itself is a setting in which a kind of perfect freedom – of intellect, soul, body – is potentially available, and Tess seems far closer to embracing it than does Angel. David Lodge's account of her natural 'sensibility' (**p. 97**) as revealed in the garden is especially striking; James Kincaid remarks briefly on the erotic yearnings she herself seems to feel (**p. 92**). Finally it should be noted that Hardy loads this passage with bibilical allusions, perhaps to underscore, by contrast, the primitivist, even pagan character of the setting.

It was a typical summer evening in June, the atmosphere being in such delicate equilibrium and so transmissive that inanimate objects seemed endowed with two or three senses, if not five. There was no distinction between the near and the far, and an auditor felt close to everything within the horizon. The soundlessness impressed her as a positive entity rather than as the mere negation of noise. It was broken by the strumming of strings.

Tess had heard those notes in the attic above her head. Dim, flattened, constrained by their confinement, they had never appealed to her as now, when they wandered in the still air with a stark quality like that of nudity. To speak absolutely, both instrument and execution were poor; but the relative is all, and as she listened Tess, like a fascinated bird, could not leave the spot. Far from leaving she drew up towards the performer, keeping behind the hedge that he might not guess her presence.

The outskirt of the garden in which Tess found herself had been left uncultivated for some years, and was now damp and rank with juicy grass which sent up mists of pollen at a touch; and with tall blooming weeds emitting offensive smells – weeds whose red and yellow and purple hues formed a polychrome as dazzling as that of cultivated flowers. She went stealthily as a cat through this profusion of growth, gathering cuckoo-spittle on her skirts, cracking snails that were underfoot, staining her hands with thistle-milk and slug-slime, and rubbing off upon her naked arms sticky blights which, though snow-white on the apple-tree trunks, made madder stains on her skin; thus she drew quite near to Clare, still unobserved of him.

Tess was conscious of neither time nor space. The exaltation which she had described as being producible at will by gazing at a star, came now without any determination of hers; she undulated upon the thin notes of the second-hand harp, and their harmonies passed like breezes through her, bringing tears into her eyes. The floating pollen seemed to be his notes made visible, and the dampness of the garden the weeping of the garden's sensibility. Though near nightfall, the rank-smelling weed-flowers glowed as if they would not close for intentness, and the waves of colour mixed with the waves of sound.

The light which still shone was derived mainly from a large hole in the western bank of cloud; it was like a piece of day left behind by accident, dusk having closed in elsewhere. He concluded his plaintive melody, a very simple performance, demanding no great skill; and she waited, thinking another might be begun. But, tired of playing, he had desultorily come round the fence, and was rambling up behind her. Tess, her cheeks on fire, moved away furtively, as if hardly moving at all.

Angel, however, saw her light summer gown, and he spoke; his low tones reaching her, though he was some distance off.

'What makes you draw off in that way, Tess?' said he. 'Are you afraid?'

'Oh no, sir . . . not of outdoor things; especially just now when the apple-blooth[1] is falling, and everything so green.'

'But you have your indoor fears – eh?'

'Well – yes, sir.'

'What of?'

'I couldn't quite say.'

---

1   Blossom.

'The milk turning sour?'

'No.'

'Life in general?'

'Yes, sir.'

'Ah – so have I, very often. This hobble[2] of being alive is rather serious, don't you think so?'

'It is – now you put it that way.'

'All the same, I shouldn't have expected a young girl like you to see it so just yet. How is it you do?'

She maintained a hesitating silence.

'Come, Tess, tell me in confidence.'

She thought that he meant what were the aspects of things to her, and replied shyly: 'The trees have inquisitive eyes, haven't they? – that is, seem as if they had. And the river says – "Why do ye trouble me with your looks?" And you seem to see numbers of to-morrows just all in a line, the first of them the biggest and clearest, the others getting smaller and smaller as they stand farther away; but they all seem very fierce and cruel and as if they said, "I'm coming! Beware of me! Beware of me!" . . . But *you*, sir, can raise up dreams with your music, and drive all such horrid fancies away!'

He was surprised to find this young woman – who though but a milkmaid had just that touch of rarity about her which might make her the envied of her house-mates – shaping such sad imaginings. She was expressing in her own native phrases – assisted a little by her Sixth Standard training[3] – feelings which might almost have been called those of the age – the ache of modernism. The perception arrested him less when he reflected that what are called advanced ideas are really in great part but the latest fashion in definition – a more accurate expression, by words in -*logy* and -*ism*, of sensations which men and women have vaguely grasped for centuries.

Still, it was strange that they should have come to her while yet so young; more than strange; it was impressive, interesting, pathetic. Not guessing the cause, there was nothing to remind him that experience is as to intensity, and not as to duration. Tess's passing corporeal blight had been her mental harvest.

Tess, on her part, could not understand why a man of clerical family and good education, and above physical want, should look upon it as a mishap to be alive. For the unhappy pilgrim herself there was very good reason. But how could this admirable and poetic man ever have descended into the Valley of Humiliation,[4] have felt with the man of Uz – as she herself had felt two or three years ago – 'My soul chooseth strangling and death rather than my life. I loathe it; I would not live alway.'[5]

It was true that he was at present out of his class. But she knew that was only because, like Peter the Great in a shipwright's yard,[6] he was studying what he

---

2 Difficulty.

3 In the standardized curriculum, the sixth standard would be the highest level of primary education.

4 John Bunyan, *The Pilgrim's Progress* (1678).

5 Job 7.15–16. The 'man of Uz' referred to earlier in the sentence is Job.

6 One of the legendary czars of Russia and a powerful naval commander, Peter the Great (1682–1725) chose to learn the trade of ship carpentry as a young man, even though, as royalty, he was not obliged to engage in such lowly work.

wanted to know. He did not milk cows because he was obliged to milk cows, but because he was learning to be a rich and prosperous dairyman, landowner, agriculturist, and breeder of cattle. He would become an American or Australian Abraham,[7] commanding like a monarch his flocks and his herds, his spotted and his ring-straked,[8] his men-servants and his maids. At times, nevertheless, it did seem unaccountable to her that a decidedly bookish, musical, thinking young man should have chosen deliberately to be a farmer, and not a clergyman, like his father and brothers.

Thus, neither having the clue to the other's secret, they were respectively puzzled at what each revealed, and awaited new knowledge of each other's character and mood without attempting to pry into each other's history.

Every day, every hour, brought to him one more little stroke of her nature, and to her one more of his. Tess was trying to lead a repressed life, but she little divined the strength of her own vitality.

At first Tess seemed to regard Angel Clare as an intelligence rather than as a man. As such she compared him with herself; and at every discovery of the abundance of his illuminations, and the unmeasurable, Andean[9] altitude of his, she became quite dejected, disheartened from all further effort on her own part whatever.

He observed her dejection one day, when he had casually mentioned something to her about pastoral life in ancient Greece. She was gathering the buds called 'lords and ladies'[10] from the bank while he spoke.

'Why do you look so woebegone all of a sudden?' he asked.

'Oh, 'tis only – about my own self,' she said, with a frail laugh of sadness, fitfully beginning to peel 'a lady' meanwhile. 'Just a sense of what might have been with me! My life looks as if it had been wasted for want of chances! When I see what you know, what you have read, and seen, and thought, I feel what a nothing I am! I'm like the poor Queen of Sheba who lived in the Bible. There is no more spirit in me.'[11]

'Bless my soul, don't go troubling about that! Why,' he said with some enthusiasm, 'I should be only too glad, my dear Tess, to help you to anything in the way of history, or any line of reading you would like to take up –'

'It is a lady again,' interrupted she, holding out the bud she had peeled.

'What?'

'I meant that there are always more ladies than lords when you come to peel them.'

'Never mind about the lords and ladies. Would you like to take up any course of study – history, for example?'

---

7 In Genesis 12 and following, Abraham follows the Lord's instructions, enters the land of Canaan and becomes rich with cattle, tents and other possessions.

8 Streaked or striped.

9 Referring to the Andean mountains of South America, perhaps a prefiguration of Angel's trip to Brazil.

10 Also called jack-in-the-pulpit.

11 After journeying to see the wealth of King Solomon, the Queen of Sheba is disconsolate regarding her own achievements: 'And when the queen of Sheba had seen all Solomon's wisdom, and the house that he had built, and the meat of his table, and the sitting of his servants, and the attendance of his ministers, and their apparel, and his cupbearers, and his ascent by which he went up unto the house of the LORD; there was no more spirit in her' (1 Kings 10.4–6).

'Sometimes I feel I don't want to know anything more about it than I know already.'

'Why not?'

'Because what's the use of learning that I am one of a long row only – finding out that there is set down in some old book somebody just like me, and to know that I shall only act her part; making me sad, that's all. The best is not to remember that your nature and your past doings have been just like thousands' and thousands', and that your coming life and doings 'll be like thousands' and thousands'.'

'What, really, then, you don't want to learn anything?'

'I shouldn't mind learning why – why the sun do shine on the just and the unjust alike,'[12] she answered, with a slight quaver in her voice. 'But that's what books will not tell me.'

'Tess, fie for such bitterness!' Of course he spoke with a conventional sense of duty only, for that sort of wondering had not been unknown to himself in bygone days. And as he looked at the unpractised mouth and lips, he thought that such a daughter of the soil could only have caught up the sentiment by rote. She went on peeling the lords and ladies till Clare, regarding for a moment the wave-like curl of her lashes as they dropped with her bent gaze on her soft cheek, lingeringly went away. When he was gone she stood awhile, thoughtfully peeling the last bud; and then, awakening from her reverie, flung it and all the crowd of floral nobility impatiently on the ground, in an ebullition[13] of displeasure with herself for her *niaiseries*,[14] and with a quickening warmth in her heart of hearts.

How stupid he must think her! In an access of hunger for his good opinion she bethought herself of what she had latterly endeavoured to forget, so unpleasant had been its issues – the identity of her family with that of the knightly d'Urbervilles. Barren attribute as it was, disastrous as its discovery had been in many ways to her, perhaps Mr Clare, as a gentleman and a student of history, would respect her sufficiently to forget her childish conduct with the lords and ladies if he knew that those Purbeck-marble[15] and alabaster people in Kingsbere Church really represented her own lineal forefathers; that she was no spurious d'Urberville, compounded of money and ambition like those at Trantridge, but true d'Urberville to the bone.

Chapter 20: The Pastoral Interlude at Talbothays

This account of the emerging attraction between Tess and Angel, who are described as 'converging, under an irresistible law, as surely as two streams in one vale', is surely one of the novel's great passages, and one of the most admired. Readers have both appreciated Hardy's flawless exercise of his grand style and felt a more visceral sense of gratitude for the happiness, beauty and

---

12 Matthew 5.45.
13 Eruption.
14 Foolish simplicities.
15 Marble quarried at Purbeck on the Dorset coast.

relative optimism the episode projects. Yet the particular terms of this happiness are crucial to an understanding of Hardy's ethos. It is tempting to focus on the characters' experience of the first blush of love; and tempting as well to revel in the unexpectedly early effacement of the Alec episode. But Hardy suggests that the happiness found here comes most fully from the characters' ability to tap into Nature's faceless, 'inhuman' processes as forces for renewal and rejuvenation. 'Nature' is not expressly hopeful; it is only Nature: but as it turns its wheel, it makes available a life-giving power to which humans can attach themselves. And, perhaps further, Nature's depersonalized indifference to human affairs can actually be read as reassuring: the landscape, at once magnificent and ordinary, does not seem to remember or care about human error. So where most of the novel alternates between suggestions of universal entropy and suggestions of bleak fatalism, here the implicit dampening-down of the human context allows humans to find a sort of happiness.

The passage is also crucial for its juxtaposition of ideal and real – or, in other terms, of the ethereal and psychological with the earthy. Its conclusion – a comic moment in which Dairyman Crick chastises one of the dairymaids for not washing her hands before milking – serves to sharply return us to the practical world of the dairy, after we have been soaring through 'luminous' realms in which Tess appears to Angel as the 'visionary essence of woman'. Thus even in what is arguably the most rapturous chapter of the novel, the seeds of disaster are sown, since it is Angel's confusion of the ideal and real that will create an expectation that Tess is powerless to undo. Hardy's poem 'The Well-Beloved' (p. 29) uses a figure reminiscent of Angel for a pointed commentary on men's idealizations of the female.

The season developed and matured. Another year's instalment of flowers, leaves, nightingales, thrushes, finches, and such ephemeral creatures, took up their positions where only a year ago others had stood in their place when these were nothing more than germs and inorganic particles. Rays from the sunrise drew forth the buds and stretched them into long stalks, lifted up sap in noiseless streams, opened petals, and sucked out scents in invisible jets and breathings.

Dairyman Crick's household of maids and men lived on comfortably, placidly, even merrily. Their position was perhaps the happiest of all positions in the social scale, being above the line at which neediness ends, and below the line at which the *convenances*[1] begin to cramp natural feelings, and the stress of threadbare modishness[2] makes too little of enough.

Thus passed the leafy time when arborescence[3] seems to be the one thing aimed at out of doors. Tess and Clare unconsciously studied each other, ever balanced on the edge of a passion, yet apparently keeping out of it. All the while they were converging, under an irresistible law, as surely as two streams in one vale.

Tess had never in her recent life been so happy as she was now, possibly never

1 Conventional modes of propriety.
2 I.e., anxiety about not being able to maintain a minimal level of fashionableness.
3 The growth of trees.

would be so happy again. She was, for one thing, physically and mentally suited among these new surroundings. The sapling which had rooted down to a poisonous stratum on the spot of its sowing had been transplanted to a deeper soil. Moreover she, and Clare also, stood as yet on the debatable land between predilection and love; where no profundities have been reached; no reflections have set in, awkwardly inquiring, 'Whither does this new current tend to carry me? What does it mean to my future? How does it stand towards my past?'

Tess was the merest stray phenomenon to Angel Clare as yet – a rosy warming apparition which had only just acquired the attribute of persistence in his consciousness. So he allowed his mind to be occupied with her, deeming his preoccupation to be no more than a philosopher's regard of an exceedingly novel, fresh, and interesting specimen of womankind.

They met continually; they could not help it. They met daily in that strange and solemn interval, the twilight of the morning, in the violet or pink dawn; for it was necessary to rise early, so very early, here. Milking was done betimes; and before the milking came the skimming, which began at a little past three. It usually fell to the lot of some one or other of them to wake the rest, the first being aroused by an alarm-clock; and, as Tess was the latest arrival, and they soon discovered that she could be depended upon not to sleep through the alarm as others did, this task was thrust most frequently upon her. No sooner had the hour of three struck and whizzed, than she left her room and ran to the dairyman's door; then up the ladder to Angel's, calling him in a loud whisper; then woke her fellow-milkmaids. By the time that Tess was dressed Clare was downstairs and out in the humid air. The remaining maids and the dairyman usually gave themselves another turn on the pillow, and did not appear till a quarter of an hour later.

The grey half-tones of daybreak are not the grey half-tones of the day's close, though the degree of their shade may be the same. In the twilight of the morning light seems active, darkness passive; in the twilight of evening it is the darkness which is active and crescent, and the light which is the drowsy reverse.

Being so often – possibly not always by chance – the first two persons to get up at the dairy-house, they seemed to themselves the first persons up of all the world. In these early days of her residence here Tess did not skim, but went out of doors at once after rising, where he was generally awaiting her. The spectral, half-compounded, aqueous light which pervaded the open mead, impressed them with a feeling of isolation, as if they were Adam and Eve. At this dim inceptive stage of the day Tess seemed to Clare to exhibit a dignified largeness both of disposition and physique, an almost regnant power, possibly because he knew that at that preternatural time hardly any woman so well endowed in person as she was likely to be walking in the open air within the boundaries of his horizon; very few in all England. Fair women are usually asleep at mid-summer dawns. She was close at hand, and the rest were nowhere.

The mixed, singular, luminous gloom in which they walked along together to the spot where the cows lay, often made him think of the Resurrection hour. He little thought that the Magdalen[4] might be at his side. Whilst all the landscape was in neutral shade his companion's face, which was the focus of his eyes, rising

---

4   Mary Magdalen, the prostitute who is reformed and sanctified by her belief in Jesus.

above the mist stratum, seemed to have a sort of phosphorescence upon it. She looked ghostly, as if she were merely a soul at large. In reality her face, without appearing to do so, had caught the cold gleam of day from the north-east; his own face, though he did not think of it, wore the same aspect to her.

It was then, as has been said, that she impressed him most deeply. She was no longer the milkmaid, but a visionary essence of woman – a whole sex condensed into one typical form. He called her Artemis, Demeter, and other fanciful names[5] half teasingly, which she did not like because she did not understand them.

'Call me Tess,' she would say askance; and he did.

Then it would grow lighter, and her features would become simply feminine; they had changed from those of a divinity who could confer bliss to those of a being who craved it.

At these non-human hours they could get quite close to the waterfowl. Herons came, with a great bold noise as of opening doors and shutters, out of the boughs of a plantation which they frequented at the side of the mead; or, if already on the spot, hardly maintained their standing in the water as the pair walked by, watching them by moving their heads round in a slow, horizontal, passionless wheel, like the turn of puppets by clockwork.

They could then see the faint summer fogs in layers, woolly, level, and apparently no thicker than counterpanes,[6] spread about the meadows in detached remnants of small extent. On the grey moisture of the grass were marks where the cows had lain through the night – dark-green islands of dry herbage the size of their carcasses, in the general sea of dew. From each island proceeded a serpentine trail, by which the cow had rambled away to feed after getting up, at the end of which trail they found her; the snoring puff from her nostrils, when she recognized them, making an intenser little fog of her own amid the prevailing one. Then they drove the animals back to the barton,[7] or sat down to milk them on the spot, as the case might require.

Or perhaps the summer fog was more general, and the meadows lay like a white sea, out of which the scattered trees rose like dangerous rocks. Birds would soar through it into the upper radiance, and hang on the wing sunning themselves, or alight on the wet rails subdividing the mead, which now shone like glass rods. Minute diamonds of moisture from the mist hung, too, upon Tess's eyelashes, and drops upon her hair, like seed pearls. When the day grew quite strong and commonplace these dried off her; moreover, Tess then lost her strange and ethereal beauty; her teeth, lips, and eyes scintillated in the sunbeams, and she was again the dazzlingly fair dairymaid only, who had to hold her own against the other women of the world.

About this time they would hear Dairyman Crick's voice, lecturing the non-resident milkers for arriving late, and speaking sharply to old Deborah Fyander for not washing her hands.

'For Heaven's sake, pop thy hands under the pump, Deb! Upon my soul, if the

---

5   The legends surrounding these Greek goddesses have very different valences. Artemis, the goddess of the hunt and the moon, protects her chastity through violence; Demeter is a fertility goddess associated with the cycle of the seasons.

6   Bedspreads or quilts.

7   Farmyard.

London folk only knowed of thee and thy slovenly ways, they'd swaller their milk and butter more mincing than they do a'ready; and that's saying a good deal.'

The milking progressed, till towards the end Tess and Clare, in common with the rest, could hear the heavy breakfast table dragged out from the wall in the kitchen by Mrs Crick, this being the invariable preliminary to each meal; the same horrible scrape accompanying its return journey when the table had been cleared.

From 'Phase the Fourth: The Consequence'

From **Chapter 34: Angel Confesses his Past**

This passage appears in the middle of Chapter 34, and shows Tess and Angel on their wedding-night, staying at an old farmhouse that was once part of the d'Urbervilles' extended manorial holdings. In the thirteen-chapter interval between the prior excerpt and this one, there are three gradual, carefully worked plot developments: the mutual discovery and profession of love between Angel and Tess; Angel's repeated proposals of marriage, which Tess resists for a long time in fears that her past will blight the union; and the worshipful attraction that Tess's three unmarried co-workers also feel toward Angel, followed by their dejection on learning definitively that he has chosen Tess. These phases of the story stretch from a sultry July to New Year's Eve, the day of the wedding. The event is surrounded by unlucky encounters and bad omens, and Tess makes two attempts to confess everything to Angel: once the night before, in a letter which by the most perverse of chances he fails to find, and again on the wedding-day itself, in a conversation he blithely cuts short.

Chapter 34 begins with a typically Hardyean turn. Expecting the delivery of their luggage, the couple receive instead a packet of diamonds willed by Angel's godmother to his future wife. Tess has just been modelling the jewellery when a messenger from Talbothays arrives with the shocking news that one of the lovelorn dairymaids has tried to drown herself, and that another was found 'dead drunk' nearby. This is the 'incident' to which the first paragraph of this excerpt refers; Tess prepares again to confess, this time impelled by a sense of obligation to her friends. (For more on this as a phenomenon of class identification see Williams, **p. 99**)

What happens next might seem simply another plot twist, but should be viewed more reflectively as laying the groundwork for the novel's profoundest emotional crisis. Angel's 'confession' is strangely jocular in tone, full of red flags as to the self-absorption and condescension that are intermixed with his love for Tess. Prefaced by his glib associations of Tess with an academic fellowship, and of the Apostle Paul with the Roman poet Horace, his 'sin' comes across as a boyish lark; indeed, when we as readers first learned of the brief love-affair in Chapter 18, it was presented as one more bump in his path toward maturity. In fact, as Angel parries Tess's replies, he sounds uncannily like Alec d'Urberville. Then, we must also take note of Tess's point of view: she seizes upon Angel's confession as miraculous evidence that he and she are after all 'double[s]', and their sins 'the same'. She will soon learn otherwise, but for the moment her reasoning strikes us, too, as perfectly sound. Finally, there are the all-important atmospherics to consider. The scene is heavily framed: the diamonds and fire-light lend 'warmth' at the beginning, and an apocalyptic 'luridness' at the end, capped with allusions not only to the Book of Revelation but also to the cautionary folktale 'Toads and Diamonds'.

This incident had turned the scale for her. They were simple and innocent girls on whom the unhappiness of unrequited love had fallen; they had deserved better at the hands of Fate. She had deserved worse – yet she was the chosen one. It was wicked of her to take all without paying. She would pay to the uttermost farthing; she would tell, there and then. This final determination she came to when she looked into the fire, he holding her hand.

A steady glare from the now flameless embers painted the sides and back of the fireplace with its colour, and the well-polished andirons,[1] and the old brass tongs that would not meet. The underside of the mantel-shelf was flushed with the high-coloured light, and the legs of the table nearest the fire. Tess's face and neck reflected the same warmth, which each gem turned into an Aldebaran or a Sirius[2] – a constellation of white, red, and green flashes, that interchanged their hues with her every pulsation.

'Do you remember what we said to each other this morning about telling our faults?' he asked abruptly, finding that she still remained immovable. 'We spoke lightly perhaps, and you may well have done so. But for me it was no light promise. I want to make a confession to you, Love.'

This, from him, so unexpectedly apposite, had the effect upon her of a Provi-dential interposition. 'You have to confess something?' she said quickly, and even with gladness and relief.

'You did not expect it? Ah – you thought too highly of me. Now listen. Put your head there, because I want you to forgive me, and not to be indignant with me for not telling you before, as perhaps I ought to have done.'

How strange it was! He seemed to be her double. She did not speak, and Clare went on:

'I did not mention it because I was afraid of endangering my chance of you, darling, the great prize of my life – my Fellowship I call you. My brother's Fellow-ship was won at his college, mine at Talbothays dairy. Well, I would not risk it. I was going to tell you a month ago – at the time you agreed to be mine, but I could not; I thought it might frighten you away from me. I put it off; then I thought I would tell you yesterday, to give you a chance at least of escaping me. But I did not. And I did not this morning, when you proposed our confessing our faults on the landing – the sinner that I was! But I must, now I see you sitting there so solemnly. I wonder if you will forgive me?'

'O yes! I am sure that –'

---

1   Metal supports used for holding up fireplace logs.
2   Two of the brightest stars in the sky; Aldebaran is known for its changing colours.

'Well, I hope so. But wait a minute. You don't know. To begin at the beginning. Though I imagine my poor father fears that I am one of the eternally lost for my doctrines, I am of course, a believer in good morals, Tess, as much as you. I used to wish to be a teacher of men, and it was a great disappointment to me when I found I could not enter the Church. I admired spotlessness, even though I could lay no claim to it, and hated impurity, as I hope I do now. Whatever one may think of plenary inspiration, one must heartily subscribe to these words of Paul: "Be thou an example – in word, in conversation, in charity, in spirit, in faith, in purity."[3] It is the only safeguard for us poor human beings. "Integer vitæ," says a Roman poet, who is strange company for St Paul –

> The man of upright life, from frailties free,
> Stands not in need of Moorish spear or bow.[4]

Well, a certain place is paved with good intentions, and having felt all that so strongly, you will see what a terrible remorse it bred in me when, in the midst of my fine aims for other people, I myself fell.'

He then told her of that time of his life to which allusion has been made when, tossed about by doubts and difficulties in London, like a cork on the waves, he plunged into eight-and-forty hours' dissipation[5] with a stranger.

'Happily I awoke almost immediately to a sense of my folly,' he continued. 'I would have no more to say to her, and I came home. I have never repeated the offence. But I felt I should like to treat you with perfect frankness and honour, and I could not do so without telling this. Do you forgive me?'

She pressed his hand tightly for an answer.

'Then we will dismiss it at once and for ever! – too painful as it is for the occasion – and talk of something lighter.'

'O, Angel – I am almost glad – because now *you* can forgive *me*! I have not made my confession. I have a confession, too – remember, I said so.'

'Ah, to be sure! Now then for it, wicked little one.'

'Perhaps, although you smile, it is as serious as yours, or more so.'

'It can hardly be more serious, dearest.'

'It cannot – O no, it cannot!' She jumped up joyfully at the hope. 'No, it cannot be more serious, certainly,' she cried, 'because 'tis just the same! I will tell you now.'

She sat down again.

Their hands were still joined. The ashes under the grate were lit by the fire vertically, like a torrid waste. Imagination might have beheld a Last Day luridness in this red-coaled glow, which fell on his face and hand, and on hers, peering into the loose hair about her brow, and firing the delicate skin underneath. A large shadow of her shape rose upon the wall and ceiling. She bent forward, at which each diamond on her neck gave a sinister wink like a toad's; and pressing her forehead against his temple she entered on her story of her acquaintance with Alec

---

3   1 Timothy 4.12.
4   The opening of Horace's Ode 22, Book 1; the words 'Integer vitæ' begin the original.
5   i.e., a sexual affair of two days' duration.

d'Urberville and its results, murmuring the words without flinching, and with her eyelids drooping down.

From 'Phase the Fifth: The Woman Pays'

From Chapter 35: Angel's Immediate Reaction to Tess's Confession

This excerpt from the beginning of Chapter 35 follows on directly from the conclusion of Chapter 34, quoted above, but after the interposition of a new 'phase', titled 'The Woman Pays'; it is as if Hardy wants his readers to pause long enough to consider the dizzying risk Tess has just taken, in telling Angel her whole story. As we take this breath, we know enough to predict Angel's disturbance at the revelations – but we may well be surprised at the massiveness of the price Tess has to 'pay' – a price that seems disproportionate even by Victorian standards. When considering Angel's repudiation of Tess as his wife, we are faced with two irreconcilable 'realities': his emotional shock, which we are asked to see as genuine, and his rationalization thereof, which is so hypocritical and inconsistent as to strain credulity. Angel's statement that 'the woman I have been loving is not you' can be taken at face value as expressing the disorientation he feels toward a person he thought he knew, but it also reveals two unpalatable presumptions on his part – first, that she deserves blame for this, and second, that his original basis for knowing her was completely honest and correct. If anything, it is his own unchecked idealization of Tess, his disinclination to see her as a fully subjective individual, that has fostered the present situation. (At the same time, it should be noted that Tess's own idealizations of Angel have played their part; and her degree of abjection in this scene – 'I will obey you like your wretched slave, even if it is to lie down and die' – is disturbing partly for what she is now, more than ever, letting him get away with.)

To take the emotional realism first: Hardy is clearly, in this scene, hitting several imagistic touchstones of the last. The second paragraph establishes this – 'the complexion even of external things seemed to suffer transmutation as her announcement progressed. The fire in the grate looked impish – demoniacally funny, as if it did not care in the least about her strait' – and thereafter, periodically, we check in with the play of light and shadow on the couple's stunned faces and stilted movements. Early on, a dull sense of nausea is evoked, along with the 'horror' and 'ghastliness' of what each person, for different reasons, is feeling. Later, Angel's benumbed and trancelike pacing, his need to get outside the house, seem pathetically believable, as is Tess's careful trailing after him and her obedient return to the house: anything, so that he will not actually leave her just yet. (These actions will be echoed later the same night, when Tess allows the sleepwalking Angel to carry her over a dangerous bridge in freezing weather, and to place her in an above-ground tomb, before cautiously leading him back to the house. Significantly, Tess does not tell Angel about any of this, the next morning.)

The dialogue, beyond the weary sense of round-and-round debate Hardy so successfully conveys (even to the touch of having Angel's few 'elaborate sarcasms' fall on deaf ears), is unsettling in a different way; there is a constant, unspoken demand to cull validity from factitiousness in Angel's analysis of the case, and we are not entirely sure we can do it. Late in the passage, when Tess timidly notes that other husbands have reconciled themselves to such circumstances as hers, Angel retorts first with a double-edged class indictment ('Different societies, different manners'; followed by a charge that she is being untrue to herself by acting like an ignorant peasant), and then with an invidious theory of heredity ('I cannot help associating your decline as a family with this other fact – of your want of firmness. Decrepit families imply decrepit wills, decrepit conduct'). These arguments do not work well together; and if we generously chalk them up to the sputterings of someone who is very upset, we must also account for their original incoherence, in Angel's flawed understanding of why he loved Tess.

Taken as a whole, this crucial passage is instructive to modern readers for another reason. It beckons to us to assume a critical mindset which we have been taught to discount as a thing of the past, and which Margaret Oliphant's remarks exemplify (pp. 58–61) – a mindset whereby literary characters are viewed as real people, and questions of literary artistry are funnelled through questions of what 'should' be done by and for them. Hardy gives us escape routes from this paradigm at various moments in the novel, but there are surely times, and this is one of them, when he seems to want us to feel entrapped or entranced by it.

Her narrative ended; even its re-assertions and secondary explanations were done. Tess's voice throughout had hardly risen higher than its opening tone; there had been no exculpatory phrase of any kind, and she had not wept.

But the complexion even of external things seemed to suffer transmutation as her announcement progressed. The fire in the grate looked impish – demoniacally funny, as if it did not care in the least about her strait. The fender[1] grinned idly, as if it too did not care. The light from the water-bottle was merely engaged in a chromatic problem. All material objects around announced their irresponsibility with terrible iteration. And yet nothing had changed since the moments when he had been kissing her; or rather, nothing in the substance of things. But the essence of things had changed.

When she ceased the auricular impressions[2] from their previous endearments seemed to hustle away into the corner of their brains, repeating themselves as echoes from a time of supremely purblind foolishness.

Clare performed the irrelevant act of stirring the fire; the intelligence had not even yet got to the bottom of him. After stirring the embers he rose to his feet; all the force of her disclosure had imparted itself now. His face had withered. In the

---

1   Fireplace frame.
2   Things heard by the ear, or perhaps in this case with Tess, endearments spoken directly into her ear by Angel.

strenuousness of his concentration he treadled[3] fitfully on the floor. He could not, by any contrivance, think closely enough; that was the meaning of his vague movement. When he spoke it was in the most inadequate, commonplace voice of the many varied tones she had heard from him.

'Tess!'

'Yes, dearest.'

'Am I to believe this? From your manner I am to take it as true. O you cannot be out of your mind! You ought to be! Yet you are not. . . . My wife, my Tess – nothing in you warrants such a supposition as that?'

'I am not out of my mind,' she said.

'And yet –' He looked vacantly at her, to resume with dazed senses: 'Why didn't you tell me before? Ah, yes, you would have told me, in a way – but I hindered you, I remember!'

These and other of his words were nothing but the perfunctory babble of the surface while the depths remained paralyzed. He turned away, and bent over a chair. Tess followed him to the middle of the room where he was, and stood there staring at him with eyes that did not weep. Presently she slid down upon her knees beside his foot, and from this position she crouched in a heap. 'In the name of our love, forgive me!' she whispered with a dry mouth. 'I have forgiven you for the same!'

And, as he did not answer, she said again; 'Forgive me as you are forgiven! *I* forgive *you*, Angel.'

'You – yes, you do.'

'But you do not forgive me?'

'O Tess, forgiveness does not apply to the case! You were one person; now you are another. My God – how can forgiveness meet such a grotesque – prestidigitation[4] as that!'

He paused, contemplating this definition; then suddenly broke into horrible laughter – as unnatural and ghastly as a laugh in hell.

'Don't – don't! It kills me quite, that!' she shrieked. 'O have mercy upon me – have mercy!'

He did not answer; and, sickly white, she jumped up. 'Angel, Angel! what do you mean by that laugh?' she cried out. 'Do you know what this is to me?'

He shook his head.

'I have been hoping, longing, praying, to make you happy! I have thought what joy it will be to do it, what an unworthy wife I shall be if I do not! That's what I have felt, Angel!'

'I know that.'

'I thought, Angel, that you loved me – me, my very self! If it is I you do love, O how can it be that you look and speak so? It frightens me! Having begun to love you, I love you for ever – in all changes, in all disgraces, because you are yourself. I ask no more. Then how can you, O my own husband, stop loving me?'

'I repeat, the woman I have been loving is not you.'

'But who?'

3 Stepped.
4 Deception.

'Another woman in your shape.'

She perceived in his words the realization of her own apprehensive foreboding in former times. He looked upon her as a species of imposter; a guilty woman in the guise of an innocent one. Terror was upon her white face as she saw it; her cheek was flaccid, and her mouth had almost the aspect of a round little hole. The horrible sense of his view of her so deadened her that she staggered; and he stepped forward, thinking she was going to fall.

'Sit down, sit down,' he said gently. 'You are ill; and it is natural that you should be.'

She did sit down, without knowing where she was, that strained look still upon her face, and her eyes such as to make his flesh creep. 'I don't belong to you any more, then; do I, Angel?' she asked helplessly. 'It is not me, but another woman like me that he loved, he says.'

The image raised caused her to take pity upon herself as one who was ill-used. Her eyes filled as she regarded her position further; she turned round and burst into a flood of self-sympathetic tears.

Clare was relieved at this change, for the effect on her of what had happened was beginning to be a trouble to him only less than the woe of the disclosure itself. He waited patiently, apathetically, till the violence of her grief had worn itself out, and her rush of weeping had lessened to a catching gasp at intervals.

'Angel,' she said suddenly, in her natural tones, the insane, dry voice of terror having left her now. 'Angel, am I too wicked for you and me to live together?'

'I have not been able to think what we can do.'

'I shan't ask you to let me live with you, Angel, because I have no right to! I shall not write to mother and sisters to say we be married, as I said I would do; and I shan't finish the good-hussif[5] I cut out and meant to make while we were in lodgings.'

'Shan't you?'

'No, I shan't do anything, unless you order me to; and if you go away from me I shall not follow 'ee; and if you never speak to me any more I shall not ask why, unless you tell me I may.'

'And if I order you to do anything?'

'I will obey you like your wretched slave, even if it is to lie down and die.'

'You are very good. But it strikes me that there is a want of harmony between your present mood of self-sacrifice and your past mood of self-preservation.'

These were the first words of antagonism. To fling elaborate sarcasms at Tess, however, was much like flinging them at a dog or cat. The charms of their subtlety passed by her unappreciated, and she only received them as inimical sounds which meant that anger ruled. She remained mute, not knowing that he was smothering his affection for her. She hardly observed that a tear descended slowly upon his cheek, a tear so large that it magnified the pores of the skin over which it rolled, like the object lens of a microscope. Meanwhile reillumination as to the terrible and total change that her confession had wrought in his life, in his universe, returned to him, and he tried desperately to advance among the new conditions in which he stood. Some consequent action was necessary; yet what?

---

5   A cloth that had been intended for some unspecified use in their household.

'Tess,' he said, as gently as he could speak, 'I cannot stay – in this room – just now. I will walk out a little way.'

He quietly left the room, and the two glasses of wine that he had poured out for their supper – one for her, one for him – remained on the table untasted. This was what their *Agape*[6] had come to. At tea, two or three hours earlier, they had, in the freakishness of affection, drunk from one cup.

The closing of the door behind him, gently as it had been pulled to, roused Tess from her stupor. He was gone; she could not stay. Hastily flinging her cloak around her she opened the door and followed, putting out the candles as if she were never coming back. The rain was over and the night was now clear.

She was soon close at his heels, for Clare walked slowly and without purpose. His form beside her light grey figure looked black, sinister, and forbidding, and she felt as sarcasm the touch of the jewels of which she had been momentarily so proud. Clare turned at hearing her footsteps, but his recognition of her presence seemed to make no difference to him, and he went on over the five yawning arches of the great bridge in front of the house.

The cow and horse tracks in the road were full of water, and rain having been enough to charge them, but not enough to wash them away. Across these minute pools the reflected stars flitted in a quick transit as she passed; she would not have known they were shining overhead if she had not seen them there – the vastest things of the universe imaged in objects so mean.

The place to which they had travelled to-day was in the same valley as Talbothays, but some miles lower down the river; and the surroundings being open she kept easily in sight of him. Away from the house the road wound through the meads, and along these she followed Clare without any attempt to come up with him or to attract him, but with dumb and vacant fidelity.

At last, however, her listless walk brought her up alongside him, and still he said nothing. The cruelty of fooled honesty is often great after enlightenment, and it was mighty in Clare now. The outdoor air had apparently taken away from him all tendency to act on impulse; she knew that he saw her without irradiation – in all her bareness; that Time was chanting his satiric psalm at her then –

> Behold, when thy face is made bare, he that loved thee shall hate;
> Thy face shall be no more fair at the fall of thy fate.
> For thy life shall fall as a leaf and be shed as the rain;
> And the veil of thine head shall be grief, and the crown shall be pain.[7]

He was still intently thinking, and her companionship had now insufficient power to break or divert the strain of thought. What a weak thing her presence must have become to him! She could not help addressing Clare.

'What have I done – what *have* I done! I have not told of anything that interferes with or belies my love for you. You don't think I planned it, do you? It is in

---

6   A Greek term denoting a love-feast; also, the highest and most spiritualized of the four kinds of love.

7   Algernon Swinburne's 'Atalanta in Calydon' (1865), ll. 1852–5.

your own mind what you are angry at, Angel; it is not in me. O, it is not in me, and I am not that deceitful woman you think me!'

'H'm – well. Not deceitful, my wife; but not the same. No, not the same. But do not make me reproach you. I have sworn that I will not; and I will do everything to avoid it.'

But she went on pleading in her distraction; and perhaps said things that would have been better left to silence. 'Angel! – Angel! I was a child – a child when it happened! I knew nothing of men.'

'You were more sinned against than sinning, that I admit.'[8]

'Then will you not forgive me?'

'I do forgive you, but forgiveness is not all.'

'And love me?'

To this question he did not answer.

'O Angel – my mother says that it sometimes happens so! – she knows several cases where they were worse than I, and the husband has not minded it much – has got over it at least. And yet the woman had not loved him as I do you!'

'Don't, Tess; don't argue. Different societies, different manners. You almost make me say you are an unapprehending peasant woman, who have never been initiated into the proportions of social things. You don't know what you say.'

'I am only a peasant by position, not by nature!'

She spoke with an impulse to anger, but it went as it came.

'So much the worse for you. I think that parson who unearthed your pedigree would have done better if he had held his tongue. I cannot help associating your decline as a family with this other fact – of your want of firmness. Decrepit families imply decrepit wills, decrepit conduct. Heaven, why did you give me a handle for despising you more by informing me of your descent! Here was I thinking you a new-sprung child of nature; there were you, the belated seedling of an effete aristocracy!'

'Lots of families are as bad as mine in that! Retty's family were once large landowners, and so were Dairyman Billett's. And the Debbyhouses, who now are carters,[9] were once the De Bayeux family. You find such as I everywhere; 'tis a feature of our county, and I can't help it.'

'So much the worse for the county.'

She took these reproaches in their bulk simply, not in their particulars; he did not love her as he had loved her hitherto, and to all else she was indifferent.

They wandered on again in silence. It was said afterwards that a cottager of Wellbridge, who went out late that night for a doctor, met two lovers in the pastures, walking very slowly, without converse, one behind the other, as in a funeral procession, and the glimpse that he obtained of their faces seemed to denote that they were anxious and sad. Returning later, he passed them again in the same field, progressing just as slowly, and as regardless of the hour and of the cheerless night as before. It was only on account of his preoccupation with his own affairs, and the illness in his house, that he did not bear in mind the curious incident, which, however, he recalled a long while after.

---

8   *King Lear*, III.ii.61.
9   Simple labourers; literally, drivers of carts.

During the interval of the cottager's going and coming, she had said to her husband –

'I don't see how I can help being the cause of much misery to you all your life. The river is down there. I can put an end to myself in it. I am not afraid.'

'I don't wish to add murder to my other follies,' he said.

'I will leave something to show that I did it myself – on account of my shame. They will not blame you then.'

'Don't speak so absurdly – I wish not to hear it. It is nonsense to have such thoughts in this kind of case, which is rather one for satirical laughter than for tragedy. You don't in the least understand the quality of the mishap. It would be viewed in the light of a joke by nine-tenths of the world if it were known. Please oblige me by returning to the house, and going to bed.'

'I will,' said she dutifully.

They had rambled round by a road which led to the well-known ruins of the Cistercian[10] abbey behind the mill, the latter having, in centuries past, been attached to the monastic establishment. The mill still worked on, food being a perennial necessity; the abbey had perished, creeds being transient. One continually sees the ministration of the temporary outlasting the ministration of the eternal. Their walk having been circuitous they were still not far from the house, and in obeying his direction she only had to reach the large stone bridge across the main river, and follow the road for a few yards. When she got back everything remained as she had left it, the fire being still burning. She did not stay downstairs for more than a minute, but proceeded to her chamber, whither the luggage had been taken. Here she sat down on the edge of the bed, looking blankly around, and presently began to undress. In removing the light towards the bedstead its rays fell upon the tester of white dimity;[11] something was hanging beneath it, and she lifted the candle to see what it was. A bough of mistletoe. Angel had put it there; she knew that in an instant. This was the explanation of that mysterious parcel which it had been so difficult to pack and bring; whose contents he would not explain to her, saying that time would soon show her the purpose thereof. In his zest and his gaiety he had hung it there. How foolish and inopportune that mistletoe looked now.

Having nothing more to fear, having scarce anything to hope, for that he would relent there seemed no promise whatever, she lay down dully. When sorrow ceases to be speculative sleep sees her opportunity. Among so many happier moods which forbid repose this was a mood which welcomed it, and in a few minutes the lonely Tess forgot existence, surrounded by the aromatic stillness of the chamber that had once, possibly, been the bride-chamber of her own ancestry.

From **Chapter 42: Initial Description of Flintcomb-Ash Farm**

After their abortive honeymoon, things change quickly for Tess and Angel. At Angel's request, Tess agrees to return to her family at Marlott, and promises not

10 A monastic order noted for its strictness.
11 A bed canopy made of cotton cloth.

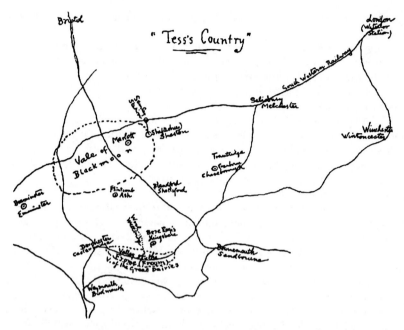

Figure 7 Hardy's map of 'Tess's Country' (By permission of the Thomas Hardy Association of America)

to try to see Angel, though she may write to him in care of his father if she needs help. He provides her £50 in cash, and leaves £30 more in the bank which she can draw upon as needed. Although historical comparisons of monetary values are notoriously difficult, it can be assumed that the £80 given to Tess is equivalent to at least £6,000 in today's currency; the effective buying power of such a sum would probably be greater. (They agree that the diamonds, which were willed to Angel's wife as a lifetime gift and not as property to be sold, should also be kept at the bank.) Angel, after taking leave of his own parents – who are curious about Tess, though they elected not to attend the wedding – leaves to seek his fortune as a farmer in Brazil. There, within a few months, he contracts a fever and almost dies. We will learn later (in Chapter 49, not excerpted here) that his time in Brazil thereafter was not only unprofitable but almost hellish: weakened by his own illness, he watched his fellow-settlers from England, all in pursuit of a better life, wasting away in the hostile climate and despairing of escape. (For a nineteenth-century observation of Brazil see Contemporary Documents, **p. 41**.) Tess, in the meantime, soon finds herself short of money and prospects. She gives half of Angel's cash gift to her parents, and a few months later is forced to draw on the banked money so that they can pay for a new roof.

Chapters 41 and 42 show Tess, some eight months after Angel's departure, living as a migrant farm worker and, with her money running out, in need of a more permanent position for the approaching winter. The opening paragraph here refers to her having been accosted on the road by a man who knows of her long-ago association with Alec d'Urberville; taking cover for the night under some low-growing trees, she awakens to strange noises, and finds in the morning that she has been surrounded by a grotesque scene of dying pheasants, shot and abandoned by recreational hunters. Chapter 41 closes with her putting the birds out of misery by strangling them, and reproaching her own lapses into self-pity.

Significant in Chapter 42, as always in Hardy, is the interplay of material realities with modes of gender-class presentation that are – albeit to varying and unpredictable degrees – under one's own control. Tess's beauty, the prior chapter has told us, brought her no trouble from wolfish men as long as she was wearing fashionable clothes; but now, the clash between her refined looks and her working attire may actually put her in danger. One wonders, though, whether Hardy intends us to view her attempts to disfigure herself as useless: *can* Tess become unbeautiful? Later, as she renews her acquaintance with a co-worker from Talbothays dairy, we rethink the question from the other direction: can she really cling meaningfully to her identity as 'Mrs Angel Clare'? Indeed, throughout this passage Tess manifests wildly varying impulses toward self-respect and self-abasement, though both impulses may suggest an even baser instinct toward simple survival.

Tess's movement into the harsher 'upland' topography of Flintcomb-Ash and its environs has been cited by critics as a prime example of how Hardy blends subjectivity with landscape. Her reunion with the former Talbothays dairymaid Marian, even given its terrible circumstances, serves to remind us, as Williams describes (**pp. 99–101**), both of the plight of female labourers and of the precious, if fragile, psychic comfort Hardy's labouring women provide one another.

It was now broad day, and she started again, emerging cautiously upon the highway. But there was no need for caution; not a soul was at hand, and Tess went onward with fortitude, her recollection of the birds' silent endurance of their night of agony impressing upon her the relativity of sorrows and the tolerable nature of her own, if she could once rise high enough to despise opinion. But that she could not do so long as it was held by Clare.

She reached Chalk-Newton, and breakfasted at an inn, where several young men were troublesomely complimentary to her good looks. Somehow she felt hopeful, for was it not possible that her husband also might say these same things to her even yet? She was bound to take care of herself on the chance of it, and keep off these casual lovers. To this end Tess resolved to run no further risks from her appearance. As soon as she got out of the village she entered a thicket and took from her basket one of the oldest field-gowns, which she had never put on even at the dairy – never since she had worked among the stubble at Marlott. She also, by a felicitous thought, took a handkerchief from her bundle and tied it round her face under her bonnet, covering her chin and half her cheeks and temples, as if she were suffering from toothache. Then with her little scissors, by the aid of a pocket looking-glass, she mercilessly nipped her eyebrows off, and thus insured against aggressive admiration she went on her uneven way.

'What a mommet[1] of a maid!' said the next man who met her to a companion. Tears came into her eyes for very pity of herself as she heard him.

'But I don't care!' she said. 'O no – I don't care! I'll always be ugly now, because Angel is not here, and I have nobody to take care of me. My husband that was is gone away, and never will love me any more; but I love him just the same, and hate all other men, and like to make 'em think scornfully of me!'

Thus Tess walks on; a figure which is part of the landscape; a fieldwoman pure and simple, in winter guise; a gray serge cape, a red woollen cravat, a stuff skirt covered by a whitey-brown rough wrapper, and buff-leather gloves. Every thread of that old attire has become faded and thin under the stroke of raindrops, the burn of sunbeams, and the stress of winds. There is no sign of young passion in her now:

> The maiden's mouth is cold
> . . .
> Fold over simple fold
> Binding her head.[2]

Inside this exterior, over which the eye might have roved as over a thing scarcely percipient,[3] almost inorganic, there was the record of a pulsing life which had learnt too well, for its years, of the dust and ashes of things, of the cruelty of lust and the fragility of love.

Next day the weather was bad, but she trudged on, the honesty, directness, and impartiality of elemental enmity disconcerting her but little. Her object being a winter's occupation and a winter's home, there was no time to lose. Her experience of short hirings had been such that she was determined to accept no more.

Thus she went forward from farm to farm in the direction of the place whence Marian had written to her, which she determined to make use of as a last shift only, its rumoured stringencies being the reverse of tempting. First she inquired for the lighter kinds of employment, and, as acceptance in any variety of these grew hopeless, applied next for the less light, till, beginning with the dairy and poultry tendance that she liked best, she ended with the heavy and coarse pursuits which she liked least – work on arable land: work of such roughness, indeed, as she would never have deliberately volunteered for.

Towards the second evening she reached the irregular chalk table-land or plateau, bosomed with semi-globular tumuli[4] – as if Cybele the Many-breasted[5] were supinely extended there – which stretched between the valley of her birth and the valley of her love. Here the air was dry and cold, and the long cart-roads were blown white and dusty within a few hours after rain. There were few trees, or none, those that would have grown in the hedges being mercilessly plashed down

---

1   A grotesquely dressed figure or doll.
2   Algernon Swinburne, 'Fragoletta', ll. 41–2; 45.
3   Having the power of perception.
4   Mounds; humps of earth; barrows.
5   In reference to the fertility goddess of Phrygian mythology, sometimes called 'mother of the gods'.

with the quickset by the tenant-farmers, the natural enemies of tree, bush and brake.[6] In the middle distance ahead of her she could see the summits of Bulbarrow and of Nettlecombe-Tout, and they seemed friendly. They had a low and unassuming aspect from this upland, though as approached on the other side from Blackmoor in her childhood they were as lofty bastions against the sky. Southerly, at many miles' distance, and over the hills and ridges coastward, she could discern a surface like polished steel: it was the English Channel at a point far out towards France.

Before her, in a slight depression, were the remains of a village. She had, in fact, reached Flintcomb-Ash, the place of Marian's sojourn. There seemed to be no help for it; hither she was doomed to come. The stubborn soil around her showed plainly enough that the kind of labour in demand here was of the roughest kind; but it was time to rest from searching, and she resolved to stay, particularly as it began to rain. At the entrance to the village was a cottage whose gable jutted into the road, and before applying for a lodging she stood under its shelter, and watched the evening close in.

'Who would think I was Mrs. Angel Clare!' she said.

The wall felt warm to her back and shoulders, and she found that immediately within the gable was the cottage fireplace, the heat of which came through the bricks. She warmed her hands upon them, and also put her cheek – red and moist with the drizzle – against their comforting surface. The wall seemed to be the only friend she had. She had so little wish to leave it that she could have stayed there all night.

Tess could hear the occupants of the cottage – gathered together after their day's labour – talking to each other within, and the rattle of their supper-plates was also audible. But in the village-street she had seen no soul as yet. The solitude was at last broken by the approach of one feminine figure, who, though the evening was cold, wore the print gown and the tilt-bonnet of summer time. Tess instinctively thought it might be Marian, and when she came near enough to be distinguishable in the gloom surely enough it was she. Marian was even stouter and redder in the face than formerly, and decidedly shabbier in attire. At any previous period of her existence Tess would hardly have cared to renew the acquaintance in such conditions; but her loneliness was excessive, and she responded readily to Marian's greeting.

Marian was quite respectful in her inquiries, but seemed much moved by the fact that Tess should still continue in no better condition than at first; though she had dimly heard of the separation.

'Tess – Mrs. Clare – the dear wife of dear he! And is it really so bad as this, my child? Why is your cwomely[7] face tied up in such a way? Anybody been beating 'ee? Not he?'

'No, no, no! I merely did it not to be clipsed or colled,[8] Marian.' She pulled off in disgust a bandage which could suggest such wild thoughts.

'And you've got no collar on' (Tess had been accustomed to wear a little white collar at the dairy).

6   Thicket.
7   Comely; beautiful.
8   i.e., so as not to attract the attention of men.

'I know it, Marian.'

'You've lost it travelling.'

'I've not lost it. The truth is, I don't care anything about my looks; and so I didn't put it on.'

'And you don't wear your wedding-ring?'

'Yes, I do; but not in public. I wear it round my neck on a ribbon. I don't wish people to think who I am by marriage, or that I am married at all; it would be so awkward while I lead my present life.'

Marian paused. 'But you *be* a gentleman's wife; and it seems hardly fair that you should live like this!'

'O yes it is, quite fair; though I am very unhappy.'

'Well, well. He married you – and you can be unhappy!'

'Wives are unhappy sometimes; from no fault of their husbands – from their own.'

'You've no faults, deary; that I'm sure of. And he's none. So it must be something outside ye both.'

'Marian, dear Marian, will you do me a good turn without asking questions? My husband has gone abroad, and somehow I have overrun my allowance, so that I have to fall back upon my old work for a time. Do not call me Mrs. Angel Clare, but Tess, as before. Do they want a hand here?'

'O yes; they'll take one always because few care to come. 'Tis a starve-acre place. Corn and swedes[9] are all they grow. Though I be here myself, I feel 'tis a pity for such as you to come.'

'But you used to be as good a dairywoman as I.'

'Yes; but I've got out o' that since I took to drink. Lord, that's the only comfort I've got now! If you engage, you'll be set swede-hacking. That's what I be doing; but you won't like it.'

'O – anything! Will you speak for me?'

'You will do better by speaking for yourself.'

'Very well. Now, Marian, remember – nothing about *him*, if I get the place. I don't wish to bring his name down to the dirt.'

Marian, who was really a trustworthy girl though of coarser grain than Tess, promised anything she asked.

'This is pay-night,' she said, 'and if you were to come with me you would know at once. I be real sorry that you are not happy; but 'tis because he's away, I know. You couldn't be unhappy if he were here, even if he gie'd ye no money – even if he used you like a drudge.'

'That's true; I could not!'

They walked on together, and soon reached the farmhouse, which was almost sublime in its dreariness. There was not a tree within sight; there was not, at this season, a green pasture – nothing but fallow and turnips everywhere; in large fields divided by hedges plashed[10] to unrelieved levels.

Tess waited outside the door of the farmhouse till the group of workfolk had received their wages, and then Marian introduced her. The farmer himself, it

---

9 Root vegetables similar to turnips, sometimes used for cattle food.
10 Interlaced with woven branches.

appeared, was not at home, but his wife, who represented him this evening, made no objection to hiring Tess, on her agreeing to remain till Old Lady-Day.[11] Female field-labour was seldom offered now, and its cheapness made it profitable for tasks which women could perform as readily as men.

Having signed the agreement, there was nothing more for Tess to do at present than to get a lodging, and she found one in the house at whose gable-wall she had warmed herself. It was a poor subsistence that she had ensured, but it would afford a shelter for the winter at any rate.

That night she wrote to inform her parents of her new address, in case a letter should arrive at Marlott from her husband. But she did not tell them of the sorriness of her situation: it might have brought reproach upon him.

From 'Phase the Sixth: The Convert'

Chapter 47: Threshing Scene; Renewal of Alec d'Urberville's Attentions to Tess

The title of *Phase the Sixth* ('The Convert') refers to an ironic subplot in which, not long after Tess has left him, Alec d'Urberville meets Angel Clare's father, an Evangelical clergyman, and — to their mutual surprise — finds his message so persuasive that he himself becomes a travelling preacher. The shallowness of his conversion is proved, however, when Alec and Tess accidentally cross paths at a tent revival he is conducting near Flintcomb-Ash. In ensuing conversations, his reawakened lust for Tess and his remorse on learning of her sufferings, along with her eloquence in voicing the religious scepticism taught her by Angel Clare, propel him to renounce his spiritual vocation and to dog Tess's footsteps in spite of her clear request that he should leave her alone.

In the famously brutal scene that follows here, we find clear reminders of at least two prior situations in the novel. One, in Chapter 14 (just prior to the excerpted 'midnight baptism' scene above, p. 136), shows a monstrous reaping-machine in a field around the village of Marlott, with Tess, an unwed mother with no better prospects, herself mechanically binding piles of grain into sheaves. Another, in Chapter 5 (in Key Passages, pp. 128–31), shows Tess's 'dreamlike' submission to the repeated action of Alec's bedecking her with roses. At the end of the following passage, these powerful forces are combined into the inexorable demands of the machine, Farmer Groby and Alec.

Critics have found in this chapter, which is included here in its entirety, a confluence of themes, motifs and narrative techniques important to *Tess*. It represents a typically Hardyean exacerbation of the already harsh conditions at Flintcomb-Ash (see the excerpt from Chapter 42 and headnote for critical references); here is one of several places in the novel where we realize that physical hardships can actually be easier to bear than the persecutions of greed, cupidity and 'progress'. As summarized by Irving Howe, 'Mechanization, impersonality, alienation, the cash nexus, dehumanisation – all these tags of modern thought, so worn and all too often true, are brought to quickened reality in Tess's ordeal' (**p. 66**). Jacobus speaks more pointedly of the threshing-machine as furthering 'the motif of sexual dominance expressed through mechanical power' (**p. 73**), and of this scene as one in which 'sexual and economic oppression are as closely identified as they had been in [Tess's] seduction' (**p. 74**). Frederick Pinion, highlighting the phrase 'the engine which was to act as the *primum mobile* of this little world' (**p. 86**), offers an extended commentary on the threshing scene as conveying Hardy's belief that the forces of universal causation must be uncaring and blind. (See also Hardy's poems 'The Lacking Sense' and 'Doom and She', reprinted in Contemporary Documents.) Bruce Johnson gestures more broadly toward the machine as an emblematic threat to the 'primeval energies' that Hardy seems to associate with Tess, and thus to 'an ideal model of consciousness' that has been largely lost with our modern alienation from nature (**pp. 104–6**).

And Tony Tanner, making a different sort of point about what we are conscious of as readers, cites Tess's smiting Alec with her heavy work-glove as an example of Hardy's artistry with concrete images: 'The man who first made her bleed now stands bleeding from the lips. Blood has blood, and it will have more blood. We need only to see the scene – there, unanalysed, unexplained; a matter of violent movements, sudden compulsions. Hardy spends more time describing the glove than attempting to unravel the hidden thoughts of these starkly confronted human beings' (**p. 83**).

It is the threshing of the last wheat-rick[1] at Flintcomb-Ash farm. The dawn of the March morning is singularly inexpressive, and there is nothing to show where the eastern horizon lies. Against the twilight rises the trapezoidal top of the stack, which has stood forlornly here through the washing and bleaching of the wintry weather.

When Izz Huett and Tess arrived at the scene of operations only a rustling denoted that others had preceded them; to which, as the light increased, there were presently added the silhouettes of two men on the summit. They were busily 'unhaling' the rick, that is, stripping off the thatch before beginning to throw down the sheaves; and while this was in progress Izz and Tess, with the other women-workers, in their whitey-brown pinners,[2] stood waiting and shivering, Farmer Groby having insisted upon their being on the spot thus early to get the job over if possible by the end of the day. Close under the eaves of the stack, and as yet barely visible, was the red tyrant that the women had come to serve – a timber-framed construction, with straps and wheels appertaining – the threshing-machine which, whilst it was going, kept up a despotic demand upon the endurance of their muscles and nerves.

---

1   A large pile or stack.
2   Snug caps with ear flaps.

A little way off there was another indistinct figure; this one black, with a sustained hiss that spoke of strength very much in reserve. The long chimney running up beside an ash-tree, and the warmth which radiated from the spot, explained without the necessity of much daylight that here was the engine which was to act as the *primum mobile*[3] of this little world. By the engine stood a dark motionless being, a sooty and grimy embodiment of tallness, in a sort of trance, with a heap of coals by his side: it was the engineman. The isolation of his manner and colour lent him the appearance of a creature from Tophet,[4] who had strayed into the pellucid smokelessness of this region of yellow grain and pale soil, with which he had nothing in common, to amaze and to discompose its aborigines.

What he looked he felt. He was in the agricultural world, but not of it. He served fire and smoke; these denizens of the fields served vegetation, weather, frost, and sun. He travelled with his engine from farm to farm, from county to county, for as yet the steam threshing-machine was itinerant in this part of Wessex. He spoke in a strange northern accent; his thoughts being turned inwards upon himself, his eye on his iron charge, hardly perceiving the scenes around him, and caring for them not at all: holding only strictly necessary intercourse with the natives, as if some ancient doom compelled him to wander here against his will in the service of his Plutonic[5] master. The long strap which ran from the driving-wheel of his engine to the red thresher under the rick was the sole tie-line between agriculture and him.

While they uncovered the sheaves he stood apathetic beside his portable repository of force, round whose hot blackness the morning air quivered. He had nothing to do with preparatory labour. His fire was waiting incandescent, his steam was at high pressure, in a few seconds he could make the long strap move at an invisible velocity. Beyond its extent the environment might be corn, straw, or chaos; it was all the same to him. If any of the autochthonous[6] idlers asked him what he called himself, he replied shortly, 'an engineer.'

The rick was unhaled by full daylight; the men then took their places, the women mounted, and the work began. Farmer Groby – or, as they called him, 'he' – had arrived ere this, and by his orders Tess was placed on the platform of the machine, close to the man who fed it, her business being to untie every sheaf of corn handed on to her by Izz Huett, who stood next, but on the rick; so that the feeder could seize it and spread it over the revolving drum, which whisked out every grain in one moment.

They were soon in full progress, after a preparatory hitch or two, which rejoiced the hearts of those who hated machinery. The work sped on till breakfast-time, when the thresher was stopped for half an hour; and on starting again after the meal the whole supplementary strength of the farm was thrown into the labour of constructing the straw-rick, which began to grow beside the stack of corn. A hasty lunch was eaten as they stood, without leaving their positions, and then another couple of hours brought them near to dinner-time; the inexorable

---

3   Prime mover. See Pinion in *Modern Criticism*, **pp. 85–6**.
4   A location near Jerusalem used for burning garbage; more broadly, a synonym for hell.
5   Of hell or the underworld.
6   Native to, or remaining in, one's place of origin, used especially in reference to sedimentary rocks.

wheel continuing to spin, and the penetrating hum of the thresher to thrill to the very marrow all who were near the revolving wire-cage.

The old men on the rising straw-rick talked of the past days when they had been accustomed to thresh with flails on the oaken barn-door; when everything, even to winnowing, was effected by hand-labour, which, to their thinking, though slow, produced better results. Those, too, on the corn-rick talked a little; but the perspiring ones at the machine, including Tess, could not lighten their duties by the exchange of many words. It was the ceaselessness of the work which tried her so severely, and began to make her wish that she had never come to Flintcomb-Ash. The women on the corn-rick – Marian, who was one of them, in particular – could stop to drink ale or cold tea from the flagon now and then, or to exchange a few gossiping remarks while they wiped their faces or cleared the fragments of straw and husk from their clothing; but for Tess there was no respite; for, as the drum never stopped, the man who fed it could not stop, and she, who had to supply the man with untied sheaves, could not stop either, unless Marian changed places with her, which she sometimes did for half an hour in spite of Groby's objections that she was too slow-handed for a feeder.

For some probably economical reason it was usually a woman who was chosen for this particular duty, and Groby gave as his motive in selecting Tess that she was one of those who best combined strength with quickness in untying, and both with staying power, and this may have been true. The hum of the thresher, which prevented speech, increased to a raving whenever the supply of corn fell short of the regular quantity. As Tess and the man who fed could never turn their heads she did not know that just before the dinner-hour a person had come silently into the field by the gate, and had been standing under a second rick watching the scene, and Tess in particular. He was dressed in a tweed suit of fashionable pattern, and he twirled a gay walking-cane.

'Who is that?' said Izz Huett to Marian. She had at first addressed the inquiry to Tess, but the latter could not hear it.

'Somebody's fancy-man, I s'pose,' said Marian laconically.

'I'll lay a guinea he's after Tess.'

'O no. 'Tis a ranter[7] pa'son who's been sniffing after her lately; not a dandy like this.'

'Well – this is the same man.'

'The same man as the preacher? But he's quite different!'

'He hev left off his black coat and white neckercher, and hev cut off his whiskers; but he's the same man for all that.'

'D'ye really think so? Then I'll tell her,' said Marian.

'Don't. She'll see him soon enough, good-now.'

'Well. I don't think it at all right for him to join his preaching to courting a married woman, even though her husband mid be abroad, and she, in a sense, a widow.'

'Oh – he can do her no harm,' said Izz drily. 'Her mind can no more be heaved from that one place where it do bide than a stooded waggon[8] from the hole he's

---

7 Generically, a bombastic preacher, but also a term applied to certain Evangelical Methodist sects.
8 A wagon sunk and/or stuck in mud.

in. Lord love 'ee, neither court-paying, nor preaching, nor the seven thunders[9] themselves, can wean a woman when 'twould be better for her that she should be weaned.'

Dinner-time came, and the whirling ceased; whereupon Tess left her post, her knees trembling so wretchedly with the shaking of the machine that she could scarcely walk. 'You ought to het a quart o' drink into 'ee, as I've done,' said Marian. 'You wouldn't look so white then. Why, souls above us, your face is as if you'd been hagrode!'[10]

It occurred to the good-natured Marian that, as Tess was so tired, her discovery of her visitor's presence might have the bad effect of taking away her appetite; and Marian was thinking of inducing Tess to descend by a ladder on the further side of the stack when the gentleman came forward and looked up.

Tess uttered a short little 'Oh!' And a moment after she said, quickly, 'I shall eat my dinner here – right on the rick.'

Sometimes, when they were so far from their cottages, they all did this; but as there was rather a keen wind going today, Marian and the rest descended, and sat under the straw-stack.

The newcomer was, indeed, Alec d'Urberville, the late Evangelist, despite his changed attire and aspect. It was obvious at a glance that the original *Weltlust*[11] had come back; that he had restored himself, as nearly as a man could do who had grown three or four years older, to the old jaunty, slap-dash guise under which Tess had first known her admirer, and cousin so-called. Having decided to remain where she was, Tess sat down among the bundles, out of sight of the ground, and began her meal; till, by-and-by, she heard footsteps on the ladder, and immediately after Alec appeared upon the stack – now an oblong and level platform of sheaves. He strode across them, and sat down opposite of her without a word.

Tess continued to eat her modest dinner, a slice of thick pancake which she had brought with her. The other workfolk were by this time all gathered under the rick, where the loose straw formed a comfortable retreat.

'I am here again, as you see,' said d'Urberville.

'Why do you trouble me so!' she cried, reproach flashing from her very finger-ends.

'*I* trouble *you*? I think I may ask, why do you trouble *me*?'

'Sure, I don't trouble you any-when!'

'You say you don't? But you do! You haunt me. Those very eyes that you turned upon my with such a bitter flash a moment ago, they come to me just as you showed them then, in the night and in the day! Tess, ever since you told me of that child of ours, it is just as if my feelings, which have been flowing in a strong puritanical stream, had suddenly found a way open in the direction of you, and had all at once gushed through. The religious channel is left dry forthwith; and it is you who have done it!'

She gazed in silence.

'What – you have given up your preaching entirely?' she asked.

---

9 Voices of the apocalypse: see Revelation 10.3–4.
10 Literally, ridden by a hag; in general terms, appearing exhausted or haunted.
11 Worldliness.

She had gathered from Angel sufficient of the incredulity of modern thought to despise flash enthusiasms; but, as a woman, she was somewhat appalled.

In affected severity d'Urberville continued –

'Entirely. I have broken every engagement since that afternoon I was to address the drunkards at Casterbridge Fair. The deuce only knows what I am thought of by the brethren. Ah-ha! The brethren! No doubt they pray for me – weep for me; for they are kind people in their way. But what do I care? How could I go on with the thing when I had lost my faith in it? – it would have been hypocrisy of the basest kind! Among them I should have stood like Hymenaeus and Alexander, who were delivered over to Satan that they might learn not to blaspheme.[12] What a grand revenge you have taken! I saw you innocent, and I deceived you. Four years after, you find me a Christian enthusiast; you then work upon me, perhaps to my complete perdition! But Tess, my coz, as I used to call you, this is only my way of talking, and you must not look so horribly concerned. Of course you have done nothing except retain your pretty face and shapely figure. I saw it on the rick before you saw me – that tight pinafore-thing sets it off, and that wing-bonnet – you field-girls should never wear those bonnets if you wish to keep out of danger.' He regarded her silently for a few moments, and with a short cynical laugh resumed: 'I believe that if the bachelor-apostle, whose deputy I thought I was, had been tempted by such a pretty face, he would have let go the plough for her sake as I do.'

Tess attempted to expostulate, but at this juncture all her fluency failed her, and without heeding he added:

'Well, this paradise that you supply is perhaps as good as any other, after all. But to speak seriously, Tess.' D'Urberville rose and came nearer, reclining sideways amid the sheaves, and resting upon his elbow. 'Since I last saw you, I have been thinking of what you said that *he* said. I have come to the conclusion that there does seem rather a want of common-sense in these threadbare old propositions; how I could have been so fired by poor Parson Clare's enthusiasm, and have gone so madly to work, transcending even him, I cannot make out! As for what you said last time, on the strength of your wonderful husband's intelligence – whose name you have never told me – about having what they call an ethical system without any dogma, I don't see my way to that at all.'

'Why, you can have the religion of loving-kindness and purity at least, if you can't have – what do you call it – dogma.'

'O no! I'm a different sort of fellow from that! If there's nobody to say, "Do this, and it will be a good thing for you after you are dead; do that, and if will be a bad thing for you," I can't warm up. Hang it, I am not going to feel responsible for my deeds and passions if there's nobody to be responsible to; and if I were you, my dear, I wouldn't either!'

She tried to argue, and tell him that he had mixed in his dull brain two matters, theology and morals, which in the primitive days of mankind had been quite distinct. But owing to Angel Clare's reticence, to her absolute want of training, and to her being a vessel of emotions rather than reasons, she could not get on.

---

12 In 1 Timothy 1. 18–20, Paul tells Timothy that Hymenaeus and Alexander are condemned for false teaching; in 2 Timothy 2. 17–18 one of Hymenaeus's errors is said to have been teaching that the resurrection has already occurred.

'Well, never mind,' he resumed. 'Here I am, my love, as in the old times!'

'Not as then – never as then – 'tis different!' she entreated. 'And there was never warmth with me! O why didn't you keep your faith, if the loss of it has brought you to speak to me like this!'

'Because you've knocked it out of me; so the evil be upon your sweet head! Your husband little thought how his teaching would recoil upon him! Ha-ha – I'm awfully glad you have made an apostate of me all the same! Tess, I am more taken with you than ever, and I pity you too. For all your closeness, I see you are in a bad way – neglected by one who ought to cherish you.'

She could not get her morsels of food down her throat; her lips were dry, and she was ready to choke. The voices and laughs of the workfolk eating and drinking under the rick came to her as if they were a quarter of a mile off.

'It is cruelty to me!' she said. 'How – how can you treat me to this talk, if you care ever so little for me?'

'True, true,' he said, wincing a little. 'I did not come to reproach you for my deeds. I came, Tess, to say that I don't like you to be working like this, and I have come on purpose for you. You say you have a husband who is not I. Well, perhaps you have; but I've never seen him, and you've not told me his name; and altogether he seems rather a mythological personage. However, even if you have one, I think I am nearer to you than he is. I, at any rate, try to help you out of trouble, but he does not, bless his invisible face! The words of the stern prophet Hosea that I used to read come back to me. Don't you know them, Tess? – "And she shall follow after her lover, but she shall not overtake him; and she shall seek him, but shall not find him; then shall she say, I will go and return to my first husband; for then was it better with me than now!" . . . Tess, my trap[13] is waiting just under the hill, and – darling mine, not his! – you know the rest.'

Her face had been rising to a dull crimson fire while he spoke; but she did not answer.

'You have been the cause of my backsliding,' he continued, stretching his arm towards her waist; 'you should be willing to share it, and leave that mule you call husband for ever.'

One of her leather gloves, which she had taken off to eat her skimmer-cake,[14] lay in her lap, and without the slightest warning she passionately swung the glove by the gauntlet directly in his face. It was heavy and thick as a warrior's, and it struck him flat on the mouth. Fancy might have regarded the act as the recrudescence[15] of a trick in which her armed progenitors were not unpractised. Alec fiercely started up from his reclining position. A scarlet oozing appeared where her blow had alighted, and in a moment the blood began dropping from his mouth upon the straw. But he soon controlled himself, calmly drew his handkerchief from his pocket, and mopped his bleeding lips.

She too had sprung up, but she sank down again. 'Now, punish me!' she said, turning up her eyes to him with the hopeless defiance of the sparrow's gaze before its captor twists its neck. 'Whip me, crush me; you need not mind those people under the rick! I shall not cry out. Once victim, always victim – that's the law!'

---

13 A two-wheeled carriage.
14 A mixture of leftovers, cooked in a shallow pan.
15 A reappearance or recurrence after a period of inactivity.

'O no, no, Tess,' he said blandly. 'I can make full allowance for this. Yet you most unjustly forget one thing, that I would have married you if you had not put it out of my power to do so. Did I not ask you flatly to be my wife – hey? Answer me.'

'You did.'

'And you cannot be. But remember one thing!' His voice hardened as his temper got the better of him with the recollection of his sincerity in asking her and her present ingratitude, and he stepped across to her side and held her by the shoulders, so that she shook under his grasp. 'Remember, my lady, I was your master once! I will be your master again. If you are any man's wife you are mine!'

The threshers now began to stir below.

'So much for our quarrel,' he said, letting her go. 'Now I shall leave you, and shall come again for your answer during the afternoon. You don't know me yet! But I know you.'

She had not spoken again, remaining as if stunned. D'Urberville retreated over the sheaves, and descended the ladder, while the workers below rose and stretched their arms, and shook down the beer they had drunk. Then the threshing-machine started afresh; and amid the renewed rustle of the straw Tess resumed her position by the buzzing drum as one in a dream, untying sheaf after sheaf in endless succession.

From 'Phase the Seventh: Fulfilment'

From **Chapter 55: Description of Sandbourne**

Hardy performs the ironic juxtapositions of this scene with a light touch that belies the portentousness of the situation: Angel Clare, finally home from Brazil after undergoing a life-threatening illness and a change of heart, has come to the seaside resort where he has been given to understand Tess now lives. Her transplantation to the slightly tawdry, overbuilt 'pleasure city' is for Angel a confusing fact; 'She was most probably engaged to do something in one of these large houses,' he speculates, and of course this is a malignant bit of dramatic irony for us, since we can easily deduce that she is here not as a domestic servant but as the reluctant companion of Alec d'Urberville.

At eleven o'clock that night, having secured a bed at one of the hotels and telegraphed his address to his father immediately on his arrival, he walked out into the streets of Sandbourne. It was too late to call on or inquire for any one, and he reluctantly postponed his purpose till the morning. But he could not retire to rest just yet.

This fashionable watering-place, with its eastern and its western stations, its piers, its groves of pines, its promenades, and its covered gardens, was, to Angel Clare, like a fairy place suddenly created by the stroke of a wand, and allowed to get a little dusty. An outlying eastern tract of the enormous Egdon Waste was close at hand, yet on the very verge of that tawny piece of antiquity such a glittering novelty as this pleasure city had chosen to spring up. Within the space of a mile from its outskirts every irregularity of the soil was prehistoric, every channel an undisturbed British trackway; not a sod having been turned there since the days of the Caesars. Yet the exotic had grown here, suddenly as the prophet's gourd;[1] and had drawn hither Tess.

By the midnight lamps he went up and down the winding way of this new world in an old one, and could discern between the trees and against the stars the lofty roofs, chimneys, gazebos, and towers of the numerous fanciful residences of which the place was composed. It was a city of detached mansions; a Mediterranean lounging-place on the English Channel; and as seen now by night it seemed even more imposing than it was.

The sea was near at hand, but not intrusive; it murmured, and he thought it was the pines; the pines murmured in precisely the same tones, and he thought they were the sea.

Where could Tess possibly be, a cottage-girl, his young wife, amidst all this wealth and fashion? The more he pondered the more was he puzzled. Were there any cows to milk here? There certainly were no fields to till. She was most probably engaged to do something in one of these large houses; and he sauntered along, looking at the chamber-windows and their lights going out one by one; and wondered which of them might be hers.

From **Chapter 55: Angel Presents Himself to Tess**

This exchange, which takes place at the 'stylish lodging-house' where Tess is staying with Alec, is in many ways painfully self-explanatory; indeed, one has to wonder whether Hardy decided to change his original title for the novel, *Too Late, Beloved!*, partly to avoid anticipating Tess's shocked utterances here in a way that might detract from their emotive power.

Some background facts, however, are important to know. When Tess refers brokenly to Alec's 'kindness' to the family 'after father's death', she greatly understates the destitution recently experienced by her mother and six siblings. Jack Durbeyfield's death followed closely upon the unexpected illness of his wife, which itself forced Tess to quit Flintcomb-Ash before her contract was up; the family were then evicted from the Marlott house, and, in irrational compliance with his aristocratic fantasy, Joan Durbeyfield insisted on transporting their possessions in an open cart to Kingsbere, the ancient seat of the d'Urbervilles, without the slightest prospect of lodging or support.

As is his habit, Hardy arranges and escalates these circumstances in such a way that Alec's earlier offer of a cottage at the Stoke-d'Urberville estate – contingent, of course, on Tess's compliance as his lover – seems not merely the lesser of two evils (for Tess can neither support the family herself nor passively allow them to starve) but almost a fated outcome toward which she is dragged despite her own considerable powers of resistance.

1 See Jonah 4.5–11.

Two documents included in this volume provoke thought about how this scene may have played in Victorian context. One is Margaret Oliphant's scathing early review of the novel which cites Tess's luxurious state of semi-dress – the very colours and textures of which signal her 'kept' womanhood – as part of a pervasive error in characterization, leading to the breakdown of Hardy's claims for Tess as a 'pure woman': such fripperies 'are not the accessories of purity, but the trappings of vice. Tess would have flung them out of the window' (**p. 60**). For Oliphant, in other words, the believability of Tess's fortitude elsewhere in the novel renders her capitulation to Alec, even under the newly desperate circumstances Hardy has carefully drawn in, flatly unbelievable. Also relevant here is Hardy's early poem 'The Ruined Maid' (**p. 31**), composed some twenty-five years before *Tess*. Though humorously matter-of-fact in tone – its speaker, a young woman enjoying the luxuries for which she has traded her virtue, counsels her friends to do likewise – the poem also comments implicitly on the starkness of the dilemma facing many a young woman, in his day, needing money.

He was shown into the front room – the dining-room – and looked out through the spring curtains at the little lawn, and the rhododendrons and other shrubs upon it. Obviously her position was by no means so bad as he had feared, and it crossed his mind that she must somehow have claimed and sold the jewels to attain it. He did not blame her for one moment. Soon his sharpened ear detected footsteps upon the stairs, at which his heart thumped so painfully that he could hardly stand firm. 'Dear me! what will she think of me, so altered as I am!' he said to himself; and the door opened.

Tess appeared on the threshold – not at all as he had expected to see her – bewilderingly otherwise, indeed. Her great natural beauty was, if not heightened, rendered more obvious by her attire. She was loosely wrapped in a cashmere dressing-gown of grey-white, embroidered in half-mourning tints, and she wore slippers of the same hue. Her neck rose out of a frill of down, and her well-remembered cable of dark-brown hair was partially coiled up in a mass at the back of her head and partly hanging on her shoulder – the evident result of haste.

He had held out his arms, but they had fallen again to his side; for she had not come forward, remaining still in the opening of the doorway. Mere yellow skeleton that he was now he felt the contrast between them, and thought his appearance distasteful to her.

'Tess!' he said huskily, 'can you forgive me for going away? Can't you – come to me? How do you get to be – like this?'

'It is too late,' said she, her voice sounding hard through the room, her eyes shining unnaturally.

'I did not think rightly of you – I did not see you as you were!' he continued to plead. 'I have learnt to since, dearest Tessy mine!'

'Too late, too late!' she said, waving her hand in the impatience of a person whose tortures cause every instant to seem an hour. 'Don't come close to me, Angel! No – you must not. Keep away.'

'But don't you love me, my dear wife, because I have been so pulled down by illness? You are not so fickle – I am come on purpose for you – my mother and father will welcome you now!'

'Yes – O, yes, yes! But I say, I say it is too late.' She seemed to feel like a fugitive in a dream, who tries to move away, but cannot. 'Don't you know all – don't you know it? Yet how do you come here if you do not know?'

'I inquired here and there, and I found the way.'

'I waited and waited for you,' she went on, her tones suddenly resuming their old fluty pathos. 'But you did not come! And I wrote to you, and you did not come! He kept on saying you would never come any more, and that I was a foolish woman. He was very kind to me, and to mother, and to all of us after father's death. He –'

'I don't understand.'

'He has won me back – to him.'

Clare looked at her keenly, then, gathering her meaning, flagged like one plague-stricken, and his glance sank; it fell on her hands, which, once rosy, were now white and more delicate.

She continued: 'He is upstairs. I hate him now, because he told me a lie – that you would not come again; and you *have* come! These clothes are what he's put upon me: I didn't care what he did wi' me! But – will you go away, Angel, please, and never come any more?'

They stood fixed, their baffled hearts looking out of their eyes with a joylessness pitiful to see. Both seemed to implore something to shelter them from reality.

'Ah – it is my fault!' said Clare.

But he could not get on. Speech was as inexpressive as silence. But he had a vague consciousness of one thing, though it was not clear to him till later; that his original Tess had spiritually ceased to recognize the body before him as hers – allowing it to drift, like a corpse upon the current, in a direction dissociated from its living will.

A few instants passed, and he found that Tess was gone. His face grew colder and more shrunken as he stood concentrated on the moment, and a minute or two after he found himself in the street, walking along he did not know whither.

From **Chapter 56: Tess's Murder of Alec**

This chapter-opening follows immediately from the passage above. Here Hardy shifts to a neutral spectator's point of view, almost as if he were anticipating the effect of a witness's testimony at a murder trial. He may also have employed this strategy to distract readers from the somewhat implausible circumstances of the killing itself. Margaret Oliphant (p. 59) was quick to point these out: 'why did Alec D'Urberville, a strong young man, allow himself to be stabbed? and how did it happen that the lodging-house carving-knife, not usually a very sharp instrument, was capable of such a blow?' The account of the stabbing, like that of the rape earlier in the novel, did present Hardy with a quandary as to the robustness of Tess's agency; here, he needed to deliver a convincing crime of passion without any hint of premeditation or skill, yet one that would dispatch Alec while driving home to readers the self-abnegating fervor of Tess's love for

Angel. Accordingly, he revised the scene several times, settling on a single post-mortem sentence that minimizes Tess's physical effort in the stabbing (see Mary Jacobus, p. 72). Ultimately, the tactic of using Mrs Brooks's point of view must be counted a success. It places us at a remove from the actual crime, while also making possible a brilliant mix of the gothic and the mundane in the landlady's slow realization of what has happened.

Mrs. Brooks, the lady who was the householder at The Herons, and owner of all the handsome furniture, was not a person of an unusually curious turn of mind. She was too deeply materialized, poor woman, by her long and enforced bondage to that arithmetical demon Profit-and-Loss, to retain much curiosity for its own sake, and apart from possible lodgers' pockets. Nevertheless, the visit of Angel Clare to her well-paying tenants, Mr. and Mrs. d'Urberville, as she deemed them, was sufficiently exceptional in point of time and manner to reinvigorate the feminine proclivity which had been stifled down as useless save in its bearings to the letting trade.

Tess had spoken to her husband from the doorway, without entering the dining-room, and Mrs. Brooks, who stood within the partly-closed door of her own sitting-room at the back of the passage, could hear fragments of the conversation – if conversation it could be called – between those two wretched souls. She heard Tess re-ascend the stairs to the first floor, and the departure of Clare, and the closing of the front door behind him. Then the door of the room above was shut, and Mrs. Brooks knew that Tess had re-entered her apartment. As the young lady was not fully dressed, Mrs. Brooks knew that she would not emerge again for some time.

She accordingly ascended the stairs softly, and stood at the door of the front room – a drawing-room, connected with the room immediately behind it (which was a bedroom) by folding-doors in the common manner. This first floor, containing Mrs. Brooks's best apartments, had been taken by the week by the d'Urbervilles. The back room was now in silence; but from the drawing-room there came sounds.

All that she could at first distinguish of them was one syllable, continually repeated in a low note of moaning, as if it came from a soul bound to some Ixionian[1] wheel:

'O – O – O!'

Then a silence, then a heavy sigh, and again,

'O – O – O!'

The landlady looked through the keyhole. Only a small space of the room inside was visible, but within that space came a corner of the breakfast table, which was already spread for the meal, and also a chair beside. Over the seat of the chair Tess's face was bowed, her posture being a kneeling one in front of it; her hands were clasped over her head, the skirts of her dressing-gown and the embroidery of her night-gown flowed upon the floor behind her, and her

---

1   A term denoting endless torment, deriving from the sufferings of Ixion, who in Greek mythology is chained for eternity to a wheel in Hades.

stockingless feet, from which the slippers had fallen, protruded upon the carpet. It was from her lips that came the murmur of unspeakable despair.

Then a man's voice from the adjoining bedroom:

'What's the matter?'

She did not answer, but went on, in a tone which was a soliloquy rather than an exclamation, and a dirge rather than a soliloquy. Mrs. Brooks could only catch a portion:

'. . . And then my dear, dear husband came home to me . . . and I did not know it! . . . And you had used your cruel persuasion upon me . . . you did not stop using it – no – you did not stop! My little sisters and brothers and my mother's needs – they were the things you moved me by . . . and you said my husband would never come back – never; and you taunted me, and said what a simpleton I was to expect him! . . . And at last I believed you and gave way! . . . And then he came back! Now he is gone. Gone a second time, and I have lost him now for ever . . . and he will not love me the littlest bit ever any more – only hate me . . . O yes, I have lost him now – again because of – you!' In writhing, with her head on the chair, she turned her face towards the door, and Mrs. Brooks could see the pain upon it; and that her lips were bleeding from the clench of her teeth upon them, and that the long lashes of her closed eyes stuck in wet tags to her cheeks. She continued: 'And he is dying – he looks as if he is dying! . . . And my sin will kill him and not kill me! . . . O, you have torn my life all to pieces . . . made me be what I prayed you in pity not to make me be again! . . . My own true husband will never, never – O God – I can't bear this! – I cannot!'

There were more and sharper words from the man; then a sudden rustle; she had sprung to her feet. Mrs. Brooks, thinking that the speaker was coming to rush out of the door, hastily retreated down the stairs.

She need not have done so, however, for the door of the sitting-room was not opened. But Mrs. Brooks felt it unsafe to watch on the landing again, and entered her own parlour below.

She could hear nothing through the floor, although she listened intently, and thereupon went to the kitchen to finish her interrupted breakfast. Coming up presently to the front room on the ground floor she took up some sewing, waiting for her lodgers to ring that she might take away the breakfast, which she meant to do herself, to discover what was the matter if possible. Overhead, as she sat, she could now hear the floor-boards slightly creak, as if some one were walking about, and presently the movement was explained by the rustle of garments against the banisters, the opening and the closing of the front door, and the form of Tess passing to the gate on her way into the street. She was fully dressed now in the walking costume of a well-to-do young lady in which she had arrived, with the sole addition that over her hat and black feathers a veil was drawn. Mrs. Brooks had not been able to catch any word of farewell, temporary or otherwise, between her tenants at the door above. They might have quarrelled, or Mr. d'Urberville might still be asleep, for he was not an early riser.

She went into the back room which was more especially her own apartment, and continued her sewing there. The lady lodger did not return, nor did the gentleman ring his bell. Mrs. Brooks pondered on the delay, and on what probable relation the visitor who had called so early bore to the couple upstairs. In reflecting she leant back in her chair.

As she did so her eyes glanced casually over the ceiling till they were arrested by a spot in the middle of its white surface which she had never noticed there before. It was about the size of a wafer when she first observed it, but it speedily grew as large as the palm of her hand, and then she could perceive that it was red. The oblong white ceiling, with this scarlet blot in the midst, had the appearance of a gigantic ace of hearts.

Mrs. Brooks had strange qualms of misgiving. She got upon the table, and touched the spot in the ceiling with her fingers. It was damp, and she fancied that it was a blood stain.

Descending from the table, she left the parlour, and went upstairs, intending to enter the room overhead, which was the bedchamber at the back of the drawing-room. But, nerveless woman as she had now become, she could not bring herself to attempt the handle. She listened. The dead silence within was broken only by a regular beat.

Drip, drip, drip.

Mrs. Brooks hastened downstairs, opened the front door, and ran into the street. A man she knew, one of the workmen employed at an adjoining villa, was passing by, and she begged him to come in and go upstairs with her; she feared something had happened to one of her lodgers. The workman assented, and followed her to the landing.

She opened the door of the drawing-room, and stood back for him to pass in, entering herself behind him. The room was empty; the breakfast – a substantial repast of coffee, eggs, and a cold ham – lay spread upon the table untouched, as when she had taken it up, excepting that the carving-knife was missing. She asked the man to go through the folding-doors into the adjoining room.

He opened the doors, entered a step or two, and came back almost instantly with a rigid face. 'My good God, the gentleman in bed is dead! I think he has been hurt with a knife – a lot of blood has run down upon the floor!'

The alarm was soon given, and the house which had lately been so quiet resounded with the tramp of many footsteps, a surgeon among the rest. The wound was small, but the point of the blade had touched the heart of the victim, who lay on his back, pale, fixed, dead, as if he had scarcely moved after the infliction of the blow. In a quarter of an hour the news that a gentleman who was a temporary visitor to the town had been stabbed in his bed, spread through every street and villa of the popular watering-place.

From **Chapters 57 and 58: The Idyll at the Deserted Mansion**

Tess, having caught up with Angel on the road out of Sandbourne, is now a fugitive from the law – yet the stunning fact of their reunion seems to override all else even for Angel, who tries to compensate for her semi-delirious state with practical thinking. On that first strange day, we are told (some paragraphs prior to the excerpt given here) that 'neither one of them seemed to consider any question of effectual escape, disguise, or long concealment. Their every idea was temporary and unforefending, like the plans of two children.' Fittingly, then, what they experience during their improvised stay at the empty mansion is a bittersweet reprise of their time at Talbothays dairy, when being alone together in the early mornings made them feel 'like Adam and Eve' (see Chapter 20, above). Even the caretaker who discovers them asleep in bed is 'struck with their innocent appearance', and inclined to view the situation sympathetically as a 'genteel elopement'. But of course, there is no going back to paradise once it has been lost, and Hardy achieves throughout these passages a poignant blend of blissful ignorance and sad, postlapsarian knowledge. (On Hardy's description of the house relative to the thematic of blindness or unconsciousness, see Janet Freeman, esp. **p. 76**.) Tess knows her fate, but has learned to cling to what she has: 'All is trouble outside there; inside here content.'

He was growing weary likewise, for they had wandered a dozen or fifteen miles, and it became necessary to consider what they should do for rest. They looked from afar at isolated cottages and little inns, and were inclined to approach one of the latter, when their hearts failed them, and they sheered off. At length their gait dragged, and they stood still.

'Could we sleep under the trees?' she asked.

He thought the season insufficiently advanced.

'I have been thinking of that empty mansion we passed,' he said. 'Let us go back towards it again.'

They retraced their steps, but it was half an hour before they stood without the entrance-gate as earlier. He then requested her to stay where she was, whilst he went to see who was within.

She sat down among the bushes within the gate, and Clare crept towards the house. His absence lasted some considerable time, and when he returned Tess was wildly anxious, not for herself, but for him. He had found out from a boy that there was only an old woman in charge as caretaker, and she only came there on fine days, from the hamlet near, to open and shut the windows. She would come to shut them at sunset. 'Now, we can get in through one of the lower windows, and rest there,' said he.

Under his escort she went tardily forward to the main front, whose shuttered windows, like sightless eyeballs, excluded the possibility of watchers. The door was reached a few steps further, and one of the windows beside it was open. Clare clambered in, and pulled Tess in after him.

Except the hall the rooms were all in darkness, and they ascended the stair-case. Up here also the shutters were tightly closed, the ventilation being perfunctorily done, for this day at least, by opening the hall-window in front and an upper window behind. Clare unlatched the door of a large chamber, felt his way across it, and parted the shutters to the width of two or three inches. A shaft of dazzling sunlight glanced into the room, revealing heavy, old-fashioned furniture, crimson damask hangings, and an enormous four-post bedstead, along the head of which were carved running figures, apparently Atalanta's race.[1]

'Rest at last!' said he, setting down his bag and the parcel of viands.[2]

They remained in great quietness till the caretaker should have come to shut the windows: as a precaution, putting themselves in total darkness by barring the shutters as before, lest the woman should open the door of their chamber for any casual reason. Between six and seven o'clock she came, but did not approach the wing they were in. They heard her close the windows, fasten them, lock the door, and go away. Then Clare again stole a chink of light from the window, and they shared another meal, till by-and-by they were enveloped in the shades of night which they had no candle to disperse.

From Chapter 58

The night was strangely solemn and still. In the small hours she whispered to him the whole story of how he had walked in his sleep with her in his arms across the Froom stream, at the imminent risk of both their lives, and laid her down in the stone coffin at the ruined abbey. He had never known of that till now.

'Why didn't you tell me next day?' he said. 'It might have prevented much misunderstanding and woe.'

'Don't think of what's past!' said she. 'I am not going to think outside of now. Why should we? Who knows what to-morrow has in store?'

But it apparently had no sorrow. The morning was wet and foggy, and Clare, rightly informed that the caretaker only opened the windows on fine days, ventured to creep out of their chamber, and explore the house, leaving Tess asleep. There was no food on the premises, but there was water, and he took advantage of the fog to emerge from the mansion, and fetch tea, bread, and butter from a shop in a little place two miles beyond, as also a small tin kettle and spirit-lamp,[3] that they might get fire without smoke. His re-entry awoke her; and they breakfasted on what he had brought.

They were indisposed to stir abroad, and the day passed, and the night following, and the next, and next; till, almost without their being aware, five days had slipped by in absolute seclusion, not a sight or sound of a human being disturbing their peacefulness, such as it was. The changes of the weather were their only events, the birds of the New Forest their only company. By tacit consent they hardly once spoke of any incident of the past subsequent to their wedding-day. The gloomy intervening time seemed to sink into chaos, over which the present and prior times closed as if it never had been. Whenever he suggested that they should leave their shelter, and go forwards towards Southampton or London, she showed a strange unwillingness to move.

'Why should we put an end to all that's sweet and lovely!' she deprecated. 'What must come will come.' And, looking through the shutter-chink: 'All is trouble outside there; inside here content.'

He peeped out also. It was quite true; within was affection, union, error forgiven: outside was the inexorable.

'And – and,' she said, pressing her cheek against his, 'I fear that what you think of me now may not last. I do not wish to outlive your present feeling for me. I

---

1 This story from Greek myth has ironic parallels to the plot of *Tess* at this moment. Atalanta is a beautiful, swift-footed huntress who will only marry a man who can beat her in a race. Milanion finally bests her, through the aid of Aphrodite, but their married happiness is quickly destroyed when they have intercourse in a sacred temple, and incur the wrath of Zeus.

2 Food.

3 Alcohol-burning, rather than oil-burning.

would rather not. I would rather be dead and buried when the time comes for you to despise me, so that it may never be known to me that you despised me.'

'I cannot ever despise you.'

'I also hope that. But considering what my life had been I cannot see why any man should, sooner or later, be able to help despising me . . . How wickedly mad I was! Yet formerly I never could bear to hurt a fly or a worm, and the sight of a bird in a cage used often to make me cry.'

They remained yet another day. In the night the dull sky cleared, and the result was that the old caretaker at the cottage awoke early. The brilliant sunrise made her unusually brisk; she decided to open the contiguous mansion immediately, and to air it thoroughly on such a day. Thus it occurred that, having arrived and opened the lower rooms before six o'clock, she ascended to the bedchambers, and was about to turn the handle of the one wherein they lay.

At that moment she fancied she could hear the breathing of persons within. Her slippers and her antiquity had rendered her progress a noiseless one so far, and she made for instant retreat; then, deeming that her hearing might have deceived her, she turned anew to the door and softly tried the handle. The lock was out of order, but a piece of furniture had been moved forward on the inside, which prevented her opening the door more than an inch or two. A stream of morning light through the shutter-chink fell upon the faces of the pair, wrapped in profound slumber, Tess's lips being parted like a half-opened flower near his cheek.

The caretaker was so struck with their innocent appearance, and with the elegance of Tess's gown hanging across a chair, her silk stockings beside it, the pretty parasol, and the other habits in which she had arrived because she had none else, that her first indignation at the effrontery of tramps and vagabonds gave way to a momentary sentimentality over this genteel elopement, as it seemed. She closed the door, and withdrew as softly as she had come, to go and consult with her neighbours on the odd discovery.

Not more than a minute had elapsed after her withdrawal when Tess woke, and then Clare. Both had a sense that something had disturbed them, though they could not say what; and the uneasy feeling which it engendered grew stronger. As soon as he was dressed he narrowly scanned the lawn through the two or three inches of shutter-chink. 'I think we will leave at once,' said he. 'It is a fine day. And I cannot help fancying somebody is about the house. At any rate, the woman will be sure to come today.'

She passively assented, and putting the room in order they took up the few articles that belonged to them, and departed noiselessly. When they had got into the forest she turned to take a last look at the house.

'Ah, happy house – goodbye!' she said. 'My life can only be a question of a few weeks. Why should we not have stayed there?'

From **Chapter 58: Tess and Angel at Stonehenge**

In this scene, Hardy twists together two threads of ongoing concern – the strange balance of assertiveness and passivity in Tess herself, and the counter-vailing forces of modernity and 'paganism' in the environments she has known;

for the latter see Johnson (**p. 104**) and Gussow (**p. 106**). Just prior to the excerpt below, Tess has insisted on resting in the open temple despite Angel's better judgement, half-humorously reminding him that he had once called her a 'heathen': what better place than Stonehenge to meet her destiny? Her understanding of the ancient stones as a site of sacrifice again indicates that she sees herself as a victim, yet there is no longer much fear or overt emotion accompanying the realization. The silence inaugurating this passage follows her having extracted a promise from Angel that after her death he will look after, and perhaps marry, her sister 'Liza-Lu, regardless of the legalities that might forbid it. The ensuing conversation, however, has her once again deferring to his theological scepticism, and, as Boumelha and Freeman have noted, falling characteristically asleep under his watch, even as the search party approaches.

As Penelope Vigar observes (see esp. **p. 70**), the Stonehenge scene (much like the 'midnight baptism') also shows Hardy's talent for balancing light and shadow, symbolic clarity and felt obscurity within a significant tableau, with the ultimate effect of promoting a sense of life's mysteriousness both for the internal witnesses and for the reader.

She ceased, and he fell into thought. In the far north-east sky he could see between the pillars a level streak of light. The uniform concavity of black cloud was lifting bodily like the lid of a pot, letting in at the earth's edge the coming day, against which the towering monoliths and trilithons[1] began to be blackly defined.

'Did they sacrifice to God here?' asked she.

'No,' said he.

'Who to?'

'I believe to the sun. That lofty stone set away by itself is in the direction of the sun, which will presently rise behind it.'

'This reminds me, dear,' she said. 'You remember you never would interfere with any belief of mine before we were married? But I knew your mind all the same, and I thought as you thought – not from any reasons of my own, but because you thought so. Tell me now, Angel, do you think we shall meet again after we are dead? I want to know.'

He kissed her to avoid a reply at such a time.

'O, Angel – I fear that means no!' said she, with a suppressed sob. 'And I wanted so to see you again – so much, so much! What – not even you and I, Angel, who love each other so well?'

Like a greater than himself, to the critical question at the critical time he did not answer; and they were again silent. In a minute or two her breathing became more regular, her clasp of his hand relaxed, and she fell asleep. The band of silver paleness along the east horizon made even the distant parts of the Great Plain appear dark and near; and the whole enormous landscape bore that impress of reserve, taciturnity, and hesitation which is usual just before day. The eastward pillars and their architraves[2] stood up blackly against the light, and the

1   i.e., the freestanding single stones, and the three-stone groupings employing two uprights and a cross-piece.
2   Stone pieces immediately atop the upright columns.

great flame-shaped Sun-stone beyond them; and the Stone of Sacrifice midway.[3] Presently the night wind died out, and the quivering little pools in the cup-like hollows of the stones lay still. At the same time something seemed to move on the verge of the dip eastward – a mere dot. It was the head of a man approaching them from the hollow beyond the Sun-stone. Clare wished they had gone onward, but in the circumstances decided to remain quiet. The figure came straight towards the circle of pillars in which they were.

He heard something behind him, the brush of feet. Turning, he saw over the prostrate columns another figure; then before he was aware, another was at hand on the right, under a trilithon, and another on the left. The dawn shone full on the front of the man westward, and Clare could discern from this that he was tall, and walked as if trained. They all closed in with evident purpose. Her story [of the murder] then was true! Springing to his feet, he looked around for a weapon, loose stone, means of escape, anything. By this time the nearest man was upon him.

From **Chapter 59: Tess's Fate, and the Novel's Closing Paragraphs**

In the last chapter of the novel, which proceeds directly from the excerpt given above, we come quickly to understand – though we are never told explicitly – that Tess has been tried and convicted for murdering Alec d'Urberville, and that

Figure 8 **Stonehenge, Salisbury, England, between c. 1890 and c. 1900 (By permission of the Library of Congress, 2002708089)**

3   Stonehenge was built over a period of more than a thousand years, and some of the design elements and uses changed over time. Although many of the stones have proven astronomical orientations, the possibility of their use in sacrificial rites is less well understood.

she is about to be executed in the cathedral town of Wintoncester. Hardy, the former architect, approaches the unspeakable here by means of a panoramic view of the town ('that fine old city, aforetime capital of Wessex') that tightens to reveal the jarring contrast of the modern prison with the centuries-old gothic structures surrounding it. He maintains a respectful distance from the mourners, as well as from Tess herself, by making Angel and 'Liza-Lu tiny, albeit emphatically human, figures in the landscape.

The novel's final paragraph has generated much comment. Most readers agree that Hardy is doing two related things here: he is placing Tess's story against a high-literary backdrop of Greek tragedy, with its entailments of divine retribution and compounded irony; and he is also voicing the broader historical irony of extinguished greatness. The questions arise, as so often in Hardy, when we try to pin down his tone: is he elevating Tess, or abandoning her? Does he mean to puncture a false system of justice, or to remind us of its enduring power as a framework of meaning? For an extended discussion of these questions, and a close reading of the final paragraph, see Ian Gregor (**pp. 101–4**), who sees the 'tragic' elements as tempered by allusions to the final scene of Milton's *Paradise Lost* – a scene that balances crushing regret against the promise of eventual redemption.

Against these far stretches of country rose, in front of the other city edifices, a large red-brick building, with level grey roofs, and rows of short barred windows bespeaking captivity, the whole contrasting greatly by its formalism with the quaint irregularities of the gothic erections. It was somewhat disguised from the road in passing it by yews and evergreen oaks, but it was visible enough up here. The wicket from which the pair had lately emerged was in the wall of this structure. From the middle of the building an ugly flat-topped octagonal tower ascended against the east horizon, and viewed from this spot, on its shady side and against the light, it seemed the one blot on the city's beauty. Yet it was with this blot, and not with the beauty, that the two gazers were concerned.

Upon the cornice of the tower a tall staff was fixed. Their eyes were riveted on it. A few minutes after the hour had struck something moved slowly up the staff, and extended itself upon the breeze. It was a black flag.

'Justice' was done, and the President of the Immortals, in Aeschylean phrase,[1] had ended his sport with Tess. And the d'Urberville knights and dames slept on in their tombs unknowing. The two speechless gazers bent themselves down to the earth, as if in prayer, and remained thus a long time, absolutely motionless: the flag continued to wave silently. As soon as they had strength they arose, joined hands again, and went on.

---

1   A translation of a phrase found in *Prometheus Bound*, by Aeschylus (525–456 BC), widely regarded as the founder of Greek tragedy.

4

Further Reading

Further Reading

Given Hardy's overall stature as a novelist and poet, and the special stature of *Tess* within his *corpus*, it is unsurprising that the novel has generated a vast quantity of scholarly work. What follows is a selective bibliography of further reading, with an emphasis on books and articles not already featured in this volume's critical excerpts. It must be noted that, because there is so much fine criticism on Hardy, decisions about works to include and exclude in such a list are, past a certain point, almost arbitrary.

Primary Sources and Biographical Studies of Hardy

There are many good editions of *Tess* currently in print. Several, including the Norton Critical Edition (ed. Scott Elledge), use the 1912 Wessex Edition as a base text; the 1998 edition published by Bedford/St Martin's (ed. John Paul Riquelme) is based on the slightly different 1920 'reimpression' of the 1912 text. The Oxford World's Classics edition, edited by Juliet Grindle and Simon Gatrell (Oxford University Press, 1998) is widely admired, and employs a text based on their earlier Clarendon Press edition of the novel (Oxford, 1983; 1986). This Oxford edition tends towards different patterns of punctuation from those present in the Wessex text, especially for passages of dialogue, and Gatrell's 'Note on the Text' should be consulted as a guide to the volume's editorial principles. The most recent Penguin text, edited by Tim Dolin with an introduction by Margaret Higgonet (1998; reprinted 2003), goes all the way back to the 1891 first edition of *Tess* for its source text. It thus presents some passages in forms that Hardy had modified by 1895.

Five notable modern biographies of Hardy are recommended, headed by Michael Millgate's magisterial *Thomas Hardy: A Biography* (Oxford: Oxford University Press, 1982). (Millgate is also the modern editor of Hardy's ghostwritten 'biography', *The Life and Work of Thomas Hardy* (London: Macmillan, 1985), which was originally published under Florence Hardy's name as *The Life of Thomas Hardy* (2 vols, 1928–30).) Millgate's works followed the appearance of two important biographical volumes by Robert Gittings, *Young*

Thomas Hardy (1975), focusing on the years 1840–75, and *The Older Hardy* (1978). The first of these has recently been re-issued (2001) under the imprint of the Penguin Classic Biography series. F.B. Pinion's *Thomas Hardy: His Life and Friends* (London: Macmillan, 1992) is lucid and informed throughout. Martin Seymour-Smith's weighty and contentious *Hardy* (New York: St Martin's, 1995) is very much conceived as addressing what he sees as negative representations and other deficiencies in Millgate and Gittings, especially Gittings's portrayals of Hardy's misogyny. Shorter, but also of merit, is James Gibson's *Thomas Hardy* (New York: Palgrave/Macmillan, 1996), published in Macmillan's *Literary Lives* series.

The standard scholarly edition of the poems is the multi-volume *The Complete Poetical Works of Thomas Hardy*, ed. Samuel Hynes (Oxford: Clarendon Press, 1982–95). A valuable shorter collection, with concise remarks on some of the difficulties the poetry presents, is *Thomas Hardy: Selected Poems*, ed. Tim Armstrong (London: Longman, 1993). Hardy's letters, which constitute an extremely useful resource, are available in *The Collected Letters of Thomas Hardy*, ed. Richard Purdy and Michael Millgate, 7 vols (Oxford: Clarendon Press, 1978–88); Millgate has also edited a one-volume selection of the letters (Clarendon, 1990). Further, it should be noted that many people consider Purdy's *Thomas Hardy: A Bibliographic Study* (Oxford: Oxford University Press, 1954) still to be one of the five or six most essential pieces of Hardyean scholarship. A valuable recent overview of several aspects of Hardy's life and art is *The Cambridge Companion to Thomas Hardy*, ed. Dale Kramer (Cambridge: Cambridge University Press, 1999).

General Studies of Hardy's Fiction and Poetry

The last three decades have seen the appearance of a number of important book-length studies of Hardy's fiction, several of which extend the feminist critiques brought to bear on *Tess*; these include Rosemarie Morgan, *Women and Sexuality in the Novels of Thomas Hardy* (London: Routledge and Kegan Paul, 1988); Marjorie Garson, *Hardy's Fables of Integrity: Woman, Body, Text* (Oxford: Clarendon Press, 1991); and Margaret Higonett, ed., *The Sense of Sex: Feminist Perspectives on Hardy* (Urbana: University of Illinois Press, 1993). Two important books from the late 1980s that seek to dissemble or problematize traditional humanist readings of Hardy are Peter Widdowson, *Hardy in History: A Study in Literary Sociology* (London: Routledge, 1989; cited in the Work in Performance), and John Goode, *Thomas Hardy: The Offensive Truth* (Oxford: Blackwell, 1988). Two discussions by the American deconstructionist J. Hillis Miller must also be registered here: his reading of *Tess* in *Fiction and Repetition* (Oxford: Blackwell, 1982), and his earlier book on Hardy's fiction, *Thomas Hardy: Distance and Desire* (Cambridge, Massachusetts: Harvard University Press, 1970). Also recommended are Dale Kramer's *Thomas Hardy: The Forms of Tragedy* (London: Macmillan, 1975); Simon Gatrell's *Hardy the Creator: A Textual Biography* (Oxford: Clarendon Press, 1988) and his new *Thomas Hardy's Vision of Wessex* (London: Palgrave, 2003); and finally Arlene M. Jackson's *Illustration and the Novels of Thomas Hardy* (Totowa, New Jersey: Rowman and Littlefield, 1981).

There are a number of fine studies of the poetry, including Donald Davie, *Thomas Hardy and British Poetry* (London: Routledge and Kegan Paul, 1973); Tom Paulin, *Thomas Hardy: The Poetry of Perception* (London: Macmillian, 1975); Dennis Taylor, *Hardy's Poetry, 1860–1928* (London: Macmillan, 1981); and Trevor Johnson, *A Critical Introduction to the Poems of Thomas Hardy* (New York: St Martin's, 1991).

Studies of *Tess*

Several recent discussions of *Tess* deserve special mention, though this list is not intended to be exhaustive. Still very useful is an older collection, *Twentieth Century Interpretations of Tess of the d'Urbervilles*, ed. Albert J. LaValley (Englewood Cliffs, New Jersey: Prentice-Hall, 1969), especially the essays by Arnold Kettle, David J. De Laura, and LaValley himself. A short and useful book intended primarily for students is Peter Casagrande, *Tess of the d'Urbervilles: Unorthodox Beauty* (New York: Twayne, 1992), published as part of Twayne's Masterwork Studies series. Essays meriting notice include Kathleen Blake, 'Pure Tess: Hardy on Knowing a Woman', *Studies in English Literature*, 22 (1982), 689–705; Kaja Silverman, 'History, Figuration and Female Subjectivity in *Tess of the d'Urbervilles*', *Novel* 18.1 (Fall 1984), 5–28; and Jerome H. Buckley, 'Tess and the d'Urbervilles', *Victorians Institute Journal*, 20 (1992), 1–12. A recent essay on the poetry that is especially helpful on explaining Hardy's mindset in the years following the publication of *Tess* is William M. Morgan, 'Hardy's Return to Verse: a New Chronology', *The Hardy Review*, 1.1 (July 1998), 117–32.

Web Resources

The Thomas Hardy Association ⟨http://www.yale.edu/hardysoc/Welcome/welcomet.htm⟩

Hardy Web Page Index ⟨http://flash.lakeheadu.ca/%7Epvalling/linksone/Links.htm⟩

The Thomas Hardy Society ⟨http://www.hardysociety.org/⟩

Victorian Web ⟨http://www.victorianweb.org/authors/hardy/hardyov.html⟩

Hardy Country Page http://www.thomashardy.co.uk/

Index

Note: page numbers in bold indicate quoted material.